Religion,
GOVERNMENT,
AND
EDUCATION

RELIGION, GOVERNMENT, AND Education

EDITED BY

William W. Brickman

Editor, School and Society;
Professor of Education, New York University

AND

Stanley Lehrer

Vice-President and Managing Editor,
School and Society

GREENWOOD PRESS, PUBLISHERS
WESTPORT, CONNECTICUT

Library of Congress Cataloging in Publication Data

Brickman, William W   ed.
  Religion, government, and education.

  Reprint of the ed. published by the Society for
the Advancement of Education, New York.
  Bibliography: p.
  1. Church and education in the United States.
I. Lehrer, Stanley, joint ed. II. Title.
[LC427.B7 1977]   377   77-24684
ISBN 0-8371-9749-X

Originally published in 1961 by Society for the Advancement
of Education, New York

Reprinted with the permission of Society for the Advancement
of Education

Reprinted in 1977 by Greenwood Press, Inc.

Library of Congress catalog card number 77-24684

ISBN 0-8371-9749-X

Printed in the United States of America

For

MARTIN and ROSE LEHRER

and to the memory of

DAVID S. and SARAH C. BRICKMAN

Preface

HISTORY HAS
been peppered with conflicts between religion
and government. Despite the popularity of the
concept of church-state separation, each challenged the other for an influential role in the
affairs of man. Each gained control of the pro-
cesses of learning. Whether church and state
should continue to remain on opposite sides of
the fence, especially in matters concerning education, has survived until today as a problem of
national and international magnitude. The
specific question of government aid for religious
schools, which is one of the main concerns of
this book, is responsible for projecting church-
state-school relations into the proportions of a
lively but serious controversy.

Such a controversy will not be resolved easily
or in a short time. Many aspects of church-state-
school co-operation — or lack of it — must be
examined and clearly understood before any
definite decisions will be reached that recommend either partnership or separationism in educational affairs. This book is designed to focus
on the issues involved and thus permit a more
rational approach to solving, if at all possible, a
dilemma that is charged with emotionalism.

Against a backdrop of notable events in history
from Biblical times to the 1960's, the book provides a comprehensive review of the church-state-
school situation in all corners of the world, with

most of the emphasis on the U. S. Of course, despite the editors' efforts to keep the contents up to date, an unexpectedly swift development such as passage of a congressional bill on Federal aid to parochial schools might tend to minimize the significance of certain viewpoints and conclusions made by contributors. Nevertheless, the statements of fact and belief cannot be dulled by changing times and always should prove enlightening as part of the historical record on the relationship of religion, government, and education.

To every contributor go the editors' thanks for excellent co-operation in preparing material when needed. The boldness of contributors to face the scorch of controversy deserves special acknowledgment. This writer owes his personal gratitude to Laurel F. Lehrer, his wife, for her patience and understanding in arranging for meals at irregular hours so that frequently during the book's progress he could work without interruption.

STANLEY LEHRER

New Hyde Park, N. Y.
August, 1961

Introduction

THE PRESIDENTIAL campaign of 1960 and its aftermath projected once more the problem of the proper interrelationship of religion, government, and education. Not that this controversial issue ever dropped out of sight or out of mind; over the years many a conflict erupted in a community concerning Bible reading, the Christmas crèche, hymn singing, and other religious practices in the public schools. However, President John F. Kennedy's pronouncements against public aid to parochial schools, as a candidate and again as Chief Executive, served again to fan the fires of conflict on a scale matching that of 1949, but without the verbal violence.

Notwithstanding the apparent popular disapproval of public financing of church-related schools on constitutional or other grounds, religious groups and individuals have shown a determination to secure favorable legislation to ease the financial burden of the parochial institutions and to obtain official recognition of the contribution by these schools to the national welfare and the national defense. In all probability, those who regard any form of public support of religious schools as a serious infringement upon the traditional principle (rather than actual practice) of maintaining a high and solid wall of separation between church and state in educational affairs will react with displeasure and active opposition.

9

The time has come when all men of good will and good intentions should restudy this controversial problem from more than one angle. It is highly essential to consider a number of basic questions: Has the principle of church-separation been honored in deed as well as in word? What is the significance of the many exceptions to the principle and do they establish or weaken the principle? Has the public school been indeed public in the sense that it has excluded religious teachings and practices, and has it been decidedly distinguishable from a religious school? Is church-state separation applicable to higher education or only to elementary-secondary education, to all religion or only to the nonsectarian and nondenominational variety? Why has there been such a concern for the "establishment of religion" clause of the First Amendment as against the neglect of the "free exercise" portion in educational matters? There also are other questions which are worthy of discussion.

In past years, much of what has been said and written about the church-state-school issue has been characterized by emotionalism and partisanship rather than by objectivity and restraint. The time has come for a new look at the problem on a foundation of fact. It is necessary to examine the historical record in detail—the laws, the court decisions, the individual and group statements, and the actual practices in the schools. The full historical context will provide the factual framework for a fair-minded appraisal of the controversial issue. It will reveal what was really in the minds of those who have had to deal with the question and thus will place the present-day problem in proper perspective. Some of the assumptions and hypotheses which govern current action may have to be seriously reassessed in the light of the cumulative evidence. Furthermore, it will be more possible for the church-state question to be regarded with reference to contemporary reality. Those whose minds are still open to the consideration of forgotten and new data will do well also to examine the theory and practice of church-state relations in education in other countries—democratic, communistic, or otherwise. The greater the variety of the data and the underlying ideas, the greater the likelihood of an objective evaluation of the controversial situation.

President Kennedy, in his press conference of March 8, 1961, used historical references to buttress his opposition to Federal aid to denominational schools. His statement about the establishment of a public school by the Massachusetts Bay Colony overlooked the religious content in these early "public" schools and the pious motives of their founders. Similarly, his reference to the Northwest Ordinance as a strengthening force in public education did not take into account the religious ideology expressed in this famous document. In point of actual fact, the historical examples cited by Mr. Kennedy lend support to a view which is at variance with the one he has taken.

To make a reasonable judgment on the church-state-school issue requires a considerable outlay of time, thought, and discussion. A quick solution is easy, but is not likely to be in accordance with the context of the question. Persons who are engaged in academic and professional pursuits owe it to themselves and to

the public whom they possibly influence to make
a many-sided study of what constitutes a rational relationship between church and state in education.

WILLIAM W. BRICKMAN

Contents

13

Appendix

14

ℛELIGION, GOVERNMENT, AND EDUCATION

ℰ1ℑ

Constitutional and Legal Aspects of the Church-State-School Problem

HAROLD H. PUNKE

THIS SUBJECT IS divided into three parts: cultural and legal framework, major court rulings, and future controversy.

Cultural and legal framework. To understand the safeguards for religious liberty in our legal structure, one must understand the cultural setting when the nation was founded—and subsequent trends. Two forms of tyranny, against which the founders especially sought protection, were arbitrary government practiced by royalty and sectarian religion dominated by a priesthood. The two were considered at their worst when joined to reinforce each other—a state church. Power of the state was then used to force acceptance and support of the established church, and religious practices were manipulated to develop awe and loyalty toward political rulers. King and bishop ruled through "divine right" and "state religion."

Safeguards against both political and religious tyranny seemed especially important to men who wanted a social system based on the personal liberties and potentialities of common people. This discussion is limited to relationships between state and church as they bear on public education. The basis for dealing with the issues concerned appears in the First and Fourteenth Amendments to the Constitution of the United States.[1]

Major court rulings. Cases seldom reach the Supreme Court of the United States before the remedies available through state and lower Federal courts have been exhausted. Since, in effect, "the Constitution of the United States means what the Supreme Court says it means," concerning religious issues in public education or other matters of Federal interest, rulings by this court become the law of the land.

The United States Supreme Court—The First Amendment embodies two concepts: prohibiting any law which would establish a religion provides for freedom from state compulsion as to religious belief; and prohibiting any law which forbids the free exercise of religion aims to guarantee freedom in practicing one's own belief. Cases involving public education, which have reached the Supreme Court, have concerned one or both prohibitions. Pertinent decisions are noted chronologically.

---

[1] The First Amendment, adopted in 1791, stipulates: "Congress shall make no law respecting an establishment of religion, or prohibiting the free exercise thereof. . . ." Pertinent aspects of the Fourteenth Amendment, adopted in 1868, stipulate: "No state shall make or enforce any law which shall abridge the privileges or immunities of citizens of the United States; nor shall any state deprive any person of life, liberty, or property, without due process of law; nor deny to any person within its jurisdiction the equal protection of the laws."

A case from Massachusetts in 1905 dealt with the compulsory vaccination against smallpox of all inhabitants in a community.[2] The decision upheld the right of a state to take compulsory measures to protect the health of persons who would not protect themselves, and to protect others who might contract disease from such persons. This included school children. A second case[3] focused on the physical and moral health of children, as related to participation with their parents in street-corner religious activities, and it pointed out that the authority and solicitude of the state for children was even greater than that for adults. The court stated that neither the family nor religious liberty was beyond regulation in the public interest. In *Zucht v. King*,[4] the nation's high court upheld a city ordinance which made vaccination a condition for attendance at public or private schools. However, in this case the opinion did not indicate whether objection to vaccination was on religious grounds.

In protecting religious liberty in 1925,[5] the court said that a state could not compel parents to send their children to a public school. A parent may send his child to a parochial school, provided it offers a type and quality of education equivalent to that of the public school in citizenship training and the usual branches of learning. Thus, the state may not deny religious instruction to a child, if parents choose a school

[2] *Jacobsen v. Massachusetts*, 197 U.S. 11, 25 S. Ct. 358, 49 L. Ed. 643, 3 Ann. Cas. 765.

[3] *Prince v. Massachusetts*, 321 U.S. 158, 64 S. Ct. 438, 88 L. Ed. 645 (1944).

[4] 260 U.S. 174, 43 S. Ct. 24, 67 L. Ed. 194.

[5] *Pierce v. Society of Sisters*, 268 U.S. 510, 45 S. 751, 39 A. L. R. 468.

which provides education in nonsectarian areas which the state considers essential.

In 1930, the court upheld[6] the use of tax funds in Louisiana to pay for school books distributed to children of parochial schools as well as those of public schools. The court accepted the reasoning of a state court that the books were for the benefit of the child and not of the school attended. The tax was for a public purpose. There was no taking of property by taxation for private use, such as would violate the "due process" clause of the Fourteenth Amendment.

The child-benefit theory indicated has been accepted to justify the use of public funds to transport children to parochial schools. A 5-4 decision in 1948 held[7] that a New Jersey statute which provided for such use of public funds did not constitute support of a church or establishment of religion, contrary to the First Amendment. The benefit and protection against highway accidents afforded by transportation accrued to parents and children, reasoned the court, not to the schools attended.

A case involving conflict between religious liberty and one manifestation of patriotism was adjudicated in 1943.[8] The court would not permit children to be expelled from a public school because of refusal to salute and pledge allegiance to the flag. The court reasoned that freedom of worship was among a small group of unusual and preferred freedoms which the state could restrict "only to prevent grave and

---

[6] *Cochran v. Louisiana State Board of Education*, 281 U.S. 370, 50 S. Ct. 335, 74 L. Ed. 913.

[7] *Everson v. Board of Education of Ewing Township*, 67 S. Ct. 500, 91 L. Ed. 711, 330 U.S. 1.

[8] *West Virginia State Board of Education v. Barnette*, 319 U.S. 624, 63 S. Ct. 1178, 147 A. L. R. 674.

immediate danger to interests which the state may lawfully protect." There are other means by which patriotism and loyalty can be as effectively shown. Hence, there was no basis for compelling flag-salutes as a means. In so ruling, the court reversed its decision of three years earlier.[9]

The Supreme Court has rendered two decisions on the "release time" method of giving sectarian instruction to public school pupils. Neither decision was unanimous. In the *McCollum Case*,[10] the instruction was given by clergymen in public school classrooms; the clergymen were approved by the superintendent of schools; pupils who were released from their regular classes were required to attend the religious classes; and pupils who did not attend religious classes were required to leave their usual classrooms and continue secular studies in other rooms. The practice constituted a use of tax-supported property for religious instruction and a use of state compulsory attendance machinery to supply pupils for religious classes. This violated the First Amendment, said the court. In the *Zorach Case*,[11] instruction was given at religious centers, attendance and costs were responsibilities of religious organizations, and pupils who were not released continued in their regular classrooms. The *Zorach Case* differed from the *McCollum Case* mainly in that the religious instruction was not given on public property or with any direct public cost. The

---

[9] *Minersville School District v. Gobitis*, 310 U.S. 586, 60 S. Ct. 1010 (1940).

[10] *Illinois* ex rel. *McCollum v. Board of Education of School District No. 71*, 333 U.S. 203, 68 S. Ct. 461, 92 L. Ed. 648 (1948).

[11] *Zorach v. Clauson*, 343 U.S. 306, 72 S. Ct. 679 96 L. Ed. 954 (1952).

use of compulsory attendance machinery to supply pupils for religious instruction was not resolved, as dissenting judges emphasized.

"Released time" should not be confused with "dismissed time." Under the latter, pupils might attend religious classes, or they might attend movies, work, go fishing, or satisfy other non-school needs and desires. There probably would be no question about the constitutionality of "dismissed time."

Lower courts—Several states make constitutional and legislative provisions concerning religious liberty, or separation of church and state, which vary somewhat from Federal provisions. Moreover, many disputes on public school practices concerning religion never reach the Supreme Court of the United States. Since the regulations and interpretations involved in such disputes vary from one jurisdiction to another, there is uncertainty on what the Supreme Court might allow if ever the disputes reach it. Because of the variation and number of cases involved, the present discussion does not examine these cases individually.

However, it is noted that such cases have related to Bible reading,[12] rental of church property for public school purposes,[13] use of school property for religious meetings, wearing of religious garb by teachers in classrooms, distribution of religious literature through pub-

---

[12] In the New Jersey case of *Doremus v. Board of Education*, 342 U.S. 429 72 S. Ct. 394, 96 L. Ed. 475 (1952), the pupil who was the basis of objection graduated before the appeal reached the Supreme Court of the United States, and the court held that taxpayer status alone was insufficient to sustain the suit.

[13] See Harold H. Punke, "The Courts and Public School Property" (Chicago: University of Chicago Press, 1936), p. 92.

lic schools,[14] holding graduation exercises in churches, sale of school property to a church at a reduced price, compulsory school attendance and religious holidays,[15] teachings which are contrary to the Bible (*e.g.*, biological evolution), social dancing as part of the school program,[16] materials in public school libraries to which religious groups object, retirement credit for teaching in parochial schools, and the right of a church to operate a Sunday school bus without paying the state vehicle license tax.[17]

Recent cases before lower courts—Eight recent cases are noted which have not produced much comment in educational literature. In some of these, there is only slight variation from established legal principles.

Four cases deal with transporting pupils who do not attend public schools. The constitution of Kentucky forbids the use, for any sectarian school, of funds raised by taxes for educational purposes. In 1942,[18] this provision was held to prohibit the use of public school funds for transporting pupils to parochial schools. By the time the *Rawlings Case*[19] was decided in 1956, legal

---

[14] *Tudor v. Board of Education*, 14 N. J. 31, 100 A. 2d. 857, 45 A. L. R. 2d. 729 (1953), reviews the history of the doctrine of separation of church and state. This case held that the distribution of Gideon Bibles in public schools showed preference for Protestantism over Judaism and Catholicism.

[15] *Ferriter v. Tyler*, 48 Vt. 444, 21 Am. Rep. 133 (1876).

[16] *Hardwick v. Board of School Trustees*, 54 Calif. App. 696, 205 p. 49 (1921).

[17] Cases on issues which are not separately footnoted were reviewed by the author in "Community Uses of Public School Facilities" (New York: King's Crown Press, 1951), pp. 35-89; also in "Religious Issues in American Public Education," *Law and Contemporary Problems*, 20: 138-168, Winter, 1955.

[18] *Sherrod v. Jefferson County Board of Education*, 294 Ky. 469, 171 S.W. 2d. 963.

[19] *Rawling v. Butler*, 290 S.W. 2d. 801.

arrangements existed which permitted the circuit court to pay for transporting pupils to parochial schools. The circuit court did not use public school funds, as the school board did when it furnished transportation. However, the real dispute in the *Rawlings Case* related to the proportion to be paid by the board of education, when some children who rode the school buses attended public schools and some attended parochial schools. In deciding the issue, the Kentucky Court of Appeals reasoned that costs in school operations usually were computed on a per-pupil basis and that the same principle should apply to paying transportation costs. Thus, if half of all pupils transported were pupils attending parochial schools, the circuit court should pay half of all transportation costs. In 1960, the formula for apportioning costs was challenged on behalf of parochial schools.[20] The court recognized that there were many cost factors, with some items being really estimates, and upheld the per-pupil basis as the most equitable way of apportioning costs.

The city council of Augusta, Me., attempted by ordinance to provide for transporting pupils to parochial schools at public expense.[21] It was defended as an exercise of police power—to conserve the health, safety, and welfare of the children. In examining the state constitution and legislative provisions on education, the court found no intention to enable a city to regulate any aspect of general education without a specific delegation of power by the legislature. There had been no such delegation, and the

---

[20] *Board of Education of Jefferson County v. Jefferson County,* 333 S.W. 2d. 746.

[21] *Squires v. City of Augusta,* 155 Me. 151, 153 A. 2d. 80 (1959).

council had no authority to pass the ordinance. The city could not do anything, under police power, unless it was provided for by constitution, statute, or city charter.[22]

Temporary use of school buildings for religious meetings during Sunday, non-school hours, while church buildings were being completed was the basis of a Florida dispute.[23] A statute authorized the use of school buildings during non-school hours "for any legal assembly." No direct expense to the district was alleged or shown. However, the constitutionality of the statute and practice was challenged. The court regarded the meetings to be "legal assemblies" and held that wear on the buildings was too small and indirect a cost to be considered a violation of constitutional provisions against using public funds to aid a church.

Divergent rulings appear in two Bible-reading cases. A Tennessee statute[24] required the teacher "to read, or cause to be read, at the opening of the school every day, a selection from the Bible." Controversy related to such reading, repeating the Lord's Prayer, and singing religious hymns. "Religious freedom" provisions

---

[22] In *Robinson Township School District v. Houghton*, 387 Pa. 236, 128 A. 2d. 58 (1956), a declaratory judgment was sought on whether the board has discretionary power to transport in public school buses, to the site of a public school, pupils who attend non-public schools. The court followed *Connell v. Kennett Township Board of School Directors*, 356 Pa. 585, 52 A. 2d. 180 (1947); appeal dismissed, 332 U.S. 748, 68 S. Ct. 26, 92 L. Ed. 335, holding that the board had no authority to transport pupils who do not attend a public school. (These cases are dealt with in an article on "Recent Court Rulings on Pupil Transportation.")

[23] *Southeast Estates Baptist Church v. Board of Trustees*, School Tax District No. 1, 115 So. 2d. 697 (1959).

[24] *Carden v. Bland*, 199 Tenn. 665, 288 S.W. 2d. 718 (1956).

25

of the state constitution were essentially the same as those of the First Amendment. The practice did not establish a religion or interfere with any student's secular beliefs. The court added, "We think that the highest duty of those who are charged with the responsibility of training the young people of this state in the public schools is in teaching both by precept and example that in the conflicts of life they should not forget God."

Unitarians in Abington, Pa.,[25] objected to religious exercises in high schools under a statute which requires a teacher to read 10 verses of the Bible, without comment, at opening exercises each day. If a teacher fails or refuses to perform this duty, continues the statute, he "shall" be discharged—on the basis of preferred and proven charges. Reciting the Lord's Prayer was sometimes involved. The court regarded the Bible to be a religious book, addressed to recognition of God. To characterize it as a work of art, literature, or history, without admitting its basically religious nature, said the court, is unrealistic. The court added that daily reading, backed by statute and teacher authority, "can hardly do less than inculcate . . . various religious doctrines in childish minds." The practice thus amounts to religious education. And since the Bible is a Christian document, the practice favors the Christian religion. To assume that reading without comment enables each pupil to make his own interpretation, continued the court, "either ignores the essentially religious nature of the Bible, or assumes that its religious quality can be disregarded by the listener. . . .

[25] *Schempp v. School District of Abington Township,* 177 F. Supp. 398 (1959).

Children cannot be expected to sift out the religious from the moral, historical, or literary content." Adult theologians engage in much dispute in trying to do so. The fact that few pupils objected, added the court, "may itself attest to the success and the subtlety of the compulsion." The statute and practice violate the First Amendment.

"Release time" was held to be compulsory if parents requested it, under an Oregon statute[26] which provided that upon a parent's application a child "may be excused" from the public school for a certain amount of time "to attend week-day schools giving instruction in religion." The statute was not void because it failed to provide for administering the program, particularly as to who grants a parent's request, or because it failed to provide a penalty for violation. Penalty might be indicated in another statute, noted the court. The ruling stipulated that "may" is to be read as "shall," with the parent having the discretion to request release, but the board having no prerogative to reject a request.

An interesting aspect of compulsory vaccination appeared in New Jersey.[27] The statute said a board "may" require immunization as a prerequisite to attending school. The board had followed a policy of excluding non-vaccinated children. The objection that the practice violated religious freedom was answered by pointing to cases cited earlier.[28]

An unusual question which arose is whether a Christian Science woman who had custody for

[26] *Dilger v. School District 24*, 352 P. 2d. 564 (1960).
[27] *Mountain Lakes Board of Education v. Maas*, 56 N. J. Super. 245, 152 A. 2d. 394 (1959).
[28] See footnotes 1-3.

12 months of three Greek orphans who had been reared in the Greek Orthodox faith could challenge the constitutionality of a statute on the ground of religious liberty—when it was her religion rather than that of the children which took offense at the practice concerned. Since constitutionality could not be attacked because of alleged interference with the rights of others, reasoned the court, there was question as to the right of Maas as a temporary foster mother to bring action. The court said that she had the right to bring up the children in their own religion, during their sojourn, not in her religion.

Future controversy. Mr. Justice Roberts stated in 1940 that the First Amendment embraces freedom to believe and freedom to act.[29] He added, "The first is absolute but, in the nature of things, the second cannot be. Conduct remains subject to regulation for the protection of society." However, conduct has been restricted only where society would suffer pronouncedly from unrestrained freedom of action. But changes in social conditions, and perhaps in court membership, bring new rulings—and reexamination of old ones. Through exploring a minor point, the court may essentially reverse an earlier decision. This may leave administrators and students of the law confused, as regarding the McCollum and Zorach decisions, and awaiting further clarification. The situation may foster religious liberty, but it reduces predictability as to what public schools may do.

Several issues concerning religion and public education have not yet reached the U.S. Supreme Court. Some of these were noted as hav-

---

[29] *Cantwell v. Connecticut,* 310 U.S. 296, 60 S. Ct. 900, 128 A. L. R. 1352, 84 L. Ed. 1213.

ing come before minor courts. Others may not appear for some time as topics of litigation. Thus, the court may be asked to define more clearly what religion is or the status of non-preferential aid in relation to a wall of separation between church and state. The religious status of certain holidays in public education, such as Christmas, Easter, or Thanksgiving, may be challenged concerning the religious liberty of non-Christian groups. As tax burdens for educational and other purposes increase, and as holdings of church property increase, there may be further urging for authority to tax church property—or certain kinds of church property. The right to teach birth control, as a part of high-school or junior colleges programs, may arouse controversy in the future. There are many other possibilities.

The status to sue may assume importance. In the *Doremus Case*,[30] the court held that taxpayer status alone was insufficient to maintain a suit which challenged Bible reading in a public school. Much may depend on the way in which the court defines what constitutes adequate standing to sue. More important, however, is the probably large number of violations of the First Amendment which never are brought to court—because offended persons are ignorant of their constitutional rights, do not have resources to carry on litigation, or fear social ostracism and perhaps injury to their persons or property if they challenge the action of powerful groups.

Will there always be controversy between church and state in American education? "Always" implies a long time. Legal controversy is

---

[30] See footnote 12. See also the *Maas Case*, footnote 27.

significant only in a society which respects both parties to an issue. Under political totalitarianism, church organization is weak. Under religious totalitarianism, the state is weak. In the United States, religion is one phase of personal and social philosophy. Other phases relate to education, health, vocation, money and investment, etc. During the past several decades, some of these other phases have become more prominent relative to religion. In a dynamic society which allows extensive individual freedom, many areas of philosophy and human values are developing and are vigorous. To assume that there will be no conflict between such individual areas and society's general regulatory agency called "government" seems unjustified. So, if the state is vigorous and developing, and also the lesser area of philosophy and values called "religion," one should expect future conflict between them. Conflict will relate to public education as well as to other functions of government.

〔2〕

Public Aid
to Religious Education

V. T. THAYER

ADVOCATES OF PUB-
lic aid to religious education have two main objectives in mind: financial assistance on the part
of the state to church-related schools and public
sanction and support of religious instruction in
public schools. Since both proposals are forbidden at present by the courts under the First
Amendment to the Federal Constitution, a consideration of these demands involves both history and the wisdom of this policy under conditions of today.

Prior to the adoption of the First Amendment
to the Federal Constitution in 1791, with its
prohibition of an establishment of religion, nine
of the original 13 states had incorporated restric-
tions in their constitutions. Four only continued
to permit multiple establishment or public assistance to religion on a "non-preferential basis."
Between 1791 and 1833, these four remaining
states likewise joined their sister states and the
Federal government in a policy of complete disestablishment.

31

This action, however, antedated general provision for public schools open and free to all under state auspices. To Connecticut in 1818 must be accorded credit (or blame?) for establishing the principle that state funds for education "shall be inviolably appropriated to the support and encouragement of the public, or common schools, throughout the State . . . and no law shall be made, authorizing said fund to be diverted to any other use than the encouragement and support of public or common schools." Other states were quick to follow Connecticut's example, with the result that, by the end of the 19th century, only two states had failed to prohibit by constitutional provision or legislative act either the use of public funds for religious schools or the teaching of sectarian doctrines in the public schools, or both. It remained for the U.S. Supreme Court in 1947, under the Fourteenth Amendment, to extend these prohibitions to state and Federal government alike in these words: "No tax in any amount, large or small, can be levied to support any religious activities or institutions, whatever they may be called, or whatever form they may adopt to teach or practice religion."[1]

This policy of "separation of church and state" as applied to education has had impressive results. Schooling that began in the colonial period as essentially a private concern and in-

---

[1] *Everson v. Board of Education of Ewing*, 330 U.S. 1 (1947). Reaffirmed in *McCollum v. Board of Education*, 333 U.S. 203 (1948). Many believe the Court modified its position significantly in *Zorach v. Clauson*, 343 U.S. 306 (1952) by sanctioning religious education of children during school hours when conducted off the school premises in this decision, however, the Court emphasized, "Government may not finance religious groups, nor undertake religious instruction nor blend secular and sectarian education to force one or some religion on any person."

tended for the few has become a public enterprise available to all young people without regard to financial circumstance or class status. To public education and its success in raising the general level of educated intelligence must be credited in large measure the phenomenal development of the material resources and the material well-being of the American people. But equally important, public education has created one people out of many diverse elements—religious, social, economic, national, even racial. This it has done by translating into educational practice a principle without which a society at once pluralistic in composition and democratic in aspiration cannot long endure. The writer refers to the principle of mutual accommodation of differences, the assumption that the absolutes which one cherishes for himself and uses to direct his own life are to be viewed as relative and suggestive only when applied to his neighbor; that in the confrontation of values and areas of controversy and conflict, the mission of the public school is to further understanding and a mutual respect for differences rather than to indoctrinate or to impose uniformity of belief and practice.

It is this principle, as public policy, that permits private groups to set up schools of their own choosing, provided they meet minimum standards as defined by the state. And private schools have not suffered from the dominance of public education. The absence of public support has meant both freedom from restrictive supervision and the opportunity for schools of a religious orientation to exercise the utmost freedom and for independent schools to experiment with unconventional methods and materials.

At no time, however, has the principle of separation of church and state in its applications to education been altogether acceptable to private groups. Despite Justice Frankfurter's assertion in *McCollum v. Board of Education* that it represents "the whole experience of our people," it is challenged today both as a valid interpretation of the Constitution and as wise public policy.

Since, in the judgment of responsible historians, neither the actions of the First Congress on the various proposed phrasings of the establishment clause, prior to its final passage, nor the status of establishments of religion within the states which participated in the adoption of the First Amendment give substance to the charge that the Supreme Court, in its present interpretation of separation, runs counter to history, the discussion here shall concentrate on the wisdom of this policy in today's world.

Opposition to the principle which denies public assistance to non-public schools may be summarized as follows: It is ethically wrong for the reason that the Constitution, as interpreted by the courts,[2] guarantees to each parent the right to decide whether to educate his child in a public or a private school. Therefore, to deny any child, whose parents may wish to educate him in a private school, a proportionate share in funds raised by general taxation in support of education is to violate "distributive justice." Moreover, to require a parent who thus exercises his "inalienable right" of choice to support both public and private education (and, there-

---

[2] See *Pierce vs. Society of Sisters*, 268 U.S. 510 (1925). Also for the Court's emphasis upon parental rights, *West Virginia State Board of Education v. Barnette*, 319 U.S. 624 (1943).

fore, to submit to "double taxation") is, in effect, to impose a handicap upon both child and parent—upon the child, in the quality of education he may receive, and upon the parent, in the exercise of religious liberty. Consequently, both freedom and justice dictate that public funds designed for education be used in a nondiscriminatory manner.

Considerations of wisdom and justice may lead, however, to a different conclusion. How wise, it may be asked, is it to reverse a policy under which so large a proportion of our people have come to enjoy the advantages of an education? Today, for example, public elementary and secondary schools enroll approximately 83% of all young people between the ages of five and 17; parochial and private schools, about 12.6%[3]; and colleges, according to recent estimates of the Department of Health, Education, and Welfare, 37.1% of the age group 18-21, inclusive.

To be sure, it is keenly recognized today that in educating the masses, quality frequently has been sacrificed to quantity. But this recognition is in response to unique and urgent requirements of the present: profound transformations in economic, social, and political relationships at home and competition with totalitarianism abroad. Changes point to the necessity of trained intelligence not only of the few but of the many in order to insure the well-being and security, if not the survival, of all. Should Americans at this most critical period in their history reverse the traditional policy of exclusive support of public schools in favor of one certain to sap their vitality and lower standards of achievement? For sap the vitality of public education it

---

[3] *Research Report*, 1959-R, National Education Association, Washington, D. C., 1959, pp. 11-12.

surely will if state and national governments undertake to divert public funds from public education to private schools.[4]

Holland frequently is cited as an example to follow in this respect, since in Holland all types of schools are assisted by the government. With what results? About 28% of all children of elementary age attend public schools; 41%, Catholic schools; 27%, Protestant schools; and one per cent, "other schools."[5]

Before we decide to follow in the footsteps of Holland, we would do well to examine the validity of the contention that a parent's right to substitute private for public education carries with it an obligation on the part of the state to finance this decision. What precedent is there in public administration for this policy? Does the state, for example, which taxes all the people in order to provide police protection for its citizens, remit the taxes of individuals who prefer to provide their own armed guards? Similarly with other fields (health, sanitation, public welfare, etc.)—indeed, in any and all areas in which the public interest clearly establishes the need for services publicly administered—are not individuals who elect to substitute private services required to bear the cost of this decision?

It is not even accurate to describe individuals who thus subject themselves to additional expense as victims of "double taxation." The costs

[4] Both religious and independent schools are mentioned, since the "right" of a parent to send his child to a non-public school applies to parents of both types of schools. If one is entitled to state subsidy, obviously the other one is, too.

[5] Quoted by Robert Gordis in "Religion and the Schools" (New York: Fund for the Republic, 1959), p. 22.

incurred are assumed voluntarily. Taxes are involuntary assessments imposed by government in order to meet needs or to insure benefits essential to all. Accordingly, in the case of education, the childless as well as those "blessed" with children are taxed alike, as are those who decide to send their children to a public school and those who do not so decide. To permit the remission of taxes to all who prefer private to public services would commit the state to a principle suicidal in its effects not only upon public education, but upon every service administered by the public at public expense.

But it is said that parents who send their children to a religiously oriented school fall within a special category and merit special consideration if the guaranteed right to religious liberty is to become a reality. This calls for a word regarding the nature of the right thus exercised.

It is not uncommon for the Catholic clergy to require Catholic parents to send their children to Catholic schools. This suggests that what is termed the parent's "inalienable right" to send his child to a parochial school is, for many, more accurately described as conformity to church discipline—as submission to an ecclesiastical injunction which the state is being asked to subsidize. Legitimate as it may be for a church to impose this discipline upon its members and for the latter to submit, it does not follow that failure of government to underwrite the conditions of such a discipline's realization constitutes a denial of an "inalienable right" or an infringment upon religious liberty.

Nowhere is clarity and consistency in the use of terms more essential than in determining the proper role of religion in public education. Take, for example, the insistence of one group of religious liberals that religion be conceived in functional rather than structural terms, as a "dedication of the entire self to the pursuit of values" in contrast with adherence to a specific creed. Surely, few would exclude the pursuit of values as such from public education! Still others define religion as "whole-hearted devotion" to values as general as the ethical principles of democracy, the concept of the brotherhood of man, and the virtues and values common to all men which tend to raise the standards of man's relation to man. Again, it is doubtful that public funds would be denied a public school which sought to promote no more than this in the way of religious faith.

On the other hand, were we to insist, with the Supreme Court in *Reynolds v. United States*, that the term *religion* "has reference to one's views of his relation to the Creator and to the obligation they impose of reverence of His being and character and of obedience to His will," we should have to insist that religion cannot properly be *taught* in public schools without violating both the Constitution and sound educational procedure. Unless, indeed, by the terms *teach* and *taught* we have in mind a process different from that of many who urge the teaching of religion in public schools; for these, in common with the average layman, equate teaching with instilling in the minds of learners ideas and conclusions of a specific character. The educator, in contrast, in areas of controversy and divided loyalties, carefully avoids weighting instruction in favor of one conclusion as against another, centering instead upon developing the discipline of free and objective inquiry. It is this difference in the concept of teaching that prompted the American Council on Education, in its report on "The Function of the Public Schools in Dealing with Religion" (1953), to advocate the "factual study of religion" in the schools rather than "the teaching of religion." It is this distinction also which prompts F. Ernest Johnson to remark that "the role of the American public school would seem to be limited to making known and understood the role which religion, as empirical fact, plays in the culture itself and in human history. To expect less of our schools is to take too narrow a view of general education; to demand more is to confuse the function of the school with that of home or church."[6]

As is so often the case, however, the role of religion in public education, as Johnson conceives it, is more easily stated than realized in practice. Were classroom instruction to deal justly with all faiths, the study of religion would include not merely the views of the orthodox faiths, but the religious convictions of dissident faiths as well; not exclusively the factors which have impelled men toward religion, but, in addition, influences that have induced others equally sincere to seek the solution to life's problems in unconventional formulae; not alone the beneficial effects of religion in the past upon men's actions, but also influences which prompted John Adams to exclaim in a letter to Thomas Jefferson, "Twenty times in the course of my late reading, have I been on the point of breaking out, 'This would be the best of all possible worlds, if there were no religion in it.'"

It is obvious that not many schools would receive community support for the study of re-

---

[6] In "Religion and the Schools," *ibid.*, p. 66.

ligion under these broad and generous conditions. Consequently, until a school, its faculty, and its sustaining community have reached the point where religion can receive genuinely objective consideration, we should view proposals for "the factual study of religion" with extreme caution.

Doubtless, the assumption that moral values require the underwriting of a religious faith prompts many to favor the introduction of religion into the curriculum of the public school. Add to this the conviction that schools at present are ineffective in educating for character and combating juvenile delinquency and we can appreciate the urgency with which reform is viewed. Witness, for example, the growing demand that "God be given a place in the curriculum"!

But this also highlights the importance of distinguishing between different levels or categories of moral injunctions; between those which have their origin in and derive authority from a parochial religious faith and those which are more expressive of the culture and the common consent of mankind. In so far as the school concerns itself with the former, it should do so with an eye to furthering information and understanding rather than commitment; whereas, with respect to the latter (principles such as the Golden Rule, the common virtues of honesty, reliability, self-control, and the like), public education cannot be neutral. The individual family and church group will wish, quite naturally, to root these virtues and values in a religious faith, but the public school, as an agency of the public, will stress their public character as the common property of all, together with the fact that they can be validated in terms of their consequences

—that is, by reference to the manner in which they ease and free and enrich relations between people.

The writer concludes that neither in the form of financial assistance to church-related schools nor in the support of religious instruction in public schools should public aid be given to religious education.

Religion and Public Education

ROLFE LANIER HUNT

FOUR KINDS OF questions are met in consideration of "Religion and Public Education." For persons committed to religion, the first is the most significant.

1. Can religious people join in support and patronage of schools not under control of the church? Does a theological position require separate schools under control of the church authorities?

Mortal man is destined for immortality, according to much religious belief. The soul's eternal destiny is important, and life in this world is significant primarily in terms of its preparation for eternal life. Children are in the care of parents, whose religious duty it is to prepare these children for life eternal.

Wherever any religious faith is in a small minority, it tends to find protection against the cultural impact of the total community by separation of its children. The theological question usually is met in a matrix of language and cultural differences, so that those inaugurating a separate religious school are often interested in maintaining a language and a national culture as well as a religious faith. To the extent that one believes that his is the only way of salvation, one is under compulsion to protect his child against error by separating him in a school in which the pure faith is taught. Every parent of religious faith will ask of the school his child attends that religious faith be left a live option for the child. He will wish the school to do nothing to offend the faith the child brings from his home and his church and that the school support rather than oppose the child's right to believe. These things are asked by humanists as well as by theists.

2. The second question is that of educational philosophy or method. How can our religious needs best be served—by a separate or a common school?

In American educational thought, there has been a strong emphasis on "the whole child." Religious leaders who accept this idea in *toto* argue that the child cannot be fragmented, that his education in religion must be part of his education in other aspects of life. Questions concerning religion come up naturally in life experience, in classrooms and playgrounds as well as at home and on the streets. Every school is thus a "religious" school, for in the school the pupil seeks answers to questions such as: "Why am I here?" "Who am I?" "What is the meaning of life?" These are questions of religion.

Appreciation for this philosophic position, when combined with belief that his is the only way of salvation, pushes one into support of separate religious schools. Yet, appreciation of this position may be combined with another theological position to argue for support of a common school. By this position, finite man never can understand the infinite God. Monopoly of education may be dangerous. He is more likely to find knowledge of the will of God by exchanging his insights with those of others than he is by isolating himself with others who see things just as he does. Within the Christian tradition, it is argued that Jesus prayed that his disciples might go into the world rather than to withdraw from it, that his followers might be a leaven in a mission to the whole world.

Thus far, we have considered only religious beliefs. Facts may have small relevance to the decision on the questions, "Shall we send our child to a common school or have a separate religious school?" "Is our religious need best served by a common or a separate school?" Indeed, few facts are available.

No objective data are available to answer a question such as, "What are the differences between products of public schools and parochial schools?" No one can say surely what the effects are when instruction in religion is given in one location, instruction in tool skills in another, and instruction in civic and vocational competence in another—or all together. We do not safely attribute to any known type of school guaranteed results in knowledge, attitudes, and character. In the light of present knowledge, those who argue that religion is valid only in so far as it is voluntary, the free choice of the individual, have free choice in the kind of school their children may attend.

But some co-ordination of efforts of the several teaching agencies to which the child is exposed becomes, for the religious parent, a necessity if responsibility for tool skills is primarily assigned to a public school, while home and church retain primary responsibility for teaching religious faith.

3. How should the common school, tax supported, serve parents of different religious faiths? How shall public schools deal with religion?

Political theory in the U.S. says that governments exist to serve the people and that the people may alter or abolish the forms of government. The public schools in the U.S., therefore, is not simply a tool of the political state, to serve its ends as an institution. The public school is, rather, the creature of the people who use the political machinery of the state to achieve their goals as persons. This wider context is significant in consideration of problems of how public schools shall deal with religion. Institutional church-state relations are part of the problem, but not all of it, as is suggested by the difference between saying "separation of church and state" and "separation of religion and education." Many persons see a substantial difference in the two phrases. The public school is the community or society in action as much as the "state," a sociologist may insist, though it cannot be overlooked that in politics they are the same. The legislature is the people, in current political science, even though signers of the Declaration of Independence said otherwise. Visitors from abroad often find our distinction difficult; it is absent in the culture from which they come.

Our tradition of separation of church and state is best understood in historic context. Refugees from religious wars helped settle these colonies. In the European tradition from which they came, the ruler's choice of faith became the established religion of subjects in his domain. The variety of religious faiths in the different colonies made political compromise useful; the new Federal government was to respect the right of the colonies to set their own policies. Proponents of religious freedom persuaded our people that such freedom was good for religion as well as good for government.

The First Amendment to the Constitution of the United States was written long before the major development of public school systems, and those who wrote it had no public school systems in mind. No wonder, then, there is disagreement among lawyers and courts when the Constitution's brief clauses are asked to bear the weight of interpretation as to whether Bibles should be read in public schools or tax funds pay for bus transportation of children to parochial schools. The gasoline engine had not even been invented when the constitutional amendment was adopted. Rather than looking altogether to the past, it is perhaps more appropriate to consider the present and the future as we consider such questions. By what policies shall we best secure a happy future for our children?

The public school which seeks to serve patrons and children from differing religious faiths has many practical problems, such as: Can a common core of religious faith be taught? What, if any, religious rituals shall be observed? What shall be taught about religious institutions and beliefs, the role of religion in history and present culture, when intrinsic to the regular school subjects, such as history, literature, music? How shall instruction in patriotic, moral, ethical, and character values be related to their ultimate sanctions in religious faiths?

Again, few facts are available on which to

base decisions. The common practice of reading the Bible may serve as an example. Nobody knows whether information is gained and what if any attitudes are changed. No objective data are available by which this practice may be compared with results in another school district in which such Bible reading is forbidden. If the public school is to serve religious people as an institution for general education, it has some responsibilities in this field which must be defined. Discussion has been inhibited by respect for freedom of religious belief. A man certainly has the right of privacy in his religious belief. Whenever any religious belief affects the policy of a public institution and the expenditure of tax funds, however, that religious belief has lost its private character and its effects must be debated in the market place and the political arena. When the questions are brought to the top of the table rather than pushed under the table, then the light of reason and experience can be brought to bear on such questions. There seems to be increasing realization of this, and the possibilities of rational discussion are improving, in the experience of this writer.

4. Shall tax moneys be used to support schools operated by churches?

Children meet requirements for compulsory education in the tool skills in schools operated by churches. Graduates of parochial schools vote alongside their fellow citizens in the community and fight alongside public school graduates in our armies. The parent who chooses a religious school in which his pure faith may be taught asks, "Why not tax support for this school?" The question becomes more pressing as the costs of education rise. This is now the billion-dollars-a-year question: "May religious schools be supported by tax funds?"

There is difficulty in answering the question because schools operated by churches serve both purposes of church and of state. Facts are not available to prove the statement, but it is commonly said that tool skills are as well taught in one school as in the other. Again without objective data, this writer believes that civic and vocational and patriotic purposes often are as well served in parochial and private schools as in public schools.

The writer believes that some parochial schools may give good service to purposes of the church. This cannot be proved either. It is said, for example, that church school students find their place in the church, but it can be argued also that children from homes willing to pay extra for religious training would find their ways into the church anyway. Objective data on the effectiveness of the church-operated school in achieving church purposes are as scanty as are those on which its efficiency in serving the purposes of the state may be evaluated.

We can only say that those who establish religious schools seem to do so less often to improve instruction and equal opportunity in the U.S. than they do to teach religious faith. A historian reports of three schools in Chicago, for example:[*]

[St. Philip's High School] aims to develop Catholic young men, prepared intellectually, morally and physically "to take their place in life as militant Catholics,

---

* "The History of Catholic Secondary Education in the Archdiocese of Chicago," Ph.D. Dissertation, by Sister Mary Innocenta Montay, C.S.F., of the Felician Sisters, Chicago, Ill. (Washington, D. C.: Catholic University of America Press, 1953).

who, conscious of their obligations to God, to their neighbor, and to themselves, work out their salvation, and help their neighbors to do likewise" (p. 155).

Fenwick boys learn to be not only good Catholics, but good American citizens. . . . The primary objective [of the Fenwick High School] is to train Catholic boys of high school age and ability in accordance with established Catholic principles of education in conformity with the Encyclical of Christian Education of Youth. . . . It aims . . . to offer a complete program of moral, intellectual, and physical training designed to perfect the student in nature and grace (pp. 172-173).

All activities of the [St. Michael High] school [for girls] are motivated by the sodality of the Blessed Virgin Mary, affiliated with Prima Primaria and active in Cisca endeavors. The entire student body attends Holy Mass and receives Holy Communion in a group on First Fridays. . . . St. Michael Central High School aims, in conformity with the Church's principles of Christian education and training, "to develop intelligent, cultured, spiritually vigorous, socially adaptable, vocationally prepared patriotic Catholic young men and women" (pp. 211-212).

The Corpus Christi High School of Chicago, established in 1945 exclusively for Negroes in Chicago, has about 10% of the students who are non-Catholic who may attend on condition that "their parents take instructions and attend Mass on Sundays" (p. 252).

The High School of St. Elizabeth Parish on the Southside of Chicago serves also Negro Catholics and non-Catholics, and parents of the 20% who are non-Catholic "are required to take instruction and to attend Sunday Mass as conditions for attendance."

St. Elizabeth's does its greatest work through religious instruction which aims to prepare the students for Christian leadership. Because many Catholic students come from non-Catholic neighborhoods, they are especially prepared to meet objections, though often sincere, to the Catholic faith (p. 264).

Since such schools serve both purposes of the state and of the church, three solutions seem obvious: the state should pay for all instruction because purposes of the state are fulfilled; the church should pay for all instruction because purposes of the church are fulfilled; the costs should be divided, with the state paying for the costs of instruction in general education and the church paying costs of religious instruction.

The first position is taken by the majority of parents in schools operated by churches, Roman Catholic in this country more often than any other. The second position is traditional in this country, presumably a result of a once substantially Protestant community. The current difficulty of assessing the third may be exemplified by the biology textbook offered for use in parochial schools and examined by this writer. "Angel life" is listed as one of the major classifications of life, with an angelic illustration. Facts are greatly needed for a division of costs to be fairly assessed, if this position is to be given the consideration it deserves. Those who argue for this position do so against the weight of the long tradition that no man in this country should be taxed for support of instruction of a religious faith not his own.

"Shared time" offers one way out. It may be described as a "part-time parochial school," with children attending for stated hours a public school for instruction in general education at tax expense and for other hours attending classes operated and paid for by the churches. Some proponents of this plan say the churches might well teach portions of history and literature, as well as church doctrine and belief, to make half-time for the child in each kind of school. Others figure that an hour a day would take care of needs for religious instruction. Still others suggest that children might attend a common school together for three or six years, then spread into sectarian schools for three months or a year of religious instruction, and then go back into a common school for vocational instruction or college preparation. The experience together would contribute to the face-to-face acquaintance useful to the unity of the country, while the recognition given by this arrangement to religious faith would be good preparation for adult life in religiously pluralistic American society. These adaptations of "released time," maintaining the principle of parental responsibility and control of the education of the child, deserve thoughtful study. They maintain our tradition that no person should be compelled to pay taxes for indoctrination of religious belief. If agreement on principle is reached, ways can be found to handle problems of physical facilities, curriculum, and teaching personnel.

Still another solution is offered by the proposal that tax funds underwrite scholarships by which the child might attend the school of his choice. Precedents are cited from G.I. benefits and welfare fields. Schools operated by the churches would thereby be supported, without necessity for direct payments to the institutions.

What will happen if tax funds support schools operated directly by grants or indirectly by scholarship plans at elementary and secondary levels? Facts are lacking, and prophecy may run wild. For what it may be worth to start the thinking of the reader, here are a few predictions:

1. If tax funds are made available, the dynamics of local churches soon will cause Protestants to have more schools than Catholics. Many substantial educational plants already are available.

2. If the interest of larger numbers of lead-ing citizens are drawn off, public schools will decline in numbers, status, and efficiency.

3. Opportunities for employment of teachers will be limited to their respective parochial school systems. Remaining public schools will tend to be more anti-church, anti-religious.

4. The several sectarian parochial school sys-tems will select their most devoted and articu-late members to teach, setting them in a situa-tion where they must justify the existence of their respective institutions, placing tax funds in support of teaching the increasingly divisive sectarian differences.

5. Fragmentation of the student body will make for less efficient instruction, less equal edu-cational opportunity.

6. If we choose that road, and go down it 100 years, the time will come when we will look back to the "good old days," when we had only two school systems based on race. Religious dif-ferences run deeper than those of race in the history of mankind.

₡4₃

Public Service of the Lutheran School

WM. A. KRAMER

CONGREGATIONS of The Lutheran Church-Missouri Synod in the United States maintain nearly 1,300 elementary schools with an enrollment of 150,000 and about 20 high schools with an enrollment approaching 10,000. Other Lutheran groups enroll more than 30,000 in their elementary schools and high schools. The total enrollment in all Lutheran elementary and secondary schools is nearly 200,000. Though more than 10% of this enrollment consists of non-Lutheran children, the schools are church institutions. The churches maintaining them believe that the home and church are jointly responsible for religious education and that the church is best able to make its contribution through parochial schools. A legitimate question is: Do these schools serve only the religious purposes of the denomination or do they also perform a "public service"—that is, do they contribute their part to their country's over-all purpose in education and to the development of a citizenry which can live together as a strong, responsible nation?

Relation of Lutheran schools to public schools. Fred F. Beach and Robert F. Will of the U.S. Office of Education state that nonpublic schools "are and have always been a significant part of the Nation's total educational resources" and that they "exert a tremendous influence in fashioning the American way of life."* While Lutheran schools constitute only a small percentage of the total nonpublic school enrollment in the United States, they contribute their part to shaping the American way of life. Their relation to the public school deserves special consideration.

Some have said that parochial schools are un-American and divisive. However, parochial schools were on the scene long before the public schools and have flourished side by side with them since the advent of the latter. They are as American as the 13 colonies and the original United States. The un-American label does not fit parents who feel bound in their consciences to provide their children with a religious education of a nature which only the parochial school can provide. Both the parochial and public schools are American, and, if they do their work well, both contribute to the unity in diversity which a democratic society permits and which is an evidence of its strength. The strength of a democracy is not in complete uniformity, but in a diversity which operates within a common love of freedom, justice, and initiative. Its strength is in a form of government which

* Fred F. Beach and Robert F. Will, "The State and Nonpublic Schools." Misc. no. 28, U.S. Office of Education (Washington: U.S. Government Printing Office, 1958), p. 1.

54

permits and encourages diverse elements to operate side by side, to influence and serve each other for the common good. It becomes weak only when the diverse elements become irresponsible and when they lose their concern for one another's welfare.

The supporters of Lutheran schools also support the public schools. Superintendents and principals of Lutheran schools work harmoniously with public school officials. Often public school officials offer advice to the representatives of Lutheran churches that are in the process of establishing their own schools.

The elementary schools of The Lutheran Church-Missouri Synod enroll about 33% of this church's eligible children. The supporters of these schools pay their school taxes as cheerfully as the average citizen. They support school bond issues. For example, the superintendent of Lutheran schools in the St. Louis, Mo., area, consistently and publicly has spoken for increases in public school taxes and for bond issues. In Deshler, Neb., where 170 grade school pupils attend Lutheran schools and only 90 the public elementary school, and where the public school district also includes two rural Lutheran schools, a $250,000 school bond issue was approved 401 to 168 in October, 1959. According to the Lincoln (Neb.) *Star* of Oct. 7, 1959, the public school superintendent stated, "This is just another evidence of the good relationship we've always had with the parochial schools here." Lutheran school supporters believe that the country needs good public schools for children who do not attend private or parochial schools, and these are the vast majority of American children. Public schools are a matter of civic importance to Lutheran school supporters.

Three types of public service. What public service does the Lutheran school perform? The fact that Lutheran schools annually save the American public millions of dollars in taxes can hardly be classed as a public service, for two reasons: Lutherans do not maintain their schools to save the public tax money; and the public does not ask Lutherans to maintain their own schools. Lutherans maintain them voluntarily to achieve certain benefits which the public schools cannot achieve at all or as well. The public schools simply cannot serve the children's religious needs because they must satisfy the many diverse elements in the community.

There are three principal types of public service in a parochial school education. The distinctive contribution of the parochial school in connection with these services lies in its unique religious concept and motivation. The three services are a thorough academic training, the development of morally responsible people, and the training for responsible citizenship.

A thorough academic training—Every citizen needs a good working knowledge of the facts and skills taught through the common school subjects. For their own welfare and for the good of their citizens, states set up standards for education in the common school subjects, and these standards apply to all schools under a given state's jurisdiction, not in detail but on an equivalent basis. Every school, and also every denominational school, is therefore expected to provide a good general education. In promoting the establishment of schools, The Lutheran Church-Missouri Synod emphasizes that just starting a school is not enough; it must be a good school —that is, it must be one that contributes to the spiritual growth of the children attending it, to the strength of the church, and to good citizenship. In every way it must be academically respectable.

It would be easy to cite examples of Lutheran schools that do outstanding work academically, that contribute far more than their share of valedictorians and salutatorians to the high schools, or that produce high standardized test scores. This would prove nothing but that some Lutheran schools are good schools academically, as some public, Roman Catholic, and other schools are good schools academically. The important question is how Lutheran schools perform generally, apart from some superior and perhaps some mediocre schools which are part of every school system.

In general education, Lutheran schools compare favorably with public schools. They are taught by teachers who are professionally trained in educational objectives, the school curriculum, teaching methods, and evaluation procedures. They use modern textbooks. The Lutheran Church-Missouri Synod maintains two fully accredited teachers colleges, one at River Forest, Ill., and another at Seward, Neb., with a combined enrollment of more than 1,800 teacher-training students. These two colleges, however, do not provide all the teachers for the Synod's schools. In the employment of those trained elsewhere, Lutheran schools also seek teachers who meet both church and state requirements. As a result, graduates of Lutheran elementary schools enter high schools on an equal basis with graduates of public elementary schools, and they hold their own as they continue their education in high school and college. Lutheran high schools encounter no greater difficulty in acquiring state and regional accreditation than public or any other schools.

The question arises how a parochial school, with a school year and a school day which correspond roughly with those of the public school, can devote time to worship and religious instruction and yet meet, and in some cases exceed, accepted academic standards. The answer is found in dedicated teachers, diligent application to the task of education, Christian attitudes toward life and work on the part of children and teachers, and concentration on the essentials of education.

The development of morally responsible people — The development of morally responsible people is not a unique objective of Lutheran schools. All schools worthy of the name pursue it. However, Lutherans believe that their schools provide a particularly effective motivation toward achievement of the objective.

Too often we see the purposes of education only in part. We are always in danger of lifting legitimate educational purposes, like economic or social competence, out of their context or of making them central instead of concentrating on the education of academically competent and morally responsible people.

Education, ordinarily, is successful in terms of its level of expectations. An education worthy of the name seeks, first of all, to produce a man who is worthy of membership in the human race, a person of high personal qualities and ideals who contributes to the spiritual and intellectual improvement of society simply because this is right and because he is determined to make the most of his interests and abilities. Such a man almost automatically will concern himself also with his own economic, political, and social needs, and with the needs of the society of which he is a part. Because of an overall balanced viewpoint and training, he is well equipped to work for the good of mankind.

There is no need to belabor the point that declining moral standards have affected adversely the stability of the family, the church, and the nation. Divorces, neglect of child training, church rolls padded with the unreconstructed in spirit, a shaky loyalty to American ideals, crime and dishonesty of every stripe are too prevalent for comfort. Our modern society has largely failed to influence youth with Christian convictions or even with common everyday morality. Lutheran schools aim for moral instruction in depth: first of all, by impressing religious convictions; second, by showing how religious belief, to be genuine, must affect all areas of life; third, by training their students in the Christian life which they advocate.

Lutherans accept the Bible view of the nature and purpose of man, and this determines their outlook in education. They believe that God made man the master of the earth within the limits which God permits and that He gave man the power for this mastery. They believe that God, in effect, says to man, "Here is the earth. It is all yours. Make it as useful as you can, using the intelligence and inventiveness which I have given you. But always exercise your mastery over the earth in keeping with My purposes and for the welfare of man." Here is where a strong moral base, and, in the Lutheran view, a strong Christian base, is of paramount importance. This moral base Lutheran schools seek to build on a religious foundation.

In the Lutheran view, life on earth becomes meaningful only if it includes a looking forward to complete joy and perfection in heaven. This view Lutheran schools regard as the real motivation for morality and for the good life generally. In teaching that man sinned, that he cannot save himself either for this life or for eternity, that he is saved by God's grace through Jesus Christ, they emphasize that man's motivation for making the most of his capacities should be gratitude for what God has done for him. They believe that the morally responsible man is the man whose first loyalty is to God and that they make their greatest contribution to the public service by training men and women who have this loyalty.

The training for responsible citizenship — Responsible citizenship comes naturally to the morally responsible person. But it deserves separate mention. In a democracy the emphasis is on freedom—freedom to worship God, freedom to live and work where one pleases, freedom to speak and write within the bounds of the law, freedom to have a voice in the government, freedom in all things to enjoy the dignity which is man's.

But freedom does not come to the irresponsible. It is maintained only through sustained effort. The person who lives lazily off others and who loves ease and pleasure above everything else is a menace to his own freedom and that of his countrymen. The freedom to be independent and useful calls for the acceptance not only of moral responsibility for being the right kind of person, but also the responsibility for working for the welfare of all. Whether a Christian or not, the good citizen accepts this responsibility. He is more interested in giving than in getting, in serving than in being served.

One contribution of Lutheran schools toward responsible citizenship is that, like other American schools, they teach democracy and train their students in democratic living. But they believe that their greatest contribution to good citizenship is in providing the Christian motivation for responsible citizenship. They emphasize that the *Christian* citizen gives and serves because he knows that God has been good to him without measure and because he wants to show his gratitude by serving God and his fellow man. This places the motivation on a much higher plane than the selfish "it is good for me" approach. Any school that succeeds in even a small measure to lessen the selfish approach in citizenship promotes a public service of high caliber.

For any school system to claim perfection in its efforts to train for general morality and good citizenship would be ridiculous. Lutheran schools have their failures as do others. But Lutheran schools "seek the peace of the city" and teach their students to "render unto Caesar the things that are Caesar's and unto God the things that are God's." Because they stress primary loyalty to God, they intensify the motivation for loyalty to their country. That they succeed in a commendable measure is apparent from frequent comments of public school officials, such as these: "The graduates of your school are consistently among our best students, scholastically, as well as in attitudes and deportment. The religious training which they have received does make a difference"; "The students you sent us last year are doing outstanding work, scholastically and socially, which reveals to us a sound Christian attitude inspired in their elementary training. Send us more of them."

Supporters of Lutheran schools believe that Christians usually excel in reverence for law, respect of government, honest payment of taxes, and other aspects of citizenship. Remembering that government exists for the benefit of the people and not people for the government, the Christian opposes evil and injustice, even if practiced by his own government. He guards against being carried away by hateful propaganda and works for justice and peace at home and abroad.

Lutheran schools teach their students responsibility for exercising voting privileges, for participation in local, state, and national services if qualified, and for defending their country even at the expense of life. All these are directly in the area of public service.

In conclusion, Lutheran schools provide a good academic training for 200,000 children and young people. They provide a religious base for moral responsibility. They aid democracy because they inculcate the religious truths which are basic to democratic living. They teach love and respect for superiors, including government officials on all levels. By their parallel system of education they also stimulate the public schools, and they help to guard against an undesirable state monopoly in education. The *church* which sponsors its own schools profits most from the fact that these schools help to propagate the Christian faith and the Christian life. The *public service* of these schools is evident in academic standards which at least match those of the public schools and in their development of responsible people who honor God and respect their fellow men. To the extent that they succeed in their purpose, and they do succeed to a notable degree, parochial schools support and strengthen the entire range of desirable human activity.

₰5₰

The Controversy Over Public Support to Parochial Schools

BERNARD J. KOHLBRENNER

ALTHOUGH THE TOPIC covered here might be considered in its manifold applications to all schools sponsored by religious bodies, the discussion will be limited to its application to Catholic schools. There are other examples of parochial schools in the U.S., but Catholics maintain by far the largest number of such schools, and the practical realities of the present time indicate a more general interest in this question as related to Catholic schools than to others.

In Catholic teaching, education is regarded as a concern of three fundamental institutions: the church, the family, and the state.[1] Rights and responsibilities in education inhere in the

[1] A brief summary of the traditional teaching is found in the Encyclical Letter of Pius XI on "Christian Education of Youth" (official and complete English text), National Catholic Welfare Conference, Washington, D. C., 1930.

church and the family, but the state also has both rights and duties, and the ideal situation to be striven for is one in which all three work harmoniously. Specifically, the state should encourage and assist the church and the family in their educational endeavors, but it also should supplement their work when necessary for the common good, as it legitimately may establish minimum requirements in the intellectual, moral, and physical development of its citizens. The state has the means "for the needs of all, and it is only right that it use these means to the advantage of those who have contributed them."[2] Pope Pius XI pointed out that the principle of distributive justice would require that financial assistance be given to "the several schools demanded by the families," but in establishing separate schools Catholics do not "intend to separate their children either from the body of the nation or its spirit, but to educate them in a perfect manner, most conducive to the prosperity of the nation."[3]

These are the most general principles, but the working out of their practical application is conditioned by the whole complex of the social, religious, economic, and political facts in the various national states. As far as this country is concerned, it is sufficient to remark that, although there were many educational efforts made by Catholics from early colonial times, the formation of a general educational policy was a long and slow process.[4] It would not be in-

---

[2] *Ibid.*, p. 17.

[3] *Ibid.*, p. 32.

[4] A summary of this development is given in James A. Burns and Bernard J. Kohlbrenner, "A History of Catholic Education in the United States" (New York: Benziger, 1937).

accurate to say that a policy of a fully developed system of parochial schools was forced upon the Catholics, first because of the generally Protestant nature of many of the public and semi-public schools of the first half of the 19th century and later because of the increasing secularism of these schools when the Protestant character was diminishing.[5] The first bishop, John Carroll, had hoped for some time that Catholics would be able to co-operate with other religious groups in opening and conducting schools, and it was not until 1884 that the general legislation requiring the establishment of a school in connection with every parish was formulated. Before this time, and indeed several times since then, various efforts were made to work out arrangements by which Catholic schools might be established within systems of local public schools. As late as 1890, Archbishop John Ireland of St. Paul, Minn., in addressing the meeting of the National Education Association, said that he regretted the necessity of parochial schools,[6] and two years later Cardinal Gibbons expressed the hope that "the Catholic schools will one day become in some way connected with the public school system."[7]

But the dynamics of our history resulted in a decreasing stress on separate religiously affiliated schools by most of the Protestant denominations with the consequent Protestant attachment to public schools at the same time that Catholics

[5] These aspects of the subject are traced in Jerome E. Diffley, "Catholic Reaction to American Public Education, 1792-1852," unpublished doctoral dissertation, University of Notre Dame, 1959.

[6] National Education Association, "Addresses and Proceedings" (1890), p. 185.

[7] Allen S. Will, "Life of Cardinal Gibbons" (New York: Dutton, 1922), p. 222.

thought it increasingly necessary to develop their own schools. One of the phases of the great public school movement that took place in the mid-19th century was the effort to eliminate the sectarian character of the schools. But this was a movement in which practically no Catholics participated; it was essentially an intra-Protestant development. What Horace Mann and his colleagues faced was primarily not a Protestant *versus* a Catholic position, but rivalries among the various Protestant denominations. Catholics were not numerous or influential in American life until after the close of the "common school awakening." Their educational efforts were concentrated on the building of their own schools, not by choice but by what they reluctantly regarded as necessity. They found themselves deserted by the leaders of the other denominations. The abandonment of the cause of denominational schools by most of the Protestant churches was probably hastened by their common opposition to the rising Catholic schools. But the public schools remained in many places generally Protestant in spirit, with Bible reading, the singing of hymns, prayers, and other activities mainly drawn from a Protestant way of life and Protestant sources. In some places, it is also true, the public schools took on the character of Catholic schools where there was a homogeneous Catholic population, but these were a small number in comparison with those that retained a generally Protestant character.

Unfortunately, there was little or no communication or contact between the leaders of public and Catholic education. The cultural isolation of the two groups led to an enormous amount of misunderstanding on both sides, from which both suffer at the present time. In the present century, Catholics often have seen in the preparation of teachers for the public schools and in the day-to-day work of the schools a vehicle for the propagation of the philosophy of secularism. It is significant that many Protestants are alarmed at the spread of this *Weltanschauung* and, as evidenced in the many discussions and publications devoted to the subject, they now are working on various efforts to relate religion to the public schools in a more substantial manner. Despite their differences in principle and outlook, many of these leaders and critics proceed from the same original basis in their thinking that Catholics follow: education that ignores religion is simply not good education, and the division of labor that would restrict religious education to other opportunities than those found in the school cannot effect a satisfactory solution to the problem. Most of the Protestant educators probably would not argue for the necessity of church-related schools but would limit their considerations to such measures as teaching about religion in the public schools, a common core of minimum essentials in religion as a school study, released-time classes in religion, or some combination of these and other proposals. The public school movement of the last century was followed by state prohibitions against the use of public funds for denominational schools. But the Catholic finds himself, in conscience, unable to make use of the public schools, as presently constituted. Hence, he upholds what most of his fellow citizens regard as a radical (in the true meaning of the term) solution of the problem of religion in education—the parochial school. In this position he is not only true to the obligations of his conscience, but he also is convinced that he is following a line of solid logical reasoning.

Although the Catholic position is that of a minority, and although the practical fulfillment of this position has been very costly to the Catholics of the country, a remarkably extensive system of parochial schools has been built. Its growth has been particularly strong in recent years. Not until 1867 did the "Catholic Directory" list separate statistics for parish schools, but by 1875 there were 1,444 such schools reported.[8] Today there are some 5,000,000 pupils enrolled in Catholic elementary and secondary schools, but an equal number of Catholic children are not in Catholic schools. Needless to say, Catholics have found the cost of the system of independent schools heavy—so heavy that they have supported measures that would give them some financial relief. The general position in these efforts might be simply stated in the following paragraphs.

Many Catholics find themselves in the position that they cannot, in conscience, enroll their children in the public schools, as presently formulated. They build parochial schools which will satisfy not only their religious commitment, but also the minimum standards at least that the state has determined. In this way they provide not only the kind of education that they believe necessary, but they also fulfill the compulsory education requirements that have been determined by the public authorities.

The right of parents to select the kind of education they wish their children to receive is a natural right that has been upheld specifically by the Supreme Court *(Pierce v. Society of Sis-*

---

[8] "Catholic Directory," 1875.

ters, 1925). In exercising this right, parents are both fulfilling a public responsibility and exercising a private option. It is absurd to say, as does Thayer,[9] that there is no more public responsibility to parents of parochial school children to implement their educational rights than there is to make facilities available to those who wish to exercise the right of free speech. The pertinent points are the difference in the two cases (for the state has legislated with regard to compulsory education but has no statutes respecting compulsory speech) and the obligation of government to the common good. Catholics as well as others have to recognize that there are constitutional and legal prohibitions in most of the states against direct financial aid to denominational schools. Consequently, they have given much attention in recent years to the support of auxiliary aids to private education, *e.g.*, school bus transportation, textbooks, health services, and other related auxiliary activities. When such services have become available to pupils in parochial schools, they often have been sustained on the "child benefit" theory. This was the distinction made in the Louisiana free textbook case[10] and in the New Jersey school bus case.[11] The courts, however, have not been consistent in the application of this principle, and in New York State a constitutional amendment was required to make legal the public support of the transportation of children in parochial schools. In a recent publication prepared by the Committee on Religion

[9] V. T. Thayer, "The Role of the School in American Society" (New York: Dodd, Mead, 1960), p. 391.

[10] *Cochran v. Louisiana Board of Education*, 281 U.S. 370 (1930).

[11] *Everson v. Board of Education*, 330 U.S. 1 (1947).

and Public Education of the National Council of the Churches of Christ in the U.S.A., the use of public funds for bus transportation and textbooks for children in non-public schools is opposed, while medical and health services, including the Federal school lunch program, are viewed as allowable. The distinction between them is made on the ground that these latter services are for the benefit of the individual and the community in general and are not "immediately related to the educational enterprise."[12] In its statements relative to the testing and guidance services provided for by the National Defense Education Act of 1958, the committee saw these services, even though extended by the Act to pupils in both public and non-public schools, as something that can be a "helpful service." But the committee pointed out that, in its view, "if the government-financed testing service . . . becomes administratively identified with the educational program of the school itself then church and state have become commingled in a manner contrary to our American traditions." It likewise stated that these Federal provisions for testing in church-supported schools should not be taken as a precedent for future "demands upon public funds for support of church-controlled education." The cautious attitude of the committee toward the operation of the Act was expressed when it said that this "needs to be carefully watched."[13]

Catholics interested in the Act probably would agree with the Committee of the National Coun-

---

[12] "Relation of Religion to Public Education," a study document prepared by the Committee on Religion and Public Education of the National Council of the Churches of Christ in the U.S.A., Feb. 18, 1960.
[13] *Ibid.*

cil of the Churches that its provisions and its administration should be "carefully watched." An examination of the various provisions of the Act convinces many of them that the Act is unnecessarily discriminatory in allowing a partial cancellation of loans for prospective teachers in the public, but not those entering teaching in the non-public, schools; in making grants to the states for the purchase of equipment for the teaching of science, mathematics, and modern foreign languages in the public schools, but providing only loans, not grants, for these purposes in private schools; in making grants for the expansion and improvement of the supervision of instruction in these critical subjects in the public schools, but not in others; and in the restriction of new Federal funds under the Act for the improvement of guidance services to public schools only. Thus, many Catholics would want to study carefully the provisions and the administration of the Act, as would the Committee of the National Council of the Churches, but the evaluation made by the two groups would differ rather fundamentally.[14] Catholics are likely to be somewhat less than enthusiastic about the provisions of the Act for pupils in non-public schools, especially in view of the purposes of the Act. An analysis and commentary of the Act published by the U.S. Office of Education, Department of Health, Education, and Welfare, speaks of the authorization of the billion dollars for "a single purpose—that every young person, from the day he first enters school, should have the opportunity to develop his gifts to the fullest. This is the

[14] A compact statement of the views held by many Catholics with reference to the Act is given by Neil G. McCluskey, "Catholic Viewpoint on Education" (New York: Hanover House, 1959), pp. 171-172.

72

emphasis that gives the Act its name, for it recognizes that in a free society the individual is the first line of defense."[15] Secretary Arthur S. Flemming of the Department characterized the Act as one that "continues a historic partnership which has demonstrated its value to the American people over many years in the past—a partnership in which the Federal government assists states, communities, and private institutions to pioneer in new educational programs and to strengthen others that have proved their worth."[16] No doubt, American Catholics do not all agree on the detailed application of the two principles stated here, but all would find in them the two basic principles governing the organization and support of education in our society: first, the primacy of the individual child to be educated; and second, the partnership of family, state, and church and of public and non-public schools in the education of the child. These principles of educational philosophy, although here expressed in a document of the U.S. Office of Education, are fundamental in Catholic educational theory. They would appear to be imperatively needed in today's pluralistic society.

The pluralisms of contemporary American society may be organized into the usual four:[17] Protestantism, Catholicism, Judaism, and secular humanism. Each has at least one more or less well-defined position with respect to education and the relations of the political state to it

[15] "Guide to the National Defense Education Act of 1958," U.S. Office of Education, Circular No. 553, (Washington: U.S. Government Printing Office, 1959), p. 1.

[16] Ibid.

[17] For a brief summary of the positions of the four on major issues in American society, cf., Leo Pfeffer, "Creeds in Competition" (New York: Harper, 1958).

as well as a point of view relating to other major concerns of modern society. It is not accurate, therefore, to think of differences with respect to the role of the family, religion, and the state in education as limited to a Protestant and a Catholic position. But the outlines of the public school system were developed in a time and a culture that were basically Protestant. Now, as Martin Luther said of another time, "a new day has dawned," and in this day it would seem necessary to put under scrutiny the institutional arrangements for the education of the young so that political activity may fully serve the common good. This will be the work not of one year or a few years; perhaps each generation will face the task in terms of its time. In the effort there will be enormous obstacles. Not only will there be prejudices and prepossessions that will hinder discussion and deliberation, but old habits will have to be replaced by new means of intergroup relations.

There are unfortunate problems that have been created by the isolation of the parochial and public school people and their patrons from each other. For the most part, the members of each group have talked only to themselves. Some of this may have been made necessary in the ongoing current of events and the lack of opportunity to do more than consider the most pressing internal problems of each group of schools. But such isolation must give way to a broadening of contact and discussion of both school persons and citizens generally. A beginning has been made in the work of the voluntary accrediting associations for the secondary schools and the many forms of contact and co-operation among colleges and universities. The most stubborn problem will be that involving

the elementary schools, for here the isolation
has been almost complete, redeemed only occa-
sionally in sporadic efforts at collaboration. The
enlargement of understanding and activity on
all levels and in all sections of the country is a
challenge to all citizens in the years ahead.

6

A Jewish Viewpoint on Church-State-School Relations

PHILIP JACOBSON

THE FIRST REQUIRE-
ment for a resolution of the problem of how
the public school may deal properly with religion as a phase of our cultural heritage, says
Dr. F. Ernest Johnson quite plausibly, "would
seem to be a clear understanding of what every
group believes to be at stake."[1] Precisely what a
"group" is, in Dr. Johnson's meaning, may not
be wholly clear, since the range of opinion in
this controversial area even within faith groups
is very wide. However, there is a very large degree of unanimity within the Jewish community on this issue, at least in principle. When
Jews differ from time to time, their disagree-
ments generally center on how to apply their
principles to a particular situation. And while
no one can speak for all Jews on this or any

[1] Ernest Johnson, "American Education and Religion"
(New York: Harper, 1952), p. 5.

76

other matter, this writer does believe the statement of views here presented is shared by the overwhelming majority of Jewish religious and secular bodies.

Certainly, there would be few demurrers to what we believe to be at stake: the vigor and freedom of religious life in America; the integrity and efficacy of our unique system of free universal public education; and the American tradition of the separation of church and state. Since the strength of religious institutional life and the stability of the public school, in our view, are dependent in large measure upon separation, we begin with a consideration of that constitutional doctrine.

As the 1960 Presidential campaign amply demonstrated, everyone favors separation. But some would apply it now and then; some prefer a "wavy line"[2] to a "wall of separation"; some insist that it merely bars a state church but permits "non-preferential aid" to all religions. Jews accept the interpretation given the religion clause of the First Amendment by the U.S. Supreme Court in the *Everson*[3] and *McCollum*[4] cases: Neither the Federal government nor the states can set up a church; aid one religion, aid all religions, or prefer one religion over another; force one to go to or remain away from church or to profess a belief or disbelief in any religion; levy a tax to support any religious activity; or openly or secretly participate in the affairs of any religious organization.

For their advocacy of this definition, Jews

---

[2] Ray Gibbons, "Protestantism and Public Education," *Social Action*, Feb. 15, 1949, pp. 4-27.

[3] *Everson v. Board of Education of Ewing*, 330 U.S. 1 (1947).

[4] *McCollum v. Board of Education*, 333 U.S. 203 (1948).

are identified as "strict separationists," an appellation that always has seemed to this writer something of a tautology, since "separate" is an absolute, not a relative term. But I cheerfully accept the designation, for I regard the separation of church and state as "best for the state and best for religion."[5]

Our system of church-state relations has enabled us to escape much of the strife that has marked the history of other lands. While religion did play a part in the Presidential election, it nevertheless was clear that most Americans considered the religious faith of a candidate for public office irrelevant to his fitness. What these Americans really were saying was that our tradition of separation establishes the political authority as an exclusively secular authority. Our real point of difference is not whether separation is best for the state, but whether it is best for religion.

Scores of religious sects and denominations flourish on the American scene. The power, the authority, the enormous influence they wield are eloquent testimony to the pervasive force of separation. At no time in the life of the nation has religion enjoyed a more authoritative voice. It reaches the largest audiences in its history not only from the pulpit, but through the radio, television, and a widely read religious press.

This amazing vitality is a product of voluntarism, imposed by the demands of separation. For a religious institution that is dependent not upon the state's bounty, but upon the devotion and loyalty of its adherents is in a far better position to realize its full potential.

Many are rapidly losing sight of that basic

---

[5] *Everson v. Board of Education, op. cit.*

fact of religious life. They look to the state to cater to the religious needs of the people, employing two patently contradictory arguments in support of their demands. First, they remind us constantly that "We are a religious people whose institutions presuppose a Supreme Being."[6] That being so, they seem to be saying, official state policy should give recognition to the fact. But what does it mean, asked John Cogley, to say "We are a religious people"? And he answers that the responses would be as divergent as the variety of opinion about religion: "Since there is no consensus about religion, there could hardly be a consensus about a religious people."[7] Cogley's reasonable conclusion is that the only sense in which Americans would agree that we are a religious people is that we are not an overtly or dogmatically anti-religious people.

It is also said that, while, to be sure, our religious institutional life is very strong, the American people nevertheless are essentially pagan in their outlook. The argument goes: We live in a spiritual wasteland; materialism is our god. If America is to play a meaningful role as the leader of the free world, there is need for a spiritual undergirding to our national life.

In the drive to enlist the state in the task of providing the necessary spiritual undergirding, there is an unfortunate casualty—the religious nonconformist who seems to be losing his status of first-class citizenship. To return to the election campaign for evidence, Vice-President Nixon made the unchallenged observation that it

<hr>

[6] *Zorach v. Clauson,* 343 U.S. 306 (1952).

[7] John Cogley, "Community Life of American Catholics," address on "The Catholic Hour," NBC, Sept. 4, 1960.

is of no importance what the religion of a candidate is so long as he has one.

Doubtless, Mr. Nixon was giving voice to the widely circulated myth that a good American is a God-fearing American. However ill-founded the belief may be, it continues to gain wide acceptance. And in the process we forget that a vital ingredient of religious liberty is the right to reject all forms of traditional religion, to be counted among the secular humanists, the agnostics, the atheists, without being regarded as a social or political pariah.

Sensitive Christians are not altogether unmindful of the plight of the religiously unaffiliated. This may be seen by the following caution included in the National Council of the Churches' study document on "Religion and Public Education": ". . . freedom of belief must be preserved. The rights of minorities, however small, must always be a matter for solicitous concern. . . ."[8] The Council's enjoinder is obviously well intended, but it seems to fall far short as a substitute for full equality.

Those who would align the state on the side of religion act on the mistaken assumption that religion is entitled to an officially preferred status on the American social scene. Religious institutions should be accorded no such advantage. They represent but one segment of thought in the market place in competition not only with one another, but with other opinion as well.[9] It would follow that the state's role in the resolution of the philosophical differences that divide us should be one of complete neu-

[8] National Council of the Churches of Christ, "Religion and Public Education—A Study Document," Part I, Feb. 18, 1960, p. 26.
[9] Cogley, *op. cit.*

trality, except merely to insure that all may enjoy full freedom to participate in the clash of opinion. To cast the state in the role of an adherent in the dispute does a grave disservice both to religion and to the state.

The third important value that Jews defend is the stability of the public school. They give it their enthusiastic support in the conviction that it is one of the chief instruments for developing an informed citizenry and achieving the goals of American democracy. They agree fully with V. T. Thayer that it is "an expression in institutional form of the democratic ideal at its best."[10]

The public schools are governmentally supported enterprises. Like every other phase of the operations of the secular political authority, they are foreclosed from intruding upon the conscience or faith of children. If our schools and educators are to continue to serve us well, like every level of governmental jurisdiction they must be free of religious entanglements.

Accordingly, Jews conclude that the "maintenance and furtherance of religion are the responsibilities of the synagogue, the church and the home, and not of the public school system"; and they stand firm against the "utilization in any manner of the time, facilities, personnel, or funds of the public school for the purposes of religious instruction. . . ."[11] They resist all efforts to assign to, or share with, the public school the function of developing religiously committed

---

[10] Vivian T. Thayer, "The Attack Upon the American Secular School" (Boston: Beacon, 1951), p. viii.

[11] "Safeguarding Religious Liberty," statements of policy and positions of the Synagogue Council of America and the National Community Relations Advisory Council, December, 1957.

boys and girls. To be sure, Jews think well of the public school teacher, but he is not their choice of instructor to insure the survival and flourishing of Judaic traditions. For that purpose, Jews constantly expand and enrich the religious educational facilities they make available to their children.

Jews think these basic principles require the acceptance of rules of conduct on the part of school administrators that will bar any program or activity that may influence or undermine the faith of any child or question the absence of religious belief in any child. All children of every shade of religious opinion, as well as those of religiously unaffiliated families, should enjoy complete equality in the classroom and school community.

If all of us could be brought to accept these simple restraints, we might come to see that prayers and religious hymns, the display of religious symbols, the observance of sectarian religious holidays, and other similar practices array the vast power and influence of the school on the side of the dominant majority in disregard of the most elementary rights of a defenseless minority of captive children. A striking example of the kind of influence that comes to mind was disclosed in the trial of *Chamberlin, et al., v. Dade County Board of Education.* In the plaintiffs' Memorandum on the Facts, the following scene is described (p. 11):

. . . The students were marched from their home rooms to the Easter assembly and the roll was taken. The program opened with the entrance of the chorus carrying candles. The story of the persecution and crucifixion of Christ was then told by two students, reading alternately. On stage, a silk screen effect was used to depict the events thus related. The nailing of Christ to the cross was enacted, with one of the students stretched out on a cross. He appeared "exactly like Christ is on any cross, a crucifix." Music was played during this action; the auditorium was darkened with the lights focussed on the Christ figure. In the words of one witness: "The lights were focussed on the boy, and then at Christ's death there was heavy breathing from the boy, and then finally collapse, and that was the end of the program, I mean then they told everyone to go back to their rooms."

Will the common-sense rules we suggest remove God or religion from the classroom? Of course not. On the contrary, believing Jews see in the influence of the public school in the lives of our children evidence of God's pervasive presence. Nor would there be excluded from the curriculum the immeasurable contributions of religion in man's tortuous rise from barbarism to civilization. Jews do want children to have an understanding of the unique tradition of religious liberty in America and of the diversified pattern that has emerged from that freedom. They see the educational importance of helping children to appreciate the role religious impulses have played in creating great social institutions—universities, hospitals, welfare agencies. They regard it as a proper function of the schools to introduce children to the world's magnificent store of religious art and literature, including the Bible. And they are aware of the ends served by the schools teaching subject matter with honesty, thoroughness, and objectivity so that when religion, both in its doctrinal and historical phases, is pertinent to the classroom lesson it will be dealt with fairly and in proper perspective. Jews do *not* want the Bible used in the schools for devotional purposes. The Bible is a source of religious inspiration, the mainspring of faith—and a recurring source of conflict between the great religions in our culture. They do *not* want the school curriculum made a vehicle for conditioning our children to a belief in God.

At this point in the discussion we are reminded—inevitably—of the abysmal lack of "religious literacy" in America's youth. But we never can be quite sure what is demanded of the school to effectuate a cure. For those who wave the banner of "religious literacy" with the greatest vigor are rather timid in advancing specifics. Are they charging that the schools are derelict in teaching about the contributions to religious thought of Martin Luther, Michael Servetus, John Wesley, and other founders of great religious movements? Are our children uninformed about what distinguishes a Protestant from a Catholic, a Christian from a Jew? If the lack of this kind of factual knowledge results in religious illiteracy, by all means let us join in seeking a remedy, possibly through revision of the school curriculum.

However, it is this observer's guess that factual knowledge will not suffice, that the other side of the coin of "religious literacy" is faith. Not, to be sure, a sectarian faith. No, the religion of the public school must be framed in nonsectarian terms.

For most Jews such an assignment to the public school presents a perfectly meaningless absurdity, fraught with the gravest danger both to religion and the public peace. Jews cannot embrace a vague, watered-down, non-Biblical, great big amalgamated public school religion, which Leo Pfeffer aptly described as ". . . a strange, new hybrid creed, an artificial religion."[12] Necessarily, they consistently reject so-

---

[12] Leo Pfeffer, "A New Religion in America," *The Churchman*, April, 1959, pp. 9-10.

called nonsectarian prayers, "interdenomination-al" versions of the Ten Commandments, and a common-denominator concept of God.

In its inception, the new public school religion may well be neither Protestant, Catholic, nor Jewish, but it is certain, in time, to become municipally colored by the numerical strength of the dominant religious majority. For a public school religion that hews to the letter of the law of nonsectarianism is doomed to be shallow and completely unsatisfying to the devout of all faiths.

Well, then, if even a neutral theism is unwelcome in the classroom, how will children learn the difference between right and wrong? Jews think basic values are best inculcated in the public school through deeds. They take a dim view of the rote recitation of a prayer or the daily recitation of the fourth stanza of *America*. (The latter program, designed to mold character, is relentlessly pursued in the New York City schools, although teachers and administrators alike acknowledge its futility.) Efforts such as these can hardly shape children's character in any way comparable to the understanding and sensitive teacher who makes her point daily through precept and example.

Yet, children do want to know why one course of action is right and another wrong, which introduces the touchy subject of sanctions. In the Jewish view, the public school may not take sides in the conflict between theistic and humanistic views of what constitutes the ultimate source of human values. The public school is committed to the task of insuring the widest possible freedom of inquiry, encouraging each pupil to think for himself. In these circumstances, can teachers reasonably be asked to inculcate religious belief? A dual goal of religious belief and independence of thought necessarily will place the teacher in an exposed position, subject to attack on either religious or educational grounds. To develop belief in God, the teacher must use persuasion and faith, skirting the edges of sectarian doctrine. To encourage free inquiry, the teacher runs the risk of challenging the faith nourished by church, synagogue, and home.

Is it not also true that if today the public school can be arrayed on the side of theism, in another age its great influence might be marshalled on the side of atheism? In assigning to the public school the task of bringing children to God, have we not established a principle from which there may be no escape?

All other considerations to one side, this writer sees no reason whatever for concern over the alleged "spiritual" shortcomings of the public school. In no institution anywhere on the American scene is the sanctity of the individual held more sacred. More successfully than any other, it has dealt with the Americanization of the foreign-born, the bridging of sharp sociological differences. "No other people demanded so much of education as have the American. None other was ever served so well by its schools and educators."[13] And today, in the face of overwhelming odds, it grapples manfully with the task of integrating children across racial lines. It continues to face up to these challenges while, year by year, its curriculum expands to meet the demands of an increasingly complex age. Yet, throughout its history it never has lost sight of the worth of the individual as a prime educa-

---

[13] Henry Steele Commager, *Life Magazine*, Oct. 16, 1950, p. 46.

tional objective. Whether one describes that objective in terms of intercultural education, or character training, or citizenship education, or moral and spiritual values instruction is of small consequence. What does matter is that the values the public school lives by and inculcates in our children are shared by all people with high moral standards, whatever their religion or lack of one. Indeed, one might ask whether the world outside the portals of the public school measures up to its standards of moral responsibility, devotion to truth, and respect for human personality.

We turn now to the second phase of church-state-school relations—the controversy over state aid for non-public educational institutions. On its outcome hinges the very future of the public school. For, if tax money should become available for church-related schools, it is certain that the landscape soon thereafter will be dotted with a wide variety of denominational systems of education—all in fierce competition with the public school for the limited tax dollars we assign to educational purposes.

The danger to the public school is very real, for today the debate is no longer centered on "fringe benefits"—lunches, medical and dental services, secular textbooks, and transportation.[14]

---

[14] Some time ago, Cardinal Spellman stated the problem in these terms: "Under the Constitution we do not ask for nor can we expect public funds to pay for the construction or repair of parochial school buildings or for the support of teachers, or for other maintenance costs. There are, however, other incidental expenses involved in education, expenses for such purposes as the transportation of children to and from the school, the purchase of non-religious textbooks and the provision of health aids. These are called "auxiliary services." The Federal-aid controversy revolves around these incidental benefits to school children and around them alone" (*The New York Times*, Aug. 6, 1949).

The issue now is whether tax funds should be provided for parochial school construction.[15] And, indeed, it has progressed to an even more advanced plateau with the recommendation of the Heald Committee for outright state grants to sectarian institutions of higher learning.[16]

The scene is thus being readied for the final assault—full tax support for the church-related school. This was evidenced with the publication of a brief prepared by the Department of Health, Education, and Welfare, holding that long-term, low-interest governnment loans to church-related elementary and secondary schools are objectionable on constitutional grounds. Commenting on the brief, Msgr. Frederick G. Hochwalt, director, National Catholic Welfare Conference education department, thereupon suggested that efforts to secure Federal loans for private schools be dropped in favor of an attempt to obtain outright grants. The government brief, he said, "has shifted the emphasis to

[15] An amendment to a school construction bill, intended to provide Federal loans of up to $150,000,000 for construction of nonprofit private schools, including parochial schools, introduced by Sen. Wayne Morse (D., Ore.), was defeated by a vote of 49-37 (*The New York Times,* Feb. 5, 1960).

[16] In the report, "Meeting the Increased Demand for Higher Education in New York State," to Gov. Nelson A. Rockefeller and the New York Board of Regents, a Committee on Higher Education suggested the following: "Private institutions of higher learning have important and unique functions to perform. They give American education a diversity and scope not possible in tax-supported institutions alone, and they have an opportunity to emphasize, if they wish, individualistic patterns of thought, courses of social action, or political or religious activity. In New York State, private colleges and universities have performed this function with great competency in the past. For the years ahead we propose that the State help to insure the continuance of their effectiveness by inaugurating a program of direct aid to private colleges and universities" (November, 1960, p. 24).

grants, since the same principle is seen as applying to both. The government brief has opened the door to the question of constitutionality all the way. It has advanced my thinking."[17] Also noteworthy is the comment by Father Virgil C. Blum, S.J., associate professor of political science at Marquette University, that there is no constitutional distinction in respect to state aid between primary, secondary, and collegiate education.[18]

Jews resist these drives, convinced that they represent backward steps along the road they have travelled to overcome the tyranny of the Old World. For the religious school is an adjunct of the church, serving sectarian ends. Indeed, religious education is the foremost responsibility of the church.[19] This was clearly confirmed by Father Neil G. McCluskey, S.J., in his listing of the benefits a Catholic parent and pastor find in a Catholic education:

1. The child learns systematically and thoroughly about his religion. He obtains a formal knowledge of the truths of Christian revelation, including the existence and nature of God, Christ's incarnation and Redemption, Christ's Church and the workings of the Holy Spirit within it, the History of the Chosen People and of the Church.
2. He enjoys regular opportunities, direct and indirect,

---

[17] *The (Brooklyn) Tablet,* April 15, 1961.
[18] *Ibid.,* Sept. 17, 1960.
[19] Mr. Justice Jackson, in *Everson v. Board of Education,* p. 24, made this point in the following words: "I should be surprised if any Catholic would deny that the parochial school is a vital, if not the most vital, part of the Roman Catholic Church. If put to the choice, that venerable institution, I should expect, would forego its whole service for mature persons before it would give up education of the young, and it would be a wise choice. Its growth and cohesion, discipline and loyalty, spring from its school. Catholic education is the rock on which the whole structure rests, and to render tax aid to its Church school is indistinguishable to me from rendering the same aid to the Church itself."

for the deepening of his sense of religious dedication. He has ready access to the Mass and the sacraments; he learns to live a fuller life of prayer; he acquires a practical knowledge and love of the Church's liturgical life.

3. The child learns an ordering of knowledge in an atmosphere in which the spiritual and the supernatural hold the primacy in the hierarchy of temporal and eternal values. He learns that his faith is not something apart but is related to the whole texture of life.

4. He acquires a "Catholic" attitude or outlook on life based upon the firm knowledge of his duties and privileges as a follower of Christ; he gains pride and love in —and loyalty to—his Catholic heritage.[20]

May it reasonably be said, as the Catholic bishops have contended, that such schools have the "full right to be considered and dealt with as components of the American educational system"[21]—in other words, as partners of the public school?

This writer thinks not and, therefore, cannot agree that parents who select church-related schools for their children are either discriminated against because these schools are denied tax aid or are the victims of "double taxation." I suggest that, quite to the contrary, if our taxes were to go to the support of such schools as Father McCluskey describes, the state would be violating *my* freedom of conscience. Support for a religious enterprise should be a matter of voluntary choice, not state compulsion.

Jews do support the expenditure of tax funds intended for the welfare of all children—school lunches and medical and dental services. They

[20] Neil G. McCluskey, S.J., "The Catholic School in Theory and Practices," *Research Consultation on the Church and State,* report of the Second Assembly, Board of Social and Economic Relations of the Methodist Church, New York East Conference, Tuxedo Park, N. Y., April 16-18, 1959.

[21] Statement of the Catholic Bishops of the U.S., National Catholic Welfare Conference, Washington, D. C., 1955.

do not believe that secular textbooks belong in the category of welfare aids. Textbooks are as essential to the operation of a school as desks and blackboards. Nor may transportation, which is equally essential to a church-related school, be deemed a child welfare benefit, since transportation is in no sense safer when paid for by the public treasurer than when paid for by parents.

Doubtless, transportation has become a major item in the school budget. One can readily sympathize with the religious school administrator who, faced with the rising cost of transportation, finds it enormously difficult to meet his bills. But to cite this difficulty as a basis for departure from principle—it is being done with increasing frequency—is palpably unfair. One might just as well point to the rising cost of teachers' salaries as justification for state aid to meet this all-important item in the religious school budget. The general public should not be required to sustain a religious school because its operation has become financially burdensome for those who conceive the need for the school.

Jews sometimes are asked, with a good deal of asperity, why their church-state policies are so negative: "You always oppose; what are you *for?*" The criticism is not nearly so devastating as it sounds, for Jews are in eminently good company: The Ten Commandments are more negative than positive. Nevertheless, this statement of views will conclude with the positive values that motivate Jewish thinking.

Jews are for religion and the unrestricted right to practice it according to the dictates of conscience. They are for free institutions of religion, completely independent of the state and truly voluntary in character. They desire a basically moral society; in the current phraseology, they are for moral and spiritual values. They are for a society in which the rights of the individual are paramount. They are for an educated citizenry steeped in the best democratic traditions. They are for free, secular public schools. They see them as the finest expression of American democracy. They favor keeping their schools independent of church control, removed from religious competition and friction. Finally, they are for freedom—freedom of the mind to flower to its fullest capacity, freedom of conscience unrestricted by the pressures of majority rule.

7

Religious Celebrations in School

J. STEPHEN SHERWIN

THE RELIGIOUS activities in public schools which are the cause of disputes are much the same in community after community, from state to state. Ironically, among the gaily wrapped Christmas gifts and amid the seasonal emphasis upon peace and goodwill comes a parcel of trouble in the form of crèches and pageants dealing with the birth of Christ. Youngsters in the lower grades compose Christmas poems, listen to Bible stories and other stories about Christmas, and tell their classmates how Christmas is celebrated in their homes. Older groups write essays on topics like "What Christmas Means to Me." One unit for secondary school students involves a study of the ways in which Christmas is observed in countries in various parts of the world. There are Bible clubs, assemblies at which hymns are sung and the Bible read, sectarian baccalaureate services, and religious symbols displayed in classrooms and elsewhere in school buildings.

An Easter program dramatizing the Crucifixion was one of several alleged violations of separation of church and state which was banned by the Circuit Court of Dade County (Miami, Fla.) in April, 1961. The American Jewish Congress, which has a long record of opposition to religious activity in public schools, described the dramatization in the opening paragraphs of its pamphlet, "The Miami Story":

In the spotlight on the darkened stage stands a child in the role of Jesus, naked except for a towel around his loins, his arms outstretched against a large wooden cross; his thin body is smeared with ketchup, simulating blood. The silence of the auditorium is broken only by the voices of two students—a boy and a girl—alternately reading the verses in the New Testament describing the Crucifixion.

". . . and he saith unto the Jews, behold your King.

"But they cried out, Away with him, away with him, crucify him. Pilate saith unto them, Shall I crucify your King? The chief priests answered, We have no king but Caesar.

"Then delivered he him therefore unto them to be crucified. And they took Jesus, and led him away.

"And he bearing his cross went forth into a place called the place of a skull, which is called in the Hebrew Golgotha;

"Where they crucified him, and two others with him, on either side one, and Jesus in the midst.

"And Pilate wrote a title, and put it on the cross. And the writing was, JESUS OF NAZARETH THE KING OF THE JEWS."

As the last verse is read the boy on the cross moans and gives a final tortured gasp. His head drops; the agony of the Crucifixion is over.

It is clear that this dramatization, which was presented without interpretation or discussion, could have contributed little to the cause of improving intergroup relations in a democratic country; its effect could only have been to re-enforce to some degree attitudes stained for centuries with the blood of innocents.

A prudent layman will handle gingerly, if at all, the question of the constitutionality of religious celebrations in the school, and he will tread warily through the morass of local and state and Federal rulings, opinions, regulations, and laws dealing with numerous specific practices affecting the relationship between religion and the public school. Therefore, this discussion will be confined to the educational and social implications of religious celebrations in the school. The particular reference will be to Christmas.

It is not enough to say that, since the citizenry are overwhelmingly Christian, the school may justifiably reflect the religious orientation of the majority, for the basic political philosophy upon which present-day American social institutions are built asserts that minority rights are as precious as majority rights and that the strength and vitality of our social organism is derived from a cross-fertilization made possible by a vigorous respect for group differences as well as likenesses. If the day of the melting pot is over and the ideal is no longer to produce a faceless uniformity among our people, then the time has come to take a hard look at the assumptions implicit in religious activities in the public school.

If the American people accept in their hearts their pluralistic society, then it is no more justifiable to celebrate the Hindu festival Durga Puja in American schools than it is to celebrate Christmas. Yet, minorities should not be trampled, and majorities should not be overridden. Because these principles cannot be applied simultaneously, the only course left would appear to be compromise. But compromise cannot possibly satisfy those who understand, cherish, and practice their religion. How can such persons agree to "general" religion in the school or to "as little religion as possible" to pacify those who want none at all? Perhaps a half-loaf is better than none, but a living religion like the living child in I Kings 3 cannot be apportioned. Solomon, in his wisdom, knew that sometimes the rightful, if difficult, solution must be found and that sometimes no compromise is possible.

Frequently it is assumed that school Christmas activities are nonsectarian and non-religious and thus "harmlessly" emphasize the Christmas symbols without touching upon the specific religious aspects and doctrinal meanings of the occasion. If the emphasis in the school is truly upon symbols stripped of their religious meanings, the emphasis is devoid of educational significance and is a mockery of legitimate religious observance. If Christmas is treated as a sort of national holiday, the school is helping to convert one of the most beautiful occasions in Christendom into a secular festival which is suitable for commercial exploitation and which emphasizes those temporal and material concerns that are the antithesis of Christian spirituality. If public school education during Christmas takes on an essentially religious character, then, by that very fact, the school can be said (even by a layman in the law) to be undermining the constitutional separation of church and state and to be acting contrary to the very law which it has every obligation to uphold. In addition, the school is transgressing upon the rights of those who worship in other ways, as well as upon the rights of those whose privilege it is not to worship at all. Many clergymen object to the school's usurping the right and duty of the church to give its young members the kind of religious education which it wishes them to have. On the other hand, non-Christian, agnostic, and atheistic parents object to their children being taught a religion in which they do not believe.

Indeed, it always has seemed strange that devout people would be willing to turn over the religious education of their children to a public agency designed, as public schools must be, to supply the educational needs of a cross-section of the community. The implicit admission is that the religious influence of the parents and the clergy is too weak to be effectual without the authority of the school to bolster it. Furthermore, what if the public school should accede to pressure and then do a creditable job of religious teaching? Would not many parents then prefer to save time, effort, and money by sending their children to public school, thereby weakening and perhaps destroying part-time and full-time parochial schools? Add to this the present inaccuracy, shallowness, and spiritual poverty of Christmas and other religious celebrations in the school and it would seem that many good parents have received little for their efforts to introduce religion into the public school and have paid much in terms of intergroup friction, social disharmony, community divisiveness, and a weakened public school system. Democracy cannot thrive in such an environment.

In a speech delivered in April, 1960, the Rev. Peter Rega, chaplain of the St. Thomas Moore Guild, University of Buffalo School of Law, recognized this danger to democracy and stressed both the opportunity which the First Amendment provides to the Catholic Church to fulfill its spiritual mission and the danger to the church in any weakening of the constitutional provision for separation of religious and civil authority:

Our constitution . . . was so utopian that no European nation believed it could ever work. But it did—for 184 years—with no sign of its death anywhere in sight. For the first time—practically speaking—in all the Church's history—the Church is left unfettered by political power to fulfill its spiritual mission. Examine all the European so-called "Catholic Countries." Their histories are full of either persecution of the Church or privilege of the Church—and . . . I am not able to say which has been more detrimental for the Church.

* * *

To strive, then, in any way (in our country) to gain any . . . "privileges" . . . would be tantamount to . . . treason to the American experience so amply proven successful and workable.

* * *

The point is that the goodness of the First Amendment . . . is manifested not only by political, but also by religious experience. By and large, it has been good for religion—for Catholicism—to have had simply the right to freedom.

If formal lessons and assembly programs containing doctrinal and theistic themes are considered objectionable, then informal observances, such as Christmas and Easter decorations, are also objectionable. The observance of a religious occasion that does not involve any formal lesson or class activity is simply a more subtle invasion of minority integrity. If a person desired a subtle means of indoctrinating majority beliefs, it would be difficult to find a more suitable technique than these informal observances.

Religious celebrations in the school have the further unhappy effect of setting minority religions apart and directing toward them a silent charge: "You are different!" Christmas observances in the school put pressure upon the youthful members of minority religious groups to conform to majority patterns of religious behavior and, through the children, put pressure upon the parents to conform. One Jewish child, for example, returned home from a school Christmas party (at which there was much talk about Santa Claus and the birth of Little Lord Jesus) and asked permission to be adopted by a Christian family "just for Christmas." To some extent, this child's reaction reveals a parental failure to supply a religious atmosphere in the home which could better withstand the pressures to which members of minority religions are inevitably subjected. But the child's reaction also reveals that the school had subjected him to unnecessary pressure. One duty of public education is to encourage a child's pride in individuality and to create an atmosphere of respect for differences among people. Christmas activities, whether formal or informal, do not bring us closer to the day when the customs and beliefs of smaller groups in society will be as respected as the ways of larger groups.

An interesting but rather odd adjunct to Christmas programs in some schools is the "Hanukkah lesson." Hanukkah is a Jewish holiday celebrating the rededication (in 165 B.C.) of the Temple which had been defiled by a Syrian king in an unsuccessful attempt to subjugate the Jews and to suppress their religion. The date varies from year to year but can be counted upon to fall within a few weeks of Christmas.

The coincidental semi-conjunction of Christmas and Hanukkah has afforded well-intentioned teachers with an opportunity to "teach tolerance." A common method is to have Jewish children, who already know about Hanukkah, prepare reports on Hanukkah while Christian children, who already know about Christmas, prepare reports about Christmas. Aside from the educational foolishness of having children investigate what they already know and aside from the fascinating problem of how religious education in the public school can be reconciled with the Federal Constitution and with most state constitutions, the major flaw in the procedure is that there is not the slightest rational connection between Christmas and Hanukkah to justify their being taught together.

The present tendency is for both proponents and opponents on the issue of religious activities in the school to harden their stands. Hope, therefore, is dim for an ingenious proposal that the public school teach not religion, but *about* religion. At Christmas time, for example, social studies teachers could introduce a unit on the customs (religious and otherwise) of majority and minority groups in America or, possibly, a unit on social customs (religious and otherwise) of people in other parts of the world. The purpose, which is educationally defensible, would be to increase students' understanding of, and appreciation for, the ways in which other people do things. Christmas, Hanukkah, and Durga Puja become, in such a study, part of a larger and more broadly meaningful pattern. Instruction is no longer directed toward a specific religious occasion but, rather, is directed toward the multitudinous ways which humanity has devised to cope with the material and spiritual problems of the universe. Stated thus generally, the goal of instruction is identical with the goal of education itself.

Unfortunately, there are certain practical difficulties with the proposal. Textbooks, unit outlines, and other instructional materials are scarce and inferior. Few teachers are capable of handling religious topics in an historical or sociological way. Teaching *about* religion may become merely an opening wedge for the teaching *of* religion. There is a real danger that the introduction of such a program would lead to a religious test for teachers as each religious group in the community presses for the employment of one of its own to assure "fair" presentation of its views. Also, objectivity in a teacher's presentation, even if it can be achieved, may well be confused in a student's mind with indifference to deep, personal, religious experience. Finally, teaching *about* religion will arouse the opposition of those to whom any religious presentation barren of efforts to win faith is false and purposeless—

> Shape without form, shade without colour,
> Paralysed force, gesture without motion.

Some of these difficulties may be overcome. For example, better textbooks can be written. But no concerted efforts to remedy the remediable have come to light, and the other difficulties are awesome. After careful study, controlled experimentation, and successful efforts to win public co-operation, conditions may favor the introduction into the public school of teaching *about* religion, but the prospect now seems no larger than a "little cloud out of the sea, like a man's hand."

The proponents of religion in the school face a painful dilemma. The freedom from governmental control which religious institutions now enjoy cannot continue if the ties to the state grow stronger. Yet, without state assistance, the religious institutions must continue their wearying struggle to find a secure place in a culture which is basically secular. The opponents of religion in the school may ask: "How long halt ye between two opinions?" Living in two worlds simultaneously is as impossible as having one's cake and eating it, too. And is not the freedom which an ecclesiastical authority apart from a civil authority possesses worth more than an alliance with government that leads to reliance on government and to the shackling of the spiritual mission by political power?

In a pluralistic and democratic society such as ours, the total education of youth cannot be safely undertaken by a single institution. The concentration of power is too great. Furthermore, since home and church emphasize the doctrinal and other differences among people, the public school must be even more zealously guarded as a place where likenesses are acknowledged and differences are given status. The public school is the common ground of the nation's children where they meet to play and to study and to discover one another face to face. The public school is the bedrock of democratic society and the single most important public agency for achieving the continuity of democratic values. As a secular institution, the public school is concerned with the education of the child as a human being and as a social being. Religious education is primarily concerned with the child as the child of God and should be willing to continue in its time-honored role as a prime contestant for the minds, hearts, and souls of the faltering and the non-believers in a world of distractions and temptations. Religious education and public education—separately and in their individual ways—can contribute to the education of those who will be the citizens, the parents, the breadwinners, and the faithful of tomorrow. However, if the proponents of religion in the public schools accomplish their aim and forsake their historical role in American society, they may live to see the dissolution of privately controlled religious education and the erection on the site of the public school of a New Babel which from its many parts speaks with many tongues about a religion grown too vacuous to support a living faith.

₰8₰

Baccalaureate in Brodhead: Interfaith Tension

WILLIAM W. BOYER

THOUGH ALL MAJOR
faiths in the U. S. support the constitutional
principle of separation of church and state, within this principle are many areas of interfaith
tension particularly when religion is meshed
with public education. One of these tension
areas concerns high-school baccalaureate exercises. The following is an account of such conflict in the community of Brodhead (population
2,016), located in a dairy-rich river valley in
southern Wisconsin.

In 1950, all ingredients for conflict were present in Brodhead. Annually, the graduating class
of Brodhead's public high school voted on which
clergyman should preside over its baccalaureate
exercise and, hence, in which church the exercise
would be held. Only a few of each class were
Catholic. The Roman Catholic faith holds to a
religious tenet which forbids its members from
attending religious ceremonies held in churches
other than its own or from participating *actively*
in joint religious exercises of any kind. Typically,

baccalaureate exercises assume a religious character with the singing of hymns and the offering of prayer. And in Brodhead at the time was a crusading and highly expressive personality in the person of the Rev. Andrew Breines, the local Catholic pastor.

Beginning in the fall of 1950, the father of one of the students to graduate from Brodhead High School approached a member of the school board and explained that the three Catholic graduates could not take part in baccalaureate services held in any church but their own without compromising their religious principles. The matter was brought to the attention of the superintendent of the high school, C. T. Pfisterer. He answered that the senior class had voted on the matter and it was, therefore, out of his hands.

The Rev. R. A. Boettcher, minister of the Evangelical Church, had been the pastor selected, and he announced meanwhile that the exercises would be held in his church. Catholic parents objected on the ground that "it was only reasonable to expect that a public school function be held in the public school auditorium without embarrassment to any of the participants." Two telephone conversations between Fr. Breines and Mr. Boettcher failed to resolve any differences. None of the three Catholic graduates, or their parents, or the six Catholic teachers in the elementary and high schools, or Fr. Breines attended the baccalaureate service in the Evangelical Church on June 6.[1]

Shortly before the baccalaureate, Fr. Breines wrote "with deep regret" to the State Superin-

[1] Letter from the Rev. A. Breines to Rebecca C. Barton, director, State of Wisconsin Governor's Commission on Human Rights, Sept. 6, 1951, in the files of the commission.

tendent of Public Instruction, George E. Watson, protesting the "ill-advised action of Mr. C. T. Pfisterer." He characterized the incident as creating "much bitter feeling and misunderstanding in the community" and as setting "a precedent of religious discrimination and intolerance in Brodhead." He added:

It has always been my understanding that the First Amendment protects American citizens from all establishments of religion and guarantees all its citizens the right to attend the church of their choice. The wisdom of the Constitution in this matter is shown in the present case for a minority of three could never successfully defend their religious rights in a class vote where the overwhelming majority is of another religious faith or where a public official arbitrarily invades the area of these basic human rights.[2]

Supt. Watson promptly replied that the matter "is within the province and power of the local school board." And he continued:

Personally, in my years as a local school administrator, I preferred to have such programs in the high school auditorium, presided over by the High School Principal, with the attendance of seniors a voluntary matter.[3]

In the *Catholic Herald Citizen*—an official Wisconsin Catholic newspaper—Fr. Breines appealed to his analysis of the American tradition of religious freedom to support his position in the Brodhead controversy:

The preservation of our God-given rights has become the number one concern of all conscientious Americans these days. Because as Americans we recognize these rights as coming from God, we view the right to worship God according to one's religious convictions as the cornerstone of our basic freedoms. Recent world experience has taught us . . . that . . . freedom of speech, freedom from fear, freedom from want, will be enjoyed and safeguarded in the measure that freedom of worship remains free. That

---

[2] Copy of letter from the Rev. A. Breines to Supt. G. E. Watson, May 31, 1951, in the files of the Wisconsin Governor's Commission on Human Rights.

[3] Copy of letter from Supt. G. E. Watson to the Rev. A. Breines, June 1, 1951, in the files of the Wisconsin Governor's Commission on Human Rights.

is what "freedom under God" means . . . . that under God the American formula of equal treatment and equal opportunity for all, regardless of race, color or creed, has preserved our freedoms for us for the past 175 years. When a public function is so arranged in a community as to make it impossible for all Americans to take part, because of race, color or creed, it can hardly be said to square with the American democratic tradition.[4]

The active interest of the State of Wisconsin Governor's Commission on Human Rights was solicited by Fr. Breines. Its director, Rebecca C. Barton, observed that the Brodhead arrangement "seems to work to the disadvantage of certain pupils who cannot participate for doctrinal reasons." Both the Catholic and Protestant members of the Governor's Commission feel strongly, Dr. Barton said, in favor of holding baccalaureate exercises on "neutral territory" (implying a place other than church or public school property) as a means of furthering better human relations.[5]

State Superintendent Watson "did not believe that the baccalaureate services as presently conducted in the typical community were illegal." He believed the problem would not be solved "if all were held in high schools . . . inasmuch as objections had been raised to *each* location for the services." And he elaborated on his position as follows:

Personally, I would like to see some spiritual aspects retained with our commencement activities. I do not think that my best contribution will come in any form of a "directive" to the schools. In order to retain this spiritual essence, and to avoid any state department or official being unfairly charged with a desire to eliminate this spiritual characteristic, I would rather proceed informally with small groups of administrators and urge them to have individual churches or synagogs plan "recognition ser-

[4] A. Breines, *Catholic Herald Citizen* (Madison), July 7, 1951.
[5] Copies of letters from R. C. Barton to Supt. G. E. Watson, Jan. 16 and March 10, 1952, in the files of the Wisconsin Governor's Commission on Human Rights.

vices" for the young people of each faith in the graduating classes.[6]

Although state administrators exerted unusual efforts to solve the problem, the graduating class of Brodhead High School again voted to hold its June, 1952, baccalaureate exercise in a Protestant church, this time in the Bethlehem Lutheran Church.

Mr. Pfisterer, apparently acting upon Supt. Watson's advice, proposed that Sunday, June 1, 1952, be designated "Baccalaureate Sunday" in all Brodhead churches and that each church observe the occasion with appropriate services rather than hold a mass baccalaureate. But this was not done. Instead, the graduating class went on record as accepting full responsibility for its action. Fr. Breines thereupon inserted a paid advertisement in the *Brodhead Independent Register* explaining the Catholic position of recognizing the baccalaureate as an "active" religious event in which Catholics could not participate. The Rev. R. W. Sachtjen, pastor of the Brodhead Methodist Church, charged that this was an "intolerable position," and asserted that, prior to the coming of Fr. Breines to Brodhead, priests always had defined baccalaureate participation as "passive participation."[7]

Meanwhile, Supt. Watson pursued the moderate policy of recognizing the matter as one of local control. "I have been bold enough," he said, "to recommend that educational and religious leaders of the community sit down together to discuss the whole problem. Some communities have abolished the service and some . . . have

[6] Letter from Supt. G. E. Watson to Mrs. Gertrude Anderson, chairman, Special Committee, Wisconsin Governor's Commission on Human Rights, April 21, 1952, in the files of the commission.

[7] *Capital Times* (Madison), June 5, 1952.

substituted several individual church services, each church recognizing the members of its congregation who are in the graduating class."[8]

Had the issue been submitted to the Wisconsin courts, the legality of holding baccalaureate exercises in churches might have been determined. Instead, the practice continued in 1953 and 1954, but the earlier tension had begun to subside. Representatives of the Governor's Commission on Human Rights talked to students, parents, and local educators about the desirability of changing the practice. More important, the Rev. Wilfred Schuster succeeded Fr. Breines as Brodhead's Catholic pastor in the spring of 1954.

Serving as pastor until 1958, Fr. Schuster did not feel that there was any animosity toward him in the community "because the aroused emotions were directed at Father Breines as an individual." Since the spring of 1955, a year after Fr. Schuster arrived, baccalaureate exercises have been held in the local high school. Ministers and priests have come and gone. Religious groups now co-operate in setting up a community crib during the Christmas season as well as planning a centennial program. Fr. Schuster credits the present Methodist minister as primarily responsible for improved interfaith relations. Other Wisconsin communities have followed Brodhead's lead by discontinuing baccalaureate exercises in churches.[9]

Certain conclusions can be drawn from this controversy. First, as stated by Fr. Breines, the

[8] Copy of letter from Supt. G. E. Watson to the Rev. L. B. Keegan, St. Patrick's Church, Sparta, Wis., June 11, 1952, in the files of the Wisconsin Department of Public Instruction.

[9] Letter from R. C. Barton, director, State of Wisconsin Governor's Commission on Human Rights, to W. W. Boyer, July 30, 1959.

Roman Catholic position adheres to a complete separation of church and state with respect to the holding of public school baccalaureate exercises in churches. This position is taken for doctrinal purposes—to maintain the Catholic right of conscience as inviolable. The outcome in Brodhead indicates that Fr. Breines won his battle, but only after he was replaced. Second, as long as the issue is withheld from the judicial process, the legality of such a contested practice remains a matter of conjecture however tempestuous may be the controversy.

Finally, and perhaps far more important, regardless of questions of doctrine and law, harmony within a community depends ultimately upon the factor of personality. Had the issue been submitted to the courts, ill feelings might have persisted. As far as the Brodhead controversy has meaning for interfaith tensions elsewhere, personality should be considered a major, if not a dominant, determinant of community interfaith conflict.

9

The Debate Over Public Aid to Religious Schools

WILLIAM W. BRICKMAN

THE TIMELY TOPIC
of Federal and state financial and other forms
of aid to schools under religious auspices has
been illustrated by a variety of arguments in behalf of, or in opposition to, this practice. Many
of these have been put forth in the past, but
some are relatively recent. It will be something
of a convenience to anyone interested in the
problem to have these statements brought together and analyzed.

Double taxation. Parents whose children
attend parochial schools often complain that
they pay twice for educational services—once for
the public school system and again for education in a religious school. This may be a hard
burden in many instances. Such parents and
their supporters, especially the Catholic clergy,
contend that the parochial school fulfills a public function in that it teaches just about what
the public school does, *mutatis mutandis*; that
many of its graduates study, teach, and serve in
public institutions and agencies; that all private

education is, as a rule, under state supervision; and that it contributes substantially to the welfare and the security of the nation. Ordinary logic and justice would demand, it would seem, that the government give help toward the secular instructional program of the religious schools.

On the other hand, opponents of public aid are quick to reply that no parent is forced by law to send his child to a parochial school. He always can withdraw the child and enroll him in a public school, thus avoiding the burden of double taxation.

Just how strong is this answer? If a substantial number of pupils are released to public education as the consequence of the closing down of financially pressed parochial schools, it is not difficult to envision the impact on local public school systems. In view of the persistent shortage of qualified teachers, of adequate school buildings, and of sufficient teaching equipment, it is likely that public education would receive a telling blow from which it might not recover for an appreciable length of time. All the present-day problems about which the educators have been complaining since World War II will be aggravated no doubt by the sudden enrollment of pupils from parochial schools. It does not seem probable that much advance notice will be given to local school boards and state education authorities. The possibility of a deluge of enrollment in some public school systems should not be dismissed as remote. In Catholic educational circles, the Rev. Neil G. McCluskey, S.J., and other educators have been urging for years the curtailment of the parochial elementary schools and the concentration upon secondary and higher education.

American tradition. It is often argued that public aid to religious schools would constitute a repudiation of the traditional American policy of tax-supported funds only for publicly controlled schools. A glance at the history of education in the U.S. will disclose Federal and state subventions to denominational schools during various periods. Thus, New York State passed a law in 1795 granting money to charity schools under religious auspices; the U.S. government made land grants to a Baptist college (1832) and a Catholic college (1833); the Freedmen's Bureau gave Federal funds to Negro schools conducted by religious groups (1865-71); the U.S. government made money grants to a Methodist university (1870), Christian missionary schools in Alaska (1888, 1892), and a denominational institution (1899); local public funds were given to Protestant colleges in Kansas and Minnesota (1909); and state support has been applied to the School of Religion of the State University of Iowa from 1927 to the present. If anything, it would seem that there is enough in American history to warrant questioning whether the tradition was not broad enough to include public financial aid to religious educational institutions. Many more examples could be cited to show how all levels of government have contributed some form of aid to schools under religious auspices.

Opponents of public support of religious schools probably will contend that, in most of these cases at least, there was some reason for the aid without involving the matter of religion. For instance, the money granted by the Federal government to the Negro religious schools was intended to provide educational opportunities to the members of a group which had been denied adequate education under slavery. In short, this was an act of social benevolence and welfare on the part of the government to a group which had suffered, rather than a move to encourage religious belief and observance. As a matter of fact, this seems to be a powerful argument, but it also can be applied to the current situation. Why should one not say, with similar cogency, that Federal funds to religious schools (where religion forms a part but certainly not all of the curriculum) are actually intended to help education rather than religion? Whatever reasons might be advanced to justify public support in particular cases, it is difficult to deny that in each instance a religious institution was involved in some way. Consequently, it is possible to conclude that the American tradition may have been other than the prevailing conception of it and that financial co-operation between government and religion in educational affairs had at least as much of a claim to being regarded as part of the American tradition as the policy of non-support.

Church-state separation. Perhaps the most frequently presented argument against Federal and state support for parochial education is its unconstitutionality. This viewpoint has been expressed time and again by President Kennedy, many Protestant and Jewish religious leaders, laymen of all faiths, and large numbers of lawyers and legislators. Certainly, everyone should be loyal to the Constitution and should fight for the integrity of the First Amendment—all of it. But it is virtually impossible to know, on the basis of the various U.S. Supreme Court decisions, the national laws in force, and the wide variety of state and local laws and actual practices, just what is or what is not in accordance with the provisions of the Constitution. To act in the spirit of the Constitution, it is necessary first of all to be enlightened on what it actually says. As nearly everyone is aware, there is no specific mention in the Constitution of the necessity of keeping a wall of separation between church and state. The Jeffersonian phrase, "wall of separation," was contained in a private message to a group of Baptists, but it appeared nowhere in the official legislative acts. In recent U.S. Supreme Court decisions, as well as in the various writings on the church-state controversy, the doctrine of separationism is treated as a dogma. Yet, there is no such thing—and there never was in American history—as a full, complete, definite, and thorough separation of church and state—decidedly not in educational matters. As the writer has stated elsewhere, when a principle, such as that of church-state separation, has been consistently violated with common consent over the years, it is reasonable to inquire if it has not been downgraded to an *un-principle* or *anti-principle*.

So long as the Supreme Court has not ruled with definitiveness—and it seems hardly likely that it would ever do so—on what the "establishment of religion" clause in the First Amendment really means, it is not exactly fair to anticipate its judgment and to prevent legislative action which would benefit the religious schools and the country in general. Even when the Supreme Court has acted with decisiveness and dispatch, as in the case of racial segregation in public education, the actual fulfillment of the decision raises many problems of interpretation which may not be solved for some time.

No one, whether he be President Kennedy, an individual legislator or judge, or an ecclesiastical or other expert is competent to give a final judgment on what is permissible or not under the Constitution in the area of church-state-school relations. In that case, it appears appropriate for all to give the Supreme Court a chance or a series of chances to come to a clear-cut conclusion concerning this controversy.

Let us take another look at the "establishment of religion" clause, the violation of which is usually cited as the major reason, or at least one major reason, for opposition to any Federal and state payments to religious schools. This disapproval even has been extended recently by many influential groups and persons to public loans to any school operated under denominational auspices.

Mr. Justice Jackson, who probably was as strict as anyone in his interpretation of the First Amendment in connection with the church-state-school problem, stated in the Everson Decision that "the prohibition against establishment of religion cannot be circumvented by a subsidy, bonus or reimbursement of expense to individuals for receiving religious instruction and indoctrination."[1] According to another dissenter, Mr. Justice Rutledge, "Not simply an established church, but any law respecting an establishment of religion is forbidden. . . . The prohibition broadly forbids state support, financial or other, of religion in any guise, form or degree. It outlaws all use of public funds for religious purposes."[2] As Mr. Justice Rutledge emphasized, the term "religion" in the First Amendment has only *one* meaning, "so that Congress and now

---

[1] *Everson v. Board of Education*, 330 U.S. 1 (1947).
[2] *Ibid.*

the states are as broadly restricted concerning the one as they are regarding the other."[3]

Put into other words, the governmental authority may not authorize free bus transportation to parochial school pupils, let alone direct grants to the schools themselves, and it also may not make any law which will diminish the freedom of religion enjoyed by an individual and the freedom of "an establishment of religion." To quote Mr. Justice Rutledge once more, the objective of the First Amendment was "to create a complete and permanent separation of the spheres of religious activity and civil authority by comprehensively forbidding every form of public aid or support of religion."[4] This reasoning appears to be at the bottom of the recent and current opposition to any form of Federal and state aid to religious schools and colleges, as well as to individuals to attend them.

Let us accept, *argumenti causa*, the Jeffersonian viewpoint of separation as applied by Justices Jackson and Rutledge and by many others. If separation must be full, complete, thorough, and permanent, then we can seriously call into question the practice of state control of secular education in the parochial schools, which already have been adjudged to constitute "an establishment of religion." Since the state is prohibited from making any law about "an establishment of religion," with reference to financial and other subsidies, it follows that under the same prohibition, as stressed by Mr. Justice Rutledge, the state cannot make any law which regulates the parochial school, which is obviously part of a religious establishment.

[3] *Loc. cit.*

How can a state authority constitutionally enforce a compulsory school attendance law when parents wish to enroll their children in a religious school? Certainly, in the free exercise of religion, a parent may decide that education minus religion is a violation of a religious precept, a view which will be supported by ecclesiastical authority. If he sends his children to a public school, they will not be taught religion, or they will be taught (unconstitutionally, of course) a form of religion not in accord with the parent's conviction, or they might be indoctrinated with secularist values. In any event, there will be a prohibition of the individual's free exercise of religion. To avoid such a situation, the parent will decide to place his children in a religious school, which is supervised but not financed by the state. He will have to spend his own money to fulfill his obligation under the state's compulsory school attendance law. Is this the "equal protection of the laws" guaranteed by the Federal and state governments under the Fourteenth Amendment? At one and the same time, the government does not give aid to religious schools but it does regulate by law and practice such religious establishments.

As Mr. Justice Jackson said in a differing context in the Everson Decision, "we cannot have it both ways." If the government insists on withholding funds from religious schools, it must, under the same First Amendment, give up its control of such religious institutions.

But, one might still argue, the state government has the constitutional right of supervising all non-religious educational content, school buildings, qualifications of teachers of secular subjects, and the like, and, consequently, can exercise its authority over the parochial schools without subsidizing them. After all, the secular content of the curriculum constitutes the major portion of what is taught in the parochial schools. However, from this standpoint, one might equally argue in behalf of public support. But leaving this matter aside, let us quote again from the opinion of Mr. Justice Rutledge in the Everson Decision: "Commingling the religious with the secular teaching does not divest the whole of its religious permeation and emphasis or make them of minor part, if proportion were material. Indeed, on any other view, the constitutional prohibition always could be brought to naught by adding a modicum of the secular."[4]

The religious school, then, is a religious establishment which is regulated and supervised by law under one interpretation and is not helped financially by the same government under another interpretation of the identical First Amendment. Here we have "a law respecting an establishment of religion" and "prohibiting the free exercise thereof" simultaneously. It would appear that the state authority lacks competence, under the Constitution, to enforce and supervise the teaching of secular subjects in a religious school once a church has set up such an institution for the education of the children of its adherents. Nor does the state government seem to have the constitutional competence even to compel parents who belong to a church to send their children to any public school when a religious school is not available. An individual has been regarded as much of "an establishment of religion" as a religious school has been.

Again, as Rutledge said in the Everson De-

---
[4] *Ibid.*

cision, " 'Religion' has the same broad significance in the twin prohibition concerning 'an establishment.' . . . The prohibition broadly forbids state support, financial or other, of religion in any guise, form or degree. It outlaws all use of public funds for religious purposes." These quotations seldom appear in discussions or in anthologies of Supreme Court cases. Rutledge often is cited as an opponent of Federal aid to religious education, but he also should be quoted with respect to the ban on public funds to religion in schools under any auspices.

It appears logical, therefore, to suppose that there should be some flexibility in the current interpretation of the "establishment of religion" clause. The state should exercise control of secular education in the religious school, but it also should subsidize it.

Public control of religious education. It is inevitable, contend the opponents of public aid, that once a governmental agency furnishes the funds, it will exercise control over the religious school, in line with the hackneyed proverb about the musician performing the compositions preferred by the philanthropist. In this connection, it is enlightening to turn once more the pages of history to discover that there is no necessary relationship between Federal aid and Federal control in education. The congressional land grants to state universities from 1862 onward, the G. I. and the Korean G. I. Bills of Rights, the National Defense Education Act of 1958, and other forms of educational financing by the U.S. government were not followed by any type of control other than the reasonable one of requiring that the monies or land grants be utilized for the purposes prescribed by the respective laws.

On the other hand, one can point to instances of Federal control *without* any aid. There may be control through suggestion or innuendo, as when schools and colleges feel that they must co-operate with the national purpose at a time that might be described as critical. Again, when a congressional group such as the Sub-committee on Un-American Affairs questioned professors and teachers with regard to their loyalty, there were sufficient institutions which conducted similar investigations without having been required or even requested to do so by any governmental body. Perhaps, in this way, those schools felt that they would be spared a possible probe by a Federal agency. Surely, the Federal government has enough resources and power to exercise some kind of control, should it choose to, over any organization. The fact is, however, that it has not controlled education in any significant way and ostensibly will not spread its power, whether or not it offers money to religious schools. Naturally, there is no guarantee with regard to any future course of action, but, in the light of the historical past, there seems little likelihood of unwarranted interference on the part of the government in the educational affairs of the religious schools.

Account also should be taken of the fact that the secular programs of the parochial schools are generally under the supervision of the state departments of education, regardless of any policy of financial aid. State authorities also influence, directly or indirectly, the selection of textbooks, the content of the curriculum, and the qualifications of the teachers of the parochial schools in virtually all areas but religious instruction. It is interesting to note that there is no record of any serious challenge of the right of the state to control the religious school as an infringement upon the doctrine of separating church and state. At the same time, it would be pertinent to raise the question whether, in view of the reality of state control, it is not fitting and proper for the state government to contribute toward the cost of the secular educational programs in the parochial schools which are under state supervision and direction. Such questions are rarely if ever discussed in legislative halls or in other circles interested in the problem of public subventions to private religious schools.

Support of undemocratic practices. Some allege that a religious school, by virtue of its very nature and its objectives and practices, is bound to foster feelings which are contrary to the democratic ideology. After all, it is an institution which tries to propagate but a single point of view and it is accordingly reserved for an elite. From this standpoint, consequently, it would be wrong to bestow public aid upon a school which is dedicated to an ideal at variance with that of the majority of the American people.

Such a definition of democracy suffers from shortsightedness and from a refusal to consider seriously the concept of cultural pluralism which many opponents of the parochial school proclaim in more or less the same breath. This narrow interpretation may be proposed by persons who approve of special schools for the gifted and handicapped children and do not seem to be conscious of any contradiction in their attitude. Significantly, there are individuals and groups who endorse separate schools for the Negroes but condemn schools for religious groups—all in the name of freedom and democracy. Strictly speaking, however, there is room in the pluralistic society characteristic of a democracy for different types of schools to serve different interests and abilities. In a multi-cultural nation there should be a broad policy in connection with the financing of educational institutions.

Something, too, might be learned from the experience of foreign countries. The proposition regarding the possible connection between parochial schools and democracy might be tested by means of an examination of the situation elsewhere than in the United States. It is enough to invite attention to the existence of religious schools which are parallel to the governmental schools in such democratic countries as Belgium, Denmark, England, France, Holland, and Israel. And while the religious schools are not supported by the government in all instances, there does not seem to be any systematic, serious opposition to them on democratic grounds. To be fully frank, it is necessary to mention the fact that even some countries which are not democratic, in the international sense of the term, may tolerate the presence of religious schools. This is the case in the Iron-Curtain area, in such countries as Rumania and Poland.

Separationism and democracy. On many occasions, the partisans of a strict policy of separating church and state in educational finance have argued that a democratic government demands that Caesar and God do not mix. Again, the other dimensions of the problem are able to cast some light. A review of close to two centuries of democratic experience in America will disclose no doubt that church and state have been something else than separate. Under any interpretation, the military chaplaincy (including its training program), the policy of exempting churches and church property from public taxation, the frequent allocation of tax monies and their equivalent for sectarian hospitals and schools, the tacit and overt approval of religious teachings and practices in the public schools, and other customs and incidents in American government and society constitute some sort of evidence that, as a nation, Americans have managed somehow to survive as a democratic people with a lack of a distinct separation of church and state. From a close consideration of the historical record, it is reasonable to doubt if there ever had existed a firm intention to achieve separationism. Let it not be forgotten, in the words of Mr. Justice Frankfurter in the Mc-Collum Decision, that "separation means separation, not something less."[5] It is evident that there never really has been a church-state separation in this country, and there is no clear reason to believe that it will be more democratic than it is at present should strict separationism become the law and the practice of the land.

Once more, attention might be focused on the situation in other nations. Any student of foreign government knows that there are established churches in the Scandinavian countries, in Great Britain, and elsewhere. Few will insist that the lack of separationism has resulted in undemocratic governmental administration. Further, there are few countries which are committed by their constitutions to a thoroughgoing policy of church-state separation as is the Soviet Union, which will be described as democratic by few who are not Communists.

---

[5] *McCollum v. Board of Education*, 333 U.S. 203 (1948).

If democracy and separationism do not necessarily go hand in hand, it becomes advisable
to rethink the objection by the devotees of
democracy to public payments to parochial
schools. It is to be hoped that a sufficient number of them will undertake a re-examination of
the question. With the religious schools making
a contribution to the democratic life of the nation, it is hard to see how any form of public
support will constitute a danger to democracy.

The existence of the public school. It may
be argued that public funds for religious schools
might jeopardize the existence of the public
school system, which is widely held to be the
foundation stone of American democratic society. According to this viewpoint, should funds
become available to the parochial school systems, the different denominations surely will be
encouraged to embark upon an expansion of
their educational systems at the expense of the
public purse. In fact, it is not at all inconceiv-
able that religious groups without schools of
their own might establish some to further their
denominational ends at a minimum cost to
themselves. The inevitable outcome would be
the fragmentation of the American educational
enterprise and effort, with the public school system becoming one among many rather than the
pre-eminent form of education.

This objection has some merit and deserves
careful consideration. Certainly, it is desirable
in a modern country to have an effective public
school system as the core of the total educational
program. However, the presence of a parallel
system of private schools does not necessarily
connote that public education is not significant.
Subsidies to the religious school, in all probability, will bring about an expansion in the num-

ber and extent of parochial institutions, but it is hardly to be expected that the public school would be eclipsed. Most likely, the preponderant percentage of parents probably will prefer the benefits of a free education in an intercultural atmosphere in which there is minimum or no religious education. Further, there are the Baptists and other religious denominations which object to parochial schools, or at least to public payments to religious education, even if they simultaneously demand the recognition of religion in the public school—all under the rubric of the separation of church and state.

If the practical monopoly of American education by the public school system is somewhat dented, this may be to the good. Competition of a healthy sort on the part of the religious school may be the life of public education. Traditionally, private schools often have started educational experiments which pointed a way toward reform in the public schools. The different types of schools have much to learn from each other.

It also is relevant to recall that the U.S. Supreme Court has decided in the Oregon Decision of 1925 that a state authority cannot constitutionally compel parents to send their children to public schools only. This influential decision established the constitutional status of private and parochial schools as legal institutions for the fulfillment of the state laws for compulsory attendance. As Mr. Justice McReynolds, writing the unanimous opinion of the court, stated, "The fundamental theory of liberty upon which all governments in this Union repose excludes any general power of the State to standardize its children by forcing them to accept instruction from public teachers only. The child is not the mere creature of the state. . . ."[6] Possibly implicit in this theory of liberty is the encouragement, to a limited extent at least, of the schools which give parents a choice, especially in the realm of religious education.

The opinion of Louis Marshall, the author of an *amicus curiae* brief which evidently served as a source for the judicial judgment in the Oregon decision, is worth citing. In presenting the brief in behalf of the American Jewish Committee, Mr. Marshall made the following point which frequently has been overlooked: "The nation is no more preserved by the public school than by the other agencies. The Fathers of the Republic and a large proportion of our finest citizens never attended a public school, and today a large number of the best exemplars of Americanism have received and are receiving their education outside of public schools."[7] Clearly, the public school can be cherished and furthered without conferring upon it the sole power of educating America's children and youth.

"Segregation" and divisiveness. Many among those who object to any public help to parochial schools do so on the ground that they do not wish to encourage institutions which will segregate groups of children from each other and from the community of children as a whole. In their judgment, the prevalence of parochial schools will reduce the chances of obtaining harmony and understanding among the religious bodies. Actually, however, divisiveness and seg-

---

[6] *Pierce v. Society of Sisters*, 268 U.S. 510 (1925).

[7] From a brief as published in Charles Reznikoff, editor, "Louis Marshall: Champion of Liberty," Volume II (Philadelphia: Jewish Publication Society of America, 1957), p. 963.

regation are less a function of religion or religious education than of economy, social status, and race. And yet, the opponents of the parochial schools are more disturbed by religious separation for several hours a day. The segregation, or rather separation, does not involve coercion and permanence, as in the matter of racial differences. There is no law which compels pupils of one faith to be kept apart from those of another. Let it also not be forgotten that pupils of various faiths mingle and will continue to mingle in the public schools.

Some religious schools enroll pupils of many different racial, ethnic, social, and economic backgrounds. On the other hand, there are public schools in some rural and even urban areas where the pupils may be of a homogeneous nature as to race, religion, economic and social level, and ethnic origin. Surely, it is of questionable logic to insist only on one sense of the term "cultural pluralism" and to ignore all the others. Consequently, it is strange to find men of good will, who think of themselves as liberals, fighting against a kind of school which contributes greatly to the pluralistic character of the country.

Furthermore, if the parochial schools are to be labeled as segregating influences, then the same judgment might be applied with more or less equal force to the churches themselves, as well as to the Sunday schools, the weekday afternoon religious schools, the vacation church schools, and other forms of religious education. But why stop here? To be consistent, one must describe children's clubs, Boy Scouts, and summer camps as segregating. The college fraternities, athletic teams, and the colleges themselves are hardly less segregating in practice. Then there are the adult fraternal groups, country clubs, and other social institutions which are specifically designed to keep certain types of people in and all others out. It can be seen, therefore, that the argument of segregation which has been leveled against the religious schools can be weakened by a *reductio ad absurdum*.

Promotion of racially segregated schools. Since about 1960, a new argument has gained ground as a variation of the objection toward segregation. Well-meaning persons state that if tax funds are given to parochial schools, then the proponents of the racially segregated schools could maintain their policies by placing their children in private parochial schools which will be closed to Negroes and will benefit from Federal funds. It must be admitted that this seems to be a powerful position, particularly since the U.S. Supreme Court has taken such a forthright stand on the issue of segregated education. Some of the southern governmental units have closed down their public schools or have threatened to discontinue operating them in an effort to prevent racial integration of public schools. The alternative would be, of course, a state-supported private school system which naturally would enjoy Federal subsidies for private education.

When this argument is closely examined, however, it loses its potency. In the first place, millions of dollars are being spent by state governments in the South for segregated schools, even with the ban by the Supreme Court. Very little is being done to achieve integration in accordance with the explicit order by the Court for "all deliberate speed."

During 1959-60, according to the report by the U.S. Commission on Civil Rights, at least

86 of the 211 public colleges and universities in the South "continued to exclude Negro applicants on the ground of race in violation of the law of the land."[8] The Commission also reported that the Federal aid to segregated colleges and universities has had "the effect of supporting racial segregation."[9] Specifically, in five Federal programs of aid, such as college housing, national defense fellowships, and agricultural research and extension, "62 percent or more of the funds expended in seven selected Southern states went to institutions which exclude applicants solely on the basis of race," while in five other Federal programs, such as the National Science Foundation grants for basic research and the National Defense Education Act's language and guidance institutes, "40 to 50 percent of the funds expended in the seven States were received by such institutions."[10]

It is obvious that a serious state of affairs is already in effect, from the standpoint of the integrity of the U.S. Constitution. Of course, another violation—that is, the making possible of more widespread Federal support of segregated education by means of a law offering funds to private and parochial schools—is clearly a matter of piling iniquity upon iniquity. However, it seems advisable to solve this impasse by following the lead of the U.S. Commission on Civil Rights. In its Recommendation No. 1, the Commission urged that "the Federal Government, either by executive or, if necessary, by congressional action, take such measures as may be required

---

[8] United States Commission on Civil Rights, "Equal Protection of the Laws in Public Higher Education: 1960" (Washington: U.S. Government Printing Office, 1961), p. 265.
[9] Ibid., p. 267.
[10] Ibid.

to assure that funds under the various programs of Federal assistance to higher education are disbursed only to such publicly controlled institutions of higher education as do not discriminate on grounds of race, color, religion, or national origin."[11] Since no mention was made of the Federal aid to private colleges and universities which practice segregation, Pres. John A. Hannah of Michigan State University, chairman of the Commission, and the Rev. Theodore M. Hesburgh, C.S.C., president of the University of Notre Dame, joined in a proposal that "the Federal Government, either by executive or, if necessary, by congressional action, take such measures as may be required to assure that funds under the various programs of Federal assistance to higher education are not disbursed to any public or private institution of higher education which discriminates on grounds of race, religion or national origin."[12] Even if the Federal power does not extend to private institutions, it can be applied in the form of a condition for the receipt of public money derived from the taxes of the entire country; thus, no part of the population might be excluded from its benefits on the sole basis of race.

This principle can be applied to the granting of public funds to private schools so that no Federal support will be given to any parochial school which practices racial segregation. The Federal law which provides money for educational purposes should include a provision that only public, private, and religious schools which obey the law of the land in matters of race would receive Federal support. In this way, the major argument of withholding Federal money

[11] *Loc. cit.*
[12] *Ibid.*, p. 273.

from parochial schools on the ground that segregation would be encouraged thereby loses its validity.

Religious parties and public funds. Some are concerned over the possibility that religious groups will enter the political arena as political parties with special interests in order to obtain the most generous grants they can through persistent pressure on legislatures. Under such circumstances, there is a reasonable fear that the religious parties would war among themselves and thus bring about a state of political imbalance, national disharmony, and possibly serious strife.

There is no proof that such parties will arise because of the payment of tax-supported money to the parochial schools. On the foundation of historical precedent, which is naturally no absolute guarantee for the future, no special religious parties have been formed as a consequence of any of the past forms of Federal or state aid to schools under denominational auspices. Nor is there any guarantee that religious parties would not be organized if public subsidies are not forthcoming.

The student of American history will recall that in the 1840's and 1850's the Native American and the Know-Nothing parties were founded with the express purpose of keeping public funds out of the Catholic school coffers, even if only a trickle actually was given by the state authorities. These parties were not interested in obtaining money for Protestant schools but rather in anti-Catholic activity in every conceivable form. It is worthy of note that the Catholics did not set up a counter-party to defend their interests. In recent decades, there seems to have been no danger of a proliferation of religious political parties in connection with Federal and state aid to religious groups or individuals with regard to lunches, secular textbooks, public bus transportation, and other benefits. Nor were any religious political parties born as a result of the court battles and the community conflicts over the issues of Bible reading, Released Time, the singing of religious hymns, the recital of prayers, Christmas observances, and the like.

The "opening wedge" theory. There is another type of opposition to public subsidies which believes that one form of aid will soon lead to demands for further aid, since the precedent already has been established. Thus, some would refuse bus transportation or any of the welfare benefits to children attending parochial schools because they believe that the religious groups which sponsor them will request in time more significant concessions. As the argument was well summed up by Leo Pfeffer, "If hot lunches, why not bus transportation? If bus transportation, why not secular textbooks? If secular textbooks, why not non-religious supplies and equipment (desks, chairs, blackboards, etc.) and why not the salaries of lay instructors teaching secular subjects?"[13] It is unfortunate that Dr. Pfeffer, who is a profound expert on church-state questions, does not accept his own air-tight logical sequence. A good Talmudic reply to his series of questions might be: *"Ain, hochi nami,"* which might be liberally translated as: "Certainly, why not?"

Not one of these benefits has been declared as contrary to the Constitution by the U.S. Supreme Court. In fact, there are decisions by the Court in favor of bus transportation and secular text-

---

[13] Leo Pfeffer, "Church, State, and Freedom" (Boston: Beacon Press, 1953), p. 438.

books. So long as the others have not been disapproved, they are apparently in the status of constitutionality. If this is so, then there seems to be no legal reason why a religious group or groups cannot make an effort to get some public relief for their educational contributions to the public welfare.

The Catholic Church as the chief beneficiary. A sizable body of opinion is reluctant to approve public funds for religious schools because most of them are conducted by the Catholic Church. There is fear that Catholic schools, thus being strengthened, would be in a position to make the church itself more powerful in religious and civil affairs. Such a situation, in the opinion of the objectors, would become a source of danger to the religious integrity and freedom of Protestants and Jews. Further, there also is displeasure over the fact that the Catholic schools are believed to inculcate in the children and adolescents certain religious outlooks and values which are detrimental to good relations with members of other faiths. Many Protestants are opposed to what is taught in the Catholic schools about the Reformation, to give but one example. Jewish groups and individuals have expressed concern and uneasiness over the Catholic teaching about the Crucifixion which they feel is a source of anti-Semitic attitudes and actions on the part of Catholics.

If the Catholics will receive more benefits than other groups, it will be because they have more schools and more children. Protestant and Jewish schools also may receive aid, since the law cannot discriminate between one faith and another. It would be interesting to analyze the statistical figures of the G. I. Bill of Rights to determine the relative percentages of the Federal money that landed in the treasuries of the Protestant, Catholic, and Jewish colleges. One has the feeling that the Protestant church-related institutions probably must have received more than the Catholic colleges.

It is necessary to try to be as objective as possible with reference to anti-denominational teachings in the respective parochial schools. It is conceivable that every faith might be guilty in some degree of such indoctrination. But it is not impossible to find public schools in which unhealthy attitudes are encouraged toward a particular religious or racial group or antipathy or even antagonism to religion as a whole. Anti-Semitism has developed not merely from some types of instruction in Christian schools, but also from that in institutions under the control of Nazi and Communist atheists. On the other hand, children have become friends of the various religions and races partly because of what they have been taught in both public and parochial schools. It is difficult, if not indeed impossible, to find reliable and conclusive evidence one way or the other.

If there is to be opposition to Catholic schools because of anti-Protestantism and anti-Semitism, then it would seem consistent to oppose Catholic hospitals and military chaplains, since it is very probable that they, too, propagate similar doctrines. At the same time, it would only be fair to stop aid to the denominational welfare institutions and individuals of the other faiths in order to avoid any possible influence which is detrimental to another group. Furthermore, since churches are also educational in nature, a campaign must be carried on, it would seem, to withdraw their privilege of exemption from governmental taxes. Finally, all public schools and all other public and private agencies with educational functions must lose public support if they teach anything which is likely to injure the feelings, reputation, or status of anyone. Clearly, here is another instance of *reductio ad absurdum*.

Safeguarding freedom of religion. A favorite argument against public help to religious schools is that any such subvention involves serious infringements upon the freedom of religion. Upholders of this view have advised religious groups that their religious liberty can only be safeguarded by a strict policy of separation of church and state. Since any receipt of funds is a violation of the principle, the religious group endangers its own position in society. If this be true, then religious liberty has long ago gone out of existence in the U.S. because of the many violations of church-state separation. Implicit in this argument is that the members of one faith or of no faith consider themselves competent to advise persons of other beliefs as to what is best for them with reference to freedom of religion.

Many parents of parochial school pupils and their ecclesiastical supporters take the position that the freedom of choice to select a school is a function of the freedom of religion. In other words, if the public authorities provide no subsidy, then there is interference with parental liberty. The parent does not, accordingly, have a free choice if he has to pay a substantial fee for religious education while the free public school beckons to him.

The other side replies that the religious parent is under no legal compulsion to send his child to either a public or a parochial school; he is merely required to send him to a school, which is subject to his personal choice. As long as he voluntarily selects the parochial school, he must exert himself to find the necessary means to defray the cost.

It must be admitted that this appears to be a powerful argument, when examined in and of itself. However, when considered in the context of other factors—such as the religious status of many public schools and the public functions of the parochial school—it is not so easy to accept it. In any event, this is about the strongest and most logical form of opposition to public payment for parochial institutions.

Another aspect of the freedom question is the objection that no one should have to pay taxes which would be used for the subvention of religious schools with which he is not in agreement. This might be regarded as compulsory support of religion and, consequently, a limitation upon freedom. It is further argued that taxpayers whose funds are used for parochial purposes ought to have a voice in the policies and in the control of the religious schools. On the face of it, this is a reasonable request. What is overlooked, however, is that the public is taxed already for the tax exemptions by the churches and by the nonprofit organizations and foundations without having a voice in their operations. Many a citizen, upon analysis, will find himself supporting governmental and nongovernmental activities which are at variance with his policies.

Still another facet of religious freedom is the view that a minority religion which favors Federal aid will jeopardize its legal position in other matters of religious concern in relation to the government. Thus, Jews are told that they should not request public support for their religious schools because in so doing they will not be able to seek exemption from the laws requiring the closing of stores on Sundays and humane-slaughter practices which are contrary to Jewish religious custom. Each problem, however, has a standing in its own right. When Jews feel that a law limits their exercise of religious freedom, they have the right to resort to the courts for relief under the provision of freedom of religious activity in the First Amendment. The same doctrine also implies the freedom to petition for public support to religious schools. No religious minority should permit itself to be intimidated, either by insiders or outsiders, from claiming its right to religious liberty.

Loans to parochial schools. Since 1958, the concept of making Federal loans to religious educational institutions has gained acceptance, especially in connection with the National Defense Education Act. There are some who would make a distinction, from the constitutional viewpoint, between loans and direct grants. Somehow, there is something less unsavory, as the separationist sees it, if the public authority merely lends money to parochial schools and later is reimbursed at a moderate rate of interest. Yet, it is difficult to discern any deep difference in principle. From one standpoint, one is as legitimate as the other; from the other view, both are equally unconstitutional. To the present writer, there is no valid reason why religious schools should not receive direct grants, loans, or both.

Religion in public schools. The last in the long line of arguments to be considered here has not been given much attention, at least in recent years, by any of the contending parties in the issue over public funds for religious schools.

A major reason why many organizations have opposed this practice has been the desire to differentiate between the public and the private religious schools in the spirit of separationism. It has been long assumed that the public schools are *public*—that is, where religion is not taught —and private schools have no recognizable public function and status. With regard to the latter assumption, the writer and others have called attention to the contributions by private and religious schools to the welfare of the nation at large. But it is high time to take a closer look at the public, particularly the non-religious, character of the public school system.

There is ample evidence that in all parts of the country there are public schools and colleges which, for all practical purposes, are religious in nature.[14] Thus, the teaching and singing of hymns, the recital of prayers, and Bible reading are to be found in many of the Michigan public schools, with "no statute, judicial opinion, or other legal prejudice prohibiting sectarian influence in public schools in Michigan."[15] Interestingly, on March 15, 1961, the Attorney General of Michigan handed down an opinion that Bible instruction in the public schools constituted a violation of both the Federal and the state constitutions and that the "local schools boards should take immediate steps to end any such programs within their jurisdictions."[16]

This decision was the result of protests against

---

[14] See the examples in William W. Brickman, "Public Aid to Religious Schools?" *Religious Education*, 55:280-282, July-August, 1960.

[15] Robert T. Anderson, "Religion in the Michigan Public Schools," *School and Society*, 88: 228, May 9, 1959.

[16] Attorney General Paul L. Adams, as quoted in Damon Stetson, "Michigan Orders Bible-Study Ban," *New York Times*, March 16, 1961.

the program of Bible teaching carried on since 1935 in the public schools of southern Michigan by the Rural Bible Mission, Inc., of Kalamazoo with the support by fundamentalist and evangelical denominations and individuals. It will be noted that it took over a quarter of a century for the state to issue a restraint order against religious teaching and practice. And while the religious society indicated that it would comply with the ruling by the Attorney General of Michigan, it is not certain that the rest of the schools of the state would discontinue forthwith all forms of religious instruction. Moreover, the situation in the other states apparently has not changed. In point of actual fact, it is highly probable that local school boards and citizens in different states may interpose their will in behalf of religion in the public schools against the laws, the court decisions, and the attorney generals' rulings. This is evident from the attitude of a representative group in Indiana,[17] and there is reason to believe that the popular will reigns in other states as well.

Let it be remembered that every state has laws which compel a parent to send his child to school. If a parent, in complying with the law, places his child in a public school in which religion is taught, then there is a clear case of compulsory attendance of religious exercises. This is an obvious violation of that part of the First Amendment (reinforced by the Fourteenth Amendment for all the states) which orders

[17] Robert L. Liggett, "An Investigation of Certain Aspects of Religious Education in the Public Schools of Indiana," abstract of Ed.D. thesis, in "Studies in Education: 1950" (Bloomington: School of Education, Indiana University, 1951), pp. 70-74.

Congress not to make any law "prohibiting the free exercise" of religion. In the words of two eminent Protestant specialists on church-state problems, "Religious instruction in the public schools, whether it consists of reading the Bible, singing hymns, or offering prayer, is, in respect to the taxpayer, a coerced support of religion."[18]

It would seem that some would like to have their cake and eat it—to keep religion in the public schools and to prevent religious schools from obtaining public funds. This is neither fair nor consistent—and very probably not constitutional. Certainly, many a court has ruled that religious practices in public schools are illegal, but they often have continued nevertheless. And what is more, public opinion has tended to become inflamed over any attempt to enforce the law which would make the public schools public in actual fact.

To be quite realistic about it, the campaign to obtain Federal and state funds for parochial schools is bound to be most difficult and protracted. There is a possibility (some would say a strong probability) that no law to this effect ever will be passed. Since a good part of the opposition is purportedly derived from constitutional considerations—the sacred status of church-state-school separation—then it is only just to ask the opponents of governmental aid to parochial schools to apply their doctrine with impartiality. If it is contrary to the Constitution to pay money to a school conducted under religious auspices, it is equally unconstitutional to give tax-supported funds to schools which promote religion under public auspices. Therefore,

---

[18] Alvin W. Johnson and Frank H. Yost, "Separation of Church and State in the United States" (Minneapolis: University of Minnesota Press, 1948), p. 72.

the writer proposes that any Congressional or state bill which would restrict public money to the public school should withhold such money at the same time from any public school in which any religious doctrine, prayer, custom, ceremony, or celebration is taught or practiced. In this way, the Constitution will be preserved from the standpoint of strict separation of church and state in educational affairs.

It is noteworthy that this proposal represents no radical innovation. Many states already have constitutional or other legal statements along these lines. In several respects, it echoes the proposed constitutional amendments by President Grover Cleveland and Rep. James G. Blaine in 1875-76. The Constitution of New York State, for example, includes the following provision: "Neither the state nor any subdivision thereof shall use its property, or credit any public money or authorize or permit either to be used, directly or indirectly, in aid . . . of any school or institution of learning wholly or in part under the control or direction of any religious denomination, or in which any denominational tenet or doctrine is taught" (Art. XI, Sect. I).

Let it especially be noted that tax-supported money is not supposed to be given to "any school or institution of learning . . . in which any denominational tenet or doctrine is taught." If the Constitution of New York State should be properly and consistently applied, many a public school would not receive any public support.

From the point of view of actual conditions, it is possible to regard the difference between the public school and the religious school as nebulous and tenuous. Consequently, unless the line of demarcation is made clear and definite, the policy regarding public support cannot, in all fairness and justice, discriminate between the public and the parochial school.

Conclusion. In the foregoing pages, the writer has attempted to assemble all the arguments known to him concerning the controverted issue of Federal and state support to schools under religious auspices or control. These statements have been derived from various writings, from questions raised during public lectures and in conferences, and from various other sources. As far as was possible, two or more sides of an argument were presented in an effort to give anyone interested in the subject some basis for further reflection and for arriving at his own judgment. It is possible that not all points have been covered and that some shades or nuances of thought have been overlooked. So far as the writer knows, however, there is no other compilation and analysis of similar scope.

The analysis in nearly all cases has been favorable to the viewpoint that governmental bodies should give support to religious schools. This is a matter of justice and equity in the light of the facts and conditions of American history and contemporary life. This is the conclusion of the present writer.

The student of the subject of church-state relations in education must spend considerable time and effort to do justice to the issue. There are many sources to be examined, appraised, and placed in total context. Prejudgment may not always be avoided, but it can be minimized. An open eye, ear, and mind would seem to be necessary for a reasonable approach toward the solution of an educational problem of great seriousness and crucial significance to the people of the United States.

ℭhurch, 𝔖tate, and 𝔖chool in 𝔍nternational 𝔓erspective

WILLIAM W. BRICKMAN

𝕿HE HISTORICAL
and international dimensions of the controversial question of the relationship between government and education must be taken into proper consideration by any serious student of the subject. Brief references in the press and in public debates have aroused public interest in the foreign experiences in the realm of church-state-school relations. A recent, detailed article, beginning on the front page of the *New York Times*, served to satisfy general curiosity.[1] Helpful as this newspaper survey was, it covered a variety of countries, some of them quite sketchily and inadequately.

More scholarly studies were made available years ago, but these need updating. I. L. Kandel's "Educational Yearbook" (1932) and

---

[1] Fred M. Hechinger, "School Aid a Thorny Issue for Many Other Nations," *New York Times*, March 27, 1961.

J. A. Lauwerys and N. Hans' "Year Book of Education" (1951) are examples of the substantial type of literature. Also useful is the detailed chapter in Leo Pfeffer's painstaking volume on "Church, State, and Freedom" (1953).

This chapter seeks to analyze the church-state issue in several countries on the basis of the historical forces and the actual current practices. The data will enable the reader to put the American problem in an international context.

HISTORICAL BACKGROUND

The history of the relation of church to state is a long and complicated one.[2] In the words of a modern Greek specialist on the question, "there are many varieties of the relations between Church and State according to different epochs and circumstances, and the various systems are of different sorts."[3] As a more recent authority has stated, "Christianity and the State have from the earliest days come into relations involving conflict, entanglement, an armed truce, active co-

---

[2] The literature on the history of church and state is an abundant one, e.g., M. Searle Bates, "Religious Liberty: An Inquiry" (New York: International Missionary Council, 1945); J. De Visser, "Kerk en Staat: Eerste Deel, Buitenland" (Leiden: Sijthoff, 1926); Frank Gavin, "Seven Centuries of the Problem of Church and State" (Princeton: Princeton University Press, 1938); Zaccaria Giacommetti, "Quellen zur Geschichte der Trennung von Staat und Kirche" (Tübingen: Mohr, 1926; reprint, 1960); Luigi Luzzatti, "Dio nella libertà," translated as "God in Freedom" (New York: Macmillan, 1930); Karl Rothenbücher, "Die Trennung von Staat und Kirche" (Munich: Beck, 1908); Francesco Ruffini, "La libertà religiosa," translated as "Religious Liberty" (London: Williams and Norgate, 1912); Paul Sabatier, "A propos de la séparation des églises de L'état" (Paris: 1906); and Luigi Sturzo, "Church and State," translated by Barbara B. Carter (New York: Longmans, Green, 1939).

[3] Chrestos Androutsos, "Ekklesia kai politeia ex epopsos Orthodoxou" (Athens, 1920), quoted in Gavin, op.cit., p. 131.

operation, or sympathetic understanding."[4] Only
some of the major events and ideas can be mentioned here.

In the Bible, God speaking through Moses to
the children of Israel promised that "if ye will
. . . keep my covenant . . . ye shall be unto me a
kingdom of priests and a holy nation."[5] The
theocratic society, which originated in the covenant with Abraham, was characteristic of the
time of Moses and Aaron, of Saul and Samuel,
of King Alexander Jannaeus and Simeon ben
Shetah, and other periods both in Biblical and
post-Biblical Jewish history. In the Talmud is
an explicit statement that, from the standpoint
of the Jewish religion, "Dina d'malkhuta dina,"
"the law of the kingdom [government] is the
law" in matters which do not contradict religious
law.[6]

Church-state relationship was exemplified in
the ancient world by the state priesthood and
the god-king in Egypt; the temple worship in
Greece, with the priest as an official of the state;
the trial and death of Socrates; the Pontifex
Maximus as head of the state religion in Rome;
the divine worship of some of the R'oman em-
perors, such as Gaius Caligula; the missionary
and other religious activities of the "St. Paul
of Buddhism," Emperor Asoka the Great of
India in the third century B. C.; and the religious political rule under Islam.

Early Christian attitudes may be illustrated by
some well-known quotations from the New
Testament. Thus, Jesus said to Simon Bar-jona,
" . . . thou art Peter, and upon this rock I will

---

[4] Anson Phelps Stokes, "Church and State in the
United States," Vol. I (New York: Harper, 1950), p. 38.
[5] Exodus, 19:5-6 (King James translation).
[6] Babylonian Talmud, Tractate Baba Kama, 113a.

146

build my church. . . . And I will give unto thee
the keys of the kingdom of heaven . . . "[7] Just
as familiar is "Render to Caesar the things that
are Caesar's, and to God the things that are
God's."[8] In his Epistle to the Romans, Paul
stated that " . . . there is no power but of God;
the powers that be are ordained of God. . . .
[The ruler] is the minister of God to thee for
good."[9] No doubt, these statements have been
and can be interpreted in several ways, theologi-
cally and otherwise, but they do seem to convey
some notion of what was regarded by the ancient
church as the right relationship between governmental and religious authority.

After the period of Roman persecution, Christianity obtained official recognition as a *religio
licita* by Emperor Constantine in 313 and in
time an even higher status in the empire. The
ideological basis for Christianity in relation to
the state was delineated by St. Augustine (354-
430), Pope Gregory the Great (540-604), and
others. The coronation by the Pope of Charle-
magne as Holy Roman Emperor in 800 was more
than a mere symbolic act. A coterminous alliance
came into existence—Pope and king, church and
state.

The medieval history of church-state relations
is familiar to students of history and needs only
to be sketched here. One thinks basically of the
struggles over the temporal power of the Pope
and lay investiture. Specifically, the church-state
controversy touched many persons, places, and
periods: Pope Gregory VII Hildebrand (1078-
85) versus Emperor Henry IV, with Canossa
(1077) and the Concordat of Worms (1122) be-

---

[7] Matthew, 16:18-19.
[8] Mark, 12:17.
[9] Romans, 13:1, 4.

ing stages; Archbishop Thomas à Becket of Canterbury versus King Henry II of England (1154-89) over the trial of priests by the state and the royal control of episcopal elections; Pope Innocent III (1198-1216), who proclaimed and successfully carried out the policy of the temporal supremacy of the papacy; and Pope Boniface VIII (1294-1303) versus King Philip IV of France over the royal taxation of the clergy, culminating in the edict, *Unam Sanctam* (1302), the last major papal effort to assert its temporal power.

In a little over two decades, the trend began to blow in the opposite direction. The periods of the Babylonian or Avignonese Captivity (1309-76) and the Great Schism (1378-1417) lowered considerably the prestige of the papacy and weakened the church in general. In the meantime, Marsiglio of Padua argued in his "Defensor Pacis" (1324) in behalf of the principle of state supremacy in secular matters and the superiority of a general church council over the Pope in religious affairs, thus paving the way for the Reformation. Before entering the modern era, it will be well to recall that in both the medieval inquisition (from 1233) and the Spanish inquisition (from 1478) the clerics handed over their victims to the secular arm for execution, an example of church-state co-operation.

During the Reformation period, the relations between church and state continued in an atmosphere of co-operation and conflict. In 1516, the Concordat of Bologna between Pope Leo X and Francis I of France was an agreement which gave to the crown the right to select bishops and abbots and gave to the papacy revenues from certain ecclesiastical property. At the Diet of Augsburg in 1530, presided over by Emperor Charles V, Philipp Melanchthon, the religious reformer and educator, presented the famous Confession, including the principle that "the ecclesiastical and civil powers are not to be confounded." However, this was by no means a statement regarding the separating of the church from the state, since Melanchthon emphasized the duty of the state to suppress with force any signs of religious heresy. The views of Martin Luther of the subordination of the church to the state and the generally contrary viewpoint of John Calvin are well known to students of history. The conflicts between Henry VIII and the papacy and the consequent establishment of Anglicanism as the state religion in England are also familiar, as are the efforts by Kings James I and James II to assert the idea of the divine right of rulers.

The doctrine of *cuius regio, eius religio,* which was promulgated in 1555 by the Religious Peace of Augsburg, had political, religious, and educational consequences. One of the results was the development of co-operation between the church authorities and the state in the control of education. "This partnership continued, especially in the field of elementary education, in most countries down to the present period, a partnership which is indicated in the subordination of educational and religious affairs to the same ministry."[10] Interestingly, as the ideas of political nationalism and the interrelationship of education and the national welfare developed, the state has tended to take over the control of the schools from the church. This practice, of course, is an argument for those who feel that governmental support must be accompanied by control.

There is another aspect of the educational

---

[10] I. L. Kandel, "Comparative Education" (Boston: Houghton Mifflin, 1933), p. 48.

impact of *cuius regio, eius religio*. By this principle, "the Protestant countries prohibited Catholic schools, and the policy of the Catholic Church in these circumstances was directed towards the defence of freedom of thought and instruction."[11] Examples of this application could be found in England and Holland during the Reformation era.

An important milestone in the history of church-state relations was the Treaty of Westphalia (1648) at the end of the Thirty Years' War. Under this agreement, there was to be equal treatment of Catholics and Protestants, including the provision of school subsidies, in the area of the Holy Roman Empire. Specifically, this treaty approved the traditional educational setup by noting that the school was an *annexum religionis* and by assuring Catholics and Protestants that they would retain the schools and churches they had possessed in 1642.[12] Another aspect of the problem in the same century was the Revocation of the Edict of Nantes in 1685 by King Louis XIV of France, and the Protestant Huguenots were forced toward conversion or exile. In the course of this and the following century, the tsars of Russia strengthened the church-state alliance in their realm, a situation which remained intact until the Revolution of 1917.

The close relationship between church and state began to wither away in the 18th century under the determined onslaught of the proponents of the Enlightenment and the leaders of

[11] Nicholas Hans, "Comparative Education" (London: Routledge & Kegan Paul, 1958), p. 114.

[12] John J. Doyle, "Education in the Recent Constitutions and Concordats" Ph.D. thesis (Washington: Catholic University of America Press, 1933), p. 22.

the French Revolution. With regard to religious freedom, Emperor Joseph II of Austria issued his famous Edict of Toleration in 1781. Although Catholicism was recognized as the dominant faith, the other religions were granted full autonomy. A parallel event in the Western Hemisphere was the dual movement in the new United States toward religious freedom and toward some type of church-state separation.

During the past century and half, there have been several significant developments. Among these were the Concordat between Napoleon and Pius VII in 1801 and the French government's act of separating church and state in 1905; the abolition of religious tests at Oxford and Cambridge Universities in 1871; the Russian Revolution of 1917, which brought about separation but not religious freedom; the Lateran Treaty between Benito Mussolini and Pope Pius XI in 1929; and the Concordat between Portugal and Pope Pius XII in 1940, by which Catholicism was designated the state religion but full freedom also was granted to all other faiths.

The French Revolution made a violent break with the dictum of Louis XIV, "Un roi, une loi, une foi," and introduced official secularism and anti-religious policy. The Concordat of 1801 between Napoleon, the First Consul, and Pope Pius VII was a form of co-operation by which the government would appoint and the papacy would confirm the French hierarchy. But this did not end at all the struggle between church and state in France. The *Loi Guizot* of 1833 may have given the church control over primary education, the *Loi Falloux* of 1850 may have extended Catholic power in other aspects of education, and Emperor Napoleon III may have strengthened the role of the church in educational matters, but there was no satisfying Rome.[13] In 1864, Pope Pius IX issued the encyclical, "Quanta cura," with the appendix, "Syllabus Errorum," which condemned, among other modern intellectual and socio-political movements, Napoleon's new policy of supremacy of the state over the church.[14] The reaction to the Pope's statement, as well as to his Dogma of Papal Infallability in 1870, was international: in Prussia, for example, Bismarck spearheaded a *Kulturkampf* against the Catholic Church; in France, anti-clericalism flourished and eventually moved toward the complete separation of church and state in 1905 *(Loi des associations)*. What separation did not change was the French law of 1882 which arranged for a free day other than Sunday during the school week, usually Thursday, when religion could be taught away from school by the various denominations.

A trend toward religious freedom in higher education developed in England during the 19th century. In 1871, Parliament passed the Universities Tests Act which allowed dissenters to obtain degrees without taking the religious tests required for three centuries. The new act abrogated the code of statutes for Oxford (1571) and Cambridge (1573) which had specified that the faculties and fellows were to be in Holy Orders and that all undergraduate students were to subscribe to the Thirty-Nine Articles of the

---

[13] For an historical survey of the French experience of church-state relations in education through the 20th century, see Paul Foulquié, "L'église et L'école" (Paris: Editions Spes, 1947), pp. 43-97.

[14] Proposition 55 condemned the principle that "the Church must be separated from the State, and the State from the Church."

Church of England.[15] This was one of the major signs of change in a higher educational system which had been closely allied to a single church.

To bring this historical sketch up to the present era, it is necessary to mention some of the developments within the Catholic Church. The encyclical, "Immortale Dei" ("The Christian Constitution of States"), by Pope Leo XIII in 1885 called attention to the principle that "to exclude the Church, founded by God Himself, from the business of life, from the power of making laws, from the training of youth, from domestic society, is a grave and fatal error . . . The Church of Christ is the true and sole teacher of virtue and guardian of morals."[16] More than four decades later, in 1929, the year of the Lateran Treaty between Italy and the papacy, Pope Pius XI issued an encyclical devoted entirely to the "Christian Education of Youth" ("Repraesentanti in terra: Divini Illius Magistri"), in which he emphasized that the only ideal and perfect education is Christian education and pointed up the motto of "Catholic education in Catholic schools for all the Catholic youth." Pius stated that " . . . first of all education belongs pre-eminently to the Church" because of the "supreme authority to teach given by her Divine Founder"[17] and because of her title to "spiritual

---

[15] S. C. Roberts, "British Universities" (London: Collins, 1947), pp. 21, 31. See also S. J. Curtis and M. E. A. Boultwood, " An Introductory History of English Education since 1800" (London: University Tutorial Press, 1960), p. 336.

[16] Translation in John A. Ryan and Francis J. Boland, "Catholic Principles of Politics" (New York: Macmillan, 1940), p. 298.

[17] "Five Great Encyclicals" (New York: Paulist Press, 1939), p. 40.

motherhood." It is not enough for a school to give some religion to make it suitable for Catholics. For a school to satisfy Catholic criteria of education, " . . . it is necessary that all the teaching and the whole organization of the school, and its teachers, syllabus and textbooks in every branch, be regulated by the Christian spirit, under the direction and maternal supervision of the Church; so that religion may be in very truth the foundation and crown of the youth's entire training; and this in every grade of school, not only the elementary, but the intermediate and the higher institutions of learning as well."[18]

The Pope recognized the financial difficulties faced by Catholic schools in countries where the church was one of several and the fact that the parochial schools may not receive public funds "as distributive justice requires."[19] At the very least, Catholic education " . . . may not be opposed by any civil authority ready to recognize the rights of the family, and the irreducible claims of legitimate liberty."[20]

It also is relevant to recall the various provisions of Canon Law which deal with education in Catholic and non-Catholic schools (Canons

---

[18] *Ibid.*, p. 60.

[19] *Ibid.*, p. 61. Distributive justice is defined as "the duty incumbent on the State, conformably to its end and purpose, to secure for each individual his right to a share in the income from products he has helped to produce, observing as far as possible the proportion which equity requires, to afford him the necessary advantages and helps due him, and finally to see that the public burdens and benefits are fairly and equitably distributed. The obligations of distributive justice rest ultimately with the State." Ryan and Boland, *op.cit.*

[20] "Five Great Encyclicals," *ibid.*

1372-1383).[21] Although Canon 1374 stresses the requirement of Catholics to attend Catholic schools, students of Catholic educational history are aware that the prohibition of studying in non-Catholic schools has not been fully enforced in all countries and is perhaps impossible of fulfillment.

This brief survey of many centuries of relations between church and state seems to indicate that, with notable modern exceptions, the two institutions have continuous contacts with each other. It might not be too much to say that a close relationship was the rule rather than the exception. The implications for the education of the past are not hard to draw.

GREAT BRITAIN

The historical advantages that the Established Church of England had in education were maintained right into the 20th century. However, the Anglican Church could not retain a monopolistic hold on education, especially since an increasingly secular state was tending to assert its authority over the church. Such events as the parliamentary act of 1871, with its abolition of the religious tests for Cambridge and Oxford, were proof that the church-state alliance was by no means one of total identity.

The modern English educational system began early in the 19th century with the voluntary efforts by philanthropists and religious groups. From 1833 onward, the government provided

---

[21] The "Codex iuris canonici" was codified early in the 20th century under the direction of St. Pius X. The Latin text and French translation are found in Foulquié, *op. cit.*, pp. 240-246. In *Everson v. Board of Education*, 330 U.S. 1 (1947), Mr. Justice Jackson of the U.S. Supreme Court cited the English translation in Stanislaus Woywod, "The New Canon Law" (New York, 1940).

funds to some religious schools, which in later years were subject to inspection by the Education Department. The Education (Forster) Act of 1870, which set up a national system of elementary schools, resulted in a "Dual System" of provided schools—that is, under public control, and under non-provided or voluntary schools, generally under the control of the church. Both types of schools were publicly supported, with the voluntary school having to provide its own building.

Under the 1870 act, the Cowper-Temple Clause stipulated that "no religious catechism or religious formulary which is distinctive of any particular denomination shall be taught in the school." In practice, this has been interpreted as allowing the teaching of the Apostle's Creed, the Lord's Prayer, and the Ten Commandments—in short, a sort of non-sectarian religion. Furthermore, a conscience clause permitted parents to withdraw their children when religion was taught, and, to make things easier, the law required that religious instruction be given only at the beginning or at the end of a school's morning or afternoon session. Religious tests for entrance into either a provided or voluntary school were forbidden. Public education inspectors were prohibited from the supervision and control of religious instruction in the voluntary schools.[22]

The Education (Balfour) Act of 1902 made more financial concessions by authorizing the allotment of local taxes to denominational

---

[22] Lord Eustace Percy, "England: General Statement," in I. L. Kandel, editor, "Educational Yearbook of the International Institute of Teachers College, Columbia University: 1932" (New York: Bureau of Publications, Teachers College, Columbia University, 1933), pp. 125-126.

schools (not including, however, the costs of buildings, structural repairs, and sites). At the same time, the law provided that the newly constituted Local Education Authorities should control the secular instruction in the voluntary schools.

The Catholic school situation was made difficult after 1870 by the "unfair competition" furnished by free and compulsory education in the provided schools. In the words of a prominent English Catholic layman, who served as chairman of the Education Committee of the London County Council, " . . . as long as the State compels Catholic parents to pay taxes and rates for public education purposes upon exactly the same basis as other citizens, and to send their children to school, Catholics claim adequate financial support from public funds for Catholic schools, to which alone they can conscientiously send their children."[23] Under the 1902 act, the "conditions of Church schools were very much improved . . . the inequality between State and Church schools was reduced but there *was* still an inequality."[24] The arguments which were put forth in the U. S. by the Catholics in the 1950's and 1960's seem to echo those of many decades ago in England.

The period between 1902 and 1914 recently has received intensive treatment in an extensively documented monograph. There was a widespread and lively controversy on the question of public financial aid to church schools and on the issue of religious instruction in the publicly

---

[23] Sir John Gilbert, "England: Roman Catholic Point of View," in Kandel, "Educational Yearbook . . . 1932," *op.cit.*, p. 150.

[24] "The Case for Catholic Schools" (London: Catholic Education Council for England and Wales, 1951), p. 11.

controlled schools. "For the people on the British Isles the controversy provoked an emotional excitement not unlike that generated in France by the contemporaneous Dreyfus affair. The strife produced court trials, prison sentences, distraint of property, election issues, exchanges between opposing church leaders, and negotiations in political circles."[25] There were divisions among and within all religious groups, and between them on the one hand and the secularists on the other; "so great was the division of opinion among Englishmen that an actual stalemate developed, dented only by partisan advantages reaped in the fluctuating fortunes of political warfare."[26] The status quo remained: religion was taught in the governmental schools and the denominational schools received public support.

During the period between the two World Wars, the place of religion in education was strengthened by the approval of the idea of the agreed syllabus, a nonsectarian outline of religious instruction, for the schools of the Local Education Authority (L. E. A.). The first of these, that of Cambridgeshire, published in 1924, served as a model for many others[27] and for the special provision in the Education (Butler) Act of 1944. Also contributing to this act were the recommendations on religious instruction in the Spens Report of 1938.

The Education (Butler) Act of 1944 gave

---

[25] Benjamin Sacks, "The Religious Issue in the State Schools of England and Wales, 1902-1914: A Nation's Quest for Human Dignity" (Albuquerque: University of New Mexico Press, 1961), p. v.

[26] *Ibid.*, p. 225.

[27] For examples, see "The London Syllabus of Religious Education" (London: London County Council, 1947) and "The Agreed Syllabus of Christian Education" (Bristol: City and County of Bristol Education Committee, 1960).

official recognition and sanction to practices which had prevailed in most English schools. The new legislation required that "the school day in every county school and in every voluntary school shall begin with collective worship on the part of all pupils in attendance at the school" and that "religious instruction shall be given in every county school and in every voluntary school."[28] The provisions of the law included the excuse from worship and religious instruction at the request of the parent, nondenominational collective worship and religious teaching in the county schools, the use of an agreed syllabus in religious education, and the safeguarding of the religious freedom of the teacher.

Of special interest is the Butler Act's reform of the Dual System. The council schools, of course, are under the full control of the L.E.A.'s. The voluntary schools, most of which are Anglican and Roman Catholic, are "maintained" or financed by the L.E.A's with respect to teachers' salaries, educational equipment, heating and lighting, cleaning, and the like. In return, the L.E.A.'s supervise the secular instruction of the voluntary schools. A special type of voluntary school is the aided school, which is under the control of the denominational managers but which receives half of the cost of building improvement and repairs from public funds. Another type is the controlled school, the full financial obligation of which is borne by the L.E.A. In return, the L.E.A.'s appoint and dismiss teachers but must consult with the managers of the controlled schools about the appointment of a headmaster or headmistress or

---

[28] "Education Act, 1944:7 and Geo. 6. Ch. 31" (London: H. M. Stationery Office, 1944), pp. 20, 21.

Reserved Teachers (instructors of the religion represented by the school managers). Finally, the special agreement school is a voluntary school which has reorganized itself with the financial support of the L.E.A. under the provisions of the Education Act of 1936 and which remains under denominational control.

Some difficulty developed later with the Catholics, who discovered that the updating of their schools cost far more than originally had been estimated when the Butler Bill was under consideration. Accordingly, the hierarchy issued a demand in 1949 for additional financial aid as well as a proposal for the permanent settlement of the problem. Their views, however, were rejected in an official memorandum from George Tomlinson, the Minister of Education. Nor did the Catholics derive any satisfaction from the attitudes of the Conservative and Labor Parties.[29] The Education Act of 1959 raised to 75% the maximum rate of grants paid by the Ministry of Education to aided and special agreement schools and also made grants of 75% for aided secondary schools.[30] Many Catholics continue to feel, however, that their schools should receive full aid with no more than the basic control by the state. As the problem recently was summed up by one Catholic educator, Canon Drinkwater, "The financial burden is very great."[31]

The English experience of the partnership between church and state in education has resulted, according to the Bishop of Peterborough, in a "record . . . of increasing friendship and

---

[29] "The Case for Catholic Schools," *op.cit.,* p. 25.
[30] "Education in Great Britain" (New York: British Information Services, 1960), p. 11.
[31] F. H. Drinkwater, "Catholic Education in England," *Religious Education,* LVI, March-April, 1961, p. 125.

co-operation" between the churches and the L.E.A.[32] A Jewish official notes that the Butler Act has brought about an improvement in religious education as well as in religious knowledge, understanding, and tolerance of other faiths. In addition, the conscience clauses have made it possible for minority groups to safeguard their religious teachings.[33]

All is not fine, however. The Bishop of Peterborough emphasizes that "as yet there is very little evidence that more boys and girls, as a result of all the care and effort given to Religious Instruction and school worship, are becoming active Christians after they have left school."[34] But this is an internal matter for the churches to solve, rather than a cause for complaint with the system of church-state relationship in England.

Whatever the weaknesses of the English system, there are lessons that may be pondered by Americans. To an American pedogogical scholar who spent a year in studying the church-state-school question in Britain, "unquestionably the most important positive lesson for Americans to be had from the English experience . . . [is] the record of protection of religious freedom. It seems undeniable that, almost without exception, the English machinery for church-state-school relations has functioned with no real in-

[32] Robert W. Stopford, "Religious Education in England: The Church's Share," *Religious Education*, March-April, 1961, p. 117.

[33] Myer Domnitz, "Religious Education and Schools in the United Kingdom—Some Jewish Aspects," *Religious Education*, March-April, 1961, p. 138.

[34] Stopford, *loc.cit.; cf.,* John Huxtable, "Church and State in Education" (Wallington, Surrey, England: Religious Education Press, 1960), p. 13.

fringement of individual rights of conscience."[35] This conclusion on the part of one who is basically a separationist is in sharp contrast to the frequently stressed viewpoint that only a policy of strict separation can guarantee religious freedom.

Religion, government, and education have been particularly close in Scotland. Six years after the Education (Scotland) Act of 1872, which recognized religious instruction in the public schools (Scottish, not English, meaning) and made grants available to voluntary religious schools, one of Her Majesty's Inspectors reported that "the public schools are to all intents and purposes denominational schools. Public and Presbyterian are practically interchangeable."[36] In point of actual fact, however, the conscience clause has operated since 1872 to safeguard the rights of religious minorities.

The Education (Scotland) Act of 1918 reaffirmed the provisions of the earlier law and placed the voluntary religious schools under the administration of the Education Authorities, which replaced the school boards. It is of special interest to note the plea for the support of religious schools made by the Secretary of State of Scotland while the new law was being considered by Parliament: "At present, one-seventh of the school population of Scotland are, owing to the inadequate resources of managers, being denied the opportunities open to children who attend our public schools. In other words, these

---

[35] Gordon C. Lee, "Church, State, and School in England: A Study in Tradition and Innovation. III. Appraisals," *Teachers College Record*, May, 1955, p. 461.

[36] Quoted in James J. Robertson, "The Scottish Solution" (Edinburgh: Church of Scotland Committee on Education, 1954), p. 4. Reprinted from the "Year Book of Education: 1951."

children are being penalized because of the religious belief of their parents. I do not think that this is expedient or just."[37] The solution, as he saw it, was for the denominational schools to be managed by public educational authorities on terms which would be satisfactory to the religious group. And this is what the law, which was passed with virtually no opposition, actually provided. Under Sect. 18, the Education Authorities fully controlled the curriculum and the appointment and dismissal of teachers. The denomination had the right to approve new teachers from the standpoint of religious belief and character and had a representative on the committee managing the former denominational school now transferred to the administration of the Education Authorities. Significantly, the time set aside for religious instruction was not to be diminished after the transfer of the school to public control. From 1920 onward, no funds were granted to any voluntary school which chose to remain independent of the official educational authority.[38] The "Scottish Solution," one of complete co-operation between church and state in educational matters, was consolidated by the Education (Scotland) Act of 1946.

Religious teaching is given in public schools of nondenominational origin according to the Syllabus of Religious Instruction, prepared by the Joint Committee on Religious Education, which represents the Scottish Churches, the Educational Institute of Scotland, and the Association of Directors of Education in Scotland. Ministers of religion may be encouraged by Education Authorities to take part in activ-

[37] *Educational News*, Jan. 18, 1918, as quoted in *ibid.*, p. 5.
[38] *Ibid.*, p. 6.

ities related to religious education.[39] On the other hand, the Secretary of State for Scotland is forbidden by law from directing, inspecting, or controlling in any way the teaching of religion in the schools so that the principle of "absolute religious freedom" can be upheld.[40]

Unlike the situation in other geographical areas, this school arrangement has won the approval of the Roman Catholics, who have tended to refer to the 1918 act as a "concordat."[41] While pointing out that the settlement is short of perfection, one Catholic educator praised it as meeting "the major dissatisfactions that are aired in England, by Catholics and Anglicans and Free Churchmen, and by the secular educationalists."[42] Yet, no successful move has been made as yet to extend the Scottish solution to England.

IRELAND

The Republic of Ireland has no single public school system, but rather denominational systems under the control of Catholics, Protestants, and Jews.[43] Although the population of Ireland is at least 95% Catholic, Art. 44 of the Constitution of 1937 also recognizes Protestants, Jews, and other denominations. The Constitution guarantees freedom of conscience, the free practice and profession of religion, freedom from religious disability or discrimination, and denominational autonomy.

With respect to schools, the Constitution

---

[39] Scottish Education Department, "Public Education in Scotland" (Edinburgh: Her Majesty's Stationery Office, 1955), p. 17.

[40] "Education in Great Britain," *op. cit.*, p. 27.

[41] Robertson, *op.cit.*, p. 7.

[42] "The Case for Catholic Schools," *op.cit.*, p. 98.

[43] John Mescal, "Religion in the Irish System of Education" (Dublin: Clonmore and Reynolds, 1957), p. 19.

specifies in Art. 42 that "the State shall provide for free primary education." Pres. Alfred O'Rahilly of University College, Cork, finding this phraseology ambiguous, quotes from the Irish language version: "The State must arrange that primary education is available gratuitously."[44] This is interpreted to mean that the government must make funds available to parents so that they may have their children educated in a school of their own choice. This school, of course, can be one which is operated by a religious group. According to Art. 44, a law providing funds for schools can neither discriminate among schools of the various denominations nor prejudice "the right of any child to attend a school receiving public money without attending religious instruction at that school."

From the standpoint of the Irish authorities, there is no single established church, even if the Constitution emphasizes that the state recognizes "the special position of the Holy, Catholic Apostolic and Roman Church as the guardian of the Faith professed by the great majority of the citizens." In the judgment of O'Rahilly, this special recognition is "merely the statement of a statistical fact which involves certain social amenities and respect,"[45] such as, apparently, the invocation of "the Most Holy Trinity" in the preamble to the Constitution.

The rationale underlying the Irish system is the firm conviction that education is, first and foremost, the fundamental responsibility of the parents. Then comes the responsibility of the

---

[44] Quoted in Alfred O'Rahilly, "The Republic of Ireland," in J. A. Lauwerys and N. Hans, editors, "The Year Book of Education: 1951" (London: Evans, 1951), p. 353. The full English text of Articles 42 and 44 may be found in "The Case for Catholic Schools," *op.cit.*, pp. 88-89.

[45] O'Rahilly, *op.cit.*, p. 350.

church, the world of scholarship, and the state, in descending order. The state's function is to assist in the educational process and effort but not to usurp the role of the other educational agencies. Apparently, the Irish educational policy has gained the approval of Protestants and Jews.[46] Even such a critic of Catholicism as Paul Blanshard admits that the government fulfills the constitutional pledges and runs the schools "with scrupulous impartiality" and that Protestants and Jews are satisfied with the Irish educational system.[47]

Whether the church in the Republic of Ireland is separated from the state has been a matter of debate, depending upon one's historical and ideological orientation. What is important is that, for most Americans, education in Ireland does not constitute separation, but neither is it an example of unjustifiable governmental control of religious minorities or interference with freedom of religion.

FRANCE

Traditionally, the Catholic Church in France exercised great power over education until about 1750, when its influence lessened and then disappeared during the Revolution of 1789. From the time of Napoleon through the *Loi Guizot* (1833) and the *Loi Falloux* (1850), its power gradually was restored, although not on the same scale as prior to 1750.[48] From about 1875 onward, the winds of secularism began to blow,

---

[46] *Ibid.*, p. 354. See also Mescal, *op.cit.*, p. 143.

[47] Paul Blanshard, "The Irish and Catholic Power" (Boston: Beacon, 1953), pp. 116-117.

[48] Clarence E. Elwell, "The Influence of the Enlightenment on the Catholic Theory of Religious Education in France: 1750-1850" (Cambridge: Harvard University Press, 1944),p. 302.

culminating in the adoption of the law of March 28, 1882, which made primary education compulsory and secular. The basic change in French national policy can be illustrated by the similar sentences from the laws of 1850 and 1882: *L'enseignement primaire comprend: l'instruction morale et religieuse* (1850); and *L'enseignement primaire comprend: L'instruction morale et civique*.[49] The new law also withdrew from priests the right to inspect, supervise, and direct public and private primary schools, and from ecclesiastical authorities the right to nominate non-Catholic teachers. In addition, the law provided for the closing of public primary schools one day a week, besides Sunday, so that parents might arrange for religious instruction for their children outside the public schools.[50]

The secularization of the French school was continued through Art. 17 of the law of Oct. 30, 1886: *Dans les écoles publiques de tout ordre, l'enseignement est exclusivement confié à un personnel laique.*[51] With primary school buildings already closed to religious instruction (1882) and to the clergy as teachers of secular subjects (1886), a circular from the Ministry of Education, April 9, 1903, stated that "no sort of religious emblems (crucifixes, pictures, statues) shall appear in school buildings."[52] The final step toward the secularized school was the enactment of the law of July 7, 1904, the first article of which forbade all members of the religious

---

[49] Quoted in Foulquié, *op.cit.*, p. 73.
[50] For the full text of the law, see Robert Brichet, "L'obligation scolaire" (Paris: La Vie Communale et Départementale [1946]), pp. 53-59. A portion of the law is given in Jean Debiesse, "Compulsory Education in France," (Paris: Unesco, 1951), pp. 105-106.
[51] Quoted in Foulquié, *op.cit.*, p. 74.
[52] Quoted in Debiesse, *op.cit.*, p. 52.

orders to teach in any kind of school: *L'enseignement de tout ordre et de toute nature est interdit en France aux congrégations.*[53]

It was obvious that the Catholics would characterize the progression of school secularization as "godless." Some, in fact, charged that a Masonic conspiracy eliminated members of the religious orders from the public schools.[54] No doubt, to counter such charges, Jules Ferry, Minister of Education, pointed out in his letter to the teachers, Nov. 17, 1887, that religion is a personal matter and has no place in public instruction, whereas knowledge is universal and therefore belongs in the public school. "Religion should be taught by the family and the Church; ethics by the school."[55] Ferry has been credited with promoting "the complete laicization of the school system."[56]

In spite of the law of separation of church and state, Dec. 9, 1905, there have been concessions and adjustments in the field of education. For one thing, secular priests have full freedom in teaching. Some outstanding ecclesiastical thinkers, in fact, have occupied chairs in public institutions such as the Ecole des Hautes Etudes and the Collège de France, "but only as scholars who have achieved distinction in a special subject, not to teach a creed."[57] Another arrangement is the granting by a commune of aid and textbooks to poor children attending private schools, the vast majority of which are Catholic. This

---

[53] Quoted in Foulquié, *op.cit.*, p. 69.
[54] Michel Glatigny, "Histoire de l'enseignement en France" (Paris: Presses Universitaires de France, 1949) p. 106.
[55] Quoted in Debiesse, *op.cit.*, p. 24.
[56] Félix Pécaut, "France," in Kandel, "Education Yearbook . . . 1932," *op.cit.*, p. 185.
[57] *Ibid.*, p. 192.

principle was particularly applied after World War I, when the government, assuming the cost of educating children of dead or wounded soldiers, granted scholarships to private elementary or secondary schools if preferred by the surviving relatives.[58] Of special interest, however, is the regulation which permits religious instruction by ministers of all faiths represented by the student bodies of lyceés and collèges, which are usually boarding schools. The religious teaching may be carried on in the public secondary school buildings, "but all religious propaganda is forbidden."[59]

Within certain reasonable limits, religious schools enjoy freedom with respect to curriculum, methods of teachings, and textbooks. The state school inspectors may enter private schools but can exercise only a few specified functions: to check the sanitary conditions of the school buildings, the required qualifications of the teachers, and the pupil notebooks to see if basic education is covered. They do not have the right to appraise the quality of instruction or the educational principles underlying them.[60]

That the question of church-state separation in French education is not a matter of distinction between white and black can be determined by a glance at the situation in Alsace-Lorraine. For various historical reasons, partly because this area was under German sovereignty in 1905 when the separation act was passed, Alsace is still governed by Napoleon's Concordat with the Pope. Catholicism, Protestantism, and Judaism

---

[58] *Ibid.*, pp. 195-96.

[59] Ministère de l'éducation national de la jeunesse et des sports, Institut Pédagogique National, "L'organisation de l'enseignement en France" (Paris: La Documentation Française, 1957), p. 6.

[60] Pécaut, *op.cit.*, p. 198.

are legally recognized and the clergymen are in the civil service. Education, accordingly, is divided along tripartite denominational lines, with a conscience clause for those not desiring religious instruction. On the other hand, the teachers, unless they express disbelief in their faith, are required to teach religion. "The result is that at the primary stage, at least, the influence of the ministers of the various sects on the young people at school, and at times on their teachers, is considerable," concludes the rector of the Académie of Strasbourg.[61] There does not seem to be any movement, even among the anti-clericals, to modify the Alsatian solution.

An important change in church-state-school relations occurred during the Vichy regime, 1940-44. As far back as 1934, Marshal Petain had condemned secularism in public education and had supported the Catholic viewpoint on religious instruction. As director of the Vichy state, Petain brought back the practices which had been abolished during the decades of secularization. Among these were the restoration of the right of religious orders to teach in the *écoles libres* (church schools which are free from government control), the teaching of religion in the public schools, public payment of the salaries of school chaplains, and public grants to the Catholic schools. While the Fourth Republic declared itself in favor of the policy of educational secularism, in actual practice there was a compromise in favor of the church.[62]

—— [61] Réne Hubert, "Schools and Education in Alsace," in Lauwerys and Hans, "The Year Book of Education: 1951," *op.cit.*, p. 467. *Cf.*, T. Noel Stern, "Church-School Conflict in France," *School and Society*, Sept. 1, 1956, p. 69; "Neutralité de l'enseignement public" (Paris: Institut Pédagogique National, 1959), p. 7.

[62] Hans, *op.cit.*, pp. 291-92; Stern, *op.cit.*, p. 69; "Neutralité de l'enseignement public," *op.cit.*, p. 6.

The new Constitution of 1946 proclaimed in its preamble that "every human being, without distinction of race, religion, or belief, possesses inalienable and sacred rights" and that "the establishment of free, secular, public education on all levels is a duty of the state." However, in guaranteeing "equal access of children and adults to education, professional training, and culture," the government in effect was holding the door open for public aid to those attending the religious schools.[63]

There were signs of a more benevolent attitude by the state toward private education in the Poinso-Chapuis Decree-Law of 1948, which subsidized poor children in private or public schools. Although this was not put into actual operation, it served as a precedent for the *Loi Marie* and the *Loi Barangé* of September, 1951, both of which allowed subsidies to children irrespective of the type of school attended.[64] Interestingly, in this land of separation, primary religious schools receive direct grants, whereas in the private secondary schools it is the students who benefit by scholarship grants.[65] Also of significance is the *Loi Laurent* of 1955 giving subsidies to private, secondary agricultural schools and placing them "under the control of the pro-church Ministry of Agriculture, rather than the lay-oriented Ministry of Education.[66] Obviously, even an explicit policy of church-state separation is capable of flexibility in practice.

---

[63] The text of the preamble is given in Herman Finer, "The Major Governments of Modern Europe" (Evanston, Ill.: Row, Peterson, 1960), p. A8.

[64] Stern, *loc. cit.*

[65] "Education in France" ([Washington:] Editions France Actuelle, 1956), p. 3; "L'organisation de l'enseignement en France," *op.cit.*, pp. 18, 42.

[66] Stern, *ibid.*

The struggle between the *cléricaux* and the *laiques* in France of educational policy is continuing into the present. There was considerable opposition and ill will during the passage of the law of Dec. 31, 1959, which gave public aid to church schools in return for some measure of control. The new law recognized that private schools, to which parents, "using one of the fundamental liberties guaranteed them," send their children, were "in a difficult financial position and cannot pay their teachers an adequate salary."[67] It provided, therefore, for a "contract of association," whereby properly qualified teachers in a private school would receive their salaries from the government on the same basis as those in the public schools. The law specified, moreover, that the private school which has signed a contract with the government may maintain its own character but must admit "all children, regardless of origins, opinions or beliefs" and give instruction "with full respect for freedom of conscience."[68] Still another significant provision is Art. 7, under which "local communities may give assistance to any child, regardless of the school he attends."[69] It is worthy of note that 1960 attendance estimates indicate that 14% of all primary school pupils attend private schools, while 57% of all secondary school students are in church institutions.[70]

The church-state situation in French education bears deeper study and careful watching on the part of everyone concerned with the meaning of the doctrine of separation, especially as

---

[67] Quoted in "Education in France," No. 9 (New York: French Cultural Services, 1960), p. 41.

[68] *Ibid.*, p. 42.

[69] *Ibid.*, p. 43.

[70] "Education in France," No. 12 (New York: French Cultural Services, 1960), p. 27.

related to democratic government and society. It is possible to observe that the French people as a whole do not take a doctrinaire, rigid, and one-sided view of private education, in spite of the fact that their constitutional and legal documents are outspoken in behalf of separation in a manner which is lacking in the U. S. Constitution.

BELGIUM

The conflict between clericals and liberals over religion in Belgian education has been going on for well over a century. The "Loi De Malheur" of 1879, as the Catholics called the liberal legislation, abolished religious instruction in the public elementary and normal schools and gave up the principle of subsidizing religious schools. In 1884, a Catholic majority in the government repealed this law, but it did not restore the compulsory Catholic instruction of 1842-79. Instead, the new law made religious education permissible in the communes, depending upon the desires of the parents of the different denominations. Then followed various compromises and adjustments in 1890, 1895, and 1911 with regard to religious teaching and subsidization of church schools. The law of October 25, 1921, set the tone for the church-state relations in education in Belgium.[71]

Since 1921, there has been compulsory religious instruction or secular moral education two hours weekly during the first or last half-hour of the day in the public primary schools and in the national-aided secondary schools. Unless a single pupil dissents, instruction of non-religious subjects is denominational in nature. Recognized schools (*écoles adoptables*) under national supervision may give rationalistic or socialistic instruction, provided they inculcate patriotism and observe the principles of tolerance.[72]

The return of the Christian Social Party (Catholic) to power in 1950 was the signal for the intensification of the effort to equalize public and private schools. The struggle continued until the adoption of the educational pact of 1958 and its parliamentary counterpart (law of May 29, 1959). The "Pacte Scolaire," which was signed by the leaders of the Christian Social, Socialist, and Liberal Parties on Nov. 28, 1958, aimed at "the growth of the cultural and material welfare, by bringing about an extension of instruction and educational peace."[73]

The new law, which was passed in the midst of much strife and violence, contains 53 articles, some of which draw upon Belgian educational experience of the past. For example, Art. 8 requires two hours weekly of religious or secular

---

[71] A. Machotte, "Belgium," in Kandel, "Educational Yearbook . . . 1932," op.cit., pp. 32-35; Centre d'Etudes Pédagogiques, "Le problème de l'école: solutions modernes, Belgique, Hollande" (Paris: Editions du Temoignage Chretien, n.d.), pp. 9-27; Marion Coulon, "Les subsides scolaires en Belgique des origines jusqu'au pacte de 1958" (Brussels: Ligue de l'Enseignement, 1959), pp. 3-13; Vernon Mallinson and Silvain de Coster, "Church and State Education in Belgium," *Comparative Education Review*, June, 1960, pp. 43, 46. See also Gommar A. De Pauw, "The Educational Rights of the Church and Elementary Schools in Belgium" (Washington: Catholic University of America Press, 1953). In general, to judge from Plancke's bibliographies, there seem to be few Belgian studies of the history of the church-state-school problem: R. L. Plancke, "De historische Paedagogiek van Belgie: Overzicht en Bibliographie" (Antwerp: De Sikkel, 1950); Marion Coulon and Rene Plancke, "Education in Belgium" (Paris: Unesco, 1957).

[72] Machotte, *op.cit.*, pp. 35-37; "L'enseignement en Belgique" (Brussels: Ministère de l'Instruction Publique, 1959), p. 10.

[73] "Pacte Scolaire" (Brussels: Ministère de l'Instruction Publique, 1958), p. 3.

174

moral instruction in the public primary and
secondary schools, while Art. 9 specifies that the
teachers of religion be ministers or instructors
approved by the denominations.[74] The law also
gives parents the right to request and obtain a
new school, whether religious or official, if they
do not live reasonably close to the type of school
they desire. The government grants teacher salaries and fringe benefits to all schools, public
and religious, but it only pays for the buildings
of the official schools.

It is noteworthy that the scholastic pact is
regarded by the rabbi of Brussels as having "all
kinds of good effects eventually" on the Jewish
school in Brussels and the two in Antwerp.
These schools, which receive at present "weak"
subsidies from the state, offer from 12 to 20
hours of religious subjects a week.[75]

Perhaps the law of 1959 will not solve all the
problems of religion in Belgian education, and
it is possible that more trouble might arise in
the future. At any rate, it is illustrative of how
a consensus may alleviate a serious question in
a country devoted to the doctrines of democracy.

HOLLAND

From the time of William the Silent, Prince of
Orange (1533-84), onward, Holland has been
identified as a country where religious toleration
is preached and practiced. Prince William, "the
apostle of tolerance,"[76] was at different times a

---

[74] "29 Mai 1959: Loi modefiant la législation relative
à l'enseignement gardien, primaire, moyen, normal, technique et artistique" (Brussels: Moniteur Belge—Belgisch
Staatsblad, 1959), p. 4. The law is published in French
and Flemish.

[75] Mark Kohlenberg, "Jewish Education in Belgium,"
Religious Education, Nov.-Dec., 1960, p. 428.

[76] Adriaan J. Barnouw, "The Pageant of Netherlands
History" (New York: Longmans, Green, 1952), p. 139.

Catholic, a Lutheran, and a Calvinist. His decree at Antwerp in 1578 proclaimed that "in the matter of religion everyone shall remain free as he shall wish to answer to God; so that no one shall trouble anyone else, but each man serve God according to the understanding given him."[77] Another practical contribution to the cause of freedom of conscience was the authorization by William of the establishment of the University of Leyden in 1575, which, although it required professors to be Calvinists, became before long a center of international learning for men of various beliefs. While it hardly can be argued that Holland was a perfect example of religious tolerance in the 16th century, the Dutch were far ahead of their time and of the rest of the world.

At the same time, there began the process of understanding between governmental and ecclesiastical authority in relation to education. A series of synods, beginning with that of Dordrecht in 1574 and including the famous Synod of Dort (Dordrecht) in 1618-19, and a number of state regulations laid down the principle of cooperation. The church recognized the authority of the state in education and the state guaranteed the right of the church to determine the qualifications and the orthodoxy of the teachers.[78] Students of American educational history can note the similarity between the Dutch idea and that of colonial America, even assuming that one did not directly influence the other.

-----

[77] Quoted in Preserved Smith, "A History of Modern Culture: Vol. I, The Great Renewal, 1543-1687" (New York: Holt, 1930), p. 472.

[78] Johan Janssen and S. Visser, "Van Plato tot Decroly: Studieboek der historische pedagogiek" (Purmerend: J. Muusses, 1951), p. 205.

Modern Dutch education begins with the French Revolution, under the influence of which the Constitution of the Batavian Republic in 1798 separated the Dutch Reformed Church from the state and banned religious instruction in the schools.[79] But this separation policy did not prohibit the Education Law of 1801 from requiring that the curriculum of the public school must contribute to the training of children "in all Christian and social virtues."[80] Some historians see in this non-denominational provision the foundation for the state's neutrality in religious educational matters.[81] Others also regard the law of 1801 as the beginning of the *schoolstrijd* (school controversy) which lasted until 1920. This law and that of 1806 recognized the *bijzonder school* (non-public school), but the law of 1803 did not.[82] Evidently, political and other conditions were exercising an influence on school policy.

Obviously, church groups could not accept the lukewarm approach to religion in education. The Calvinists and Catholics, consequently, opened and paid for their own schools in order to ensure the perpetuation of their doctrines. The problem of proper financial recognition would absorb the efforts of the religious leaders for a long time to come.

The Constitution of 1848 emphasized the idea

---

[79] *Ibid.*, p. 214; D. H. Rodriques, "Education, Fountainhead of Freedom," *Netherlands News Letter*, December, 1948, p. 6.

[80] Quoted in P. A. Diels, "Holland," in Kandel, "Educational Yearbook . . . 1932," *op.cit.*, p. 266.

[81] D. Wouters and W. J. Visser, "Geschiednis van de opvoeding en het onderwijs, vooral in Nederland" (Groningen: Noordhoff, 1927), p. 229.

[82] Br. O. Mandigers, "Leerboek der opvoedkunde: IV, Schoolstelsels" ('s-Hertogenbosch: Malmberg, 1955), pp. 118-21.

that public education must respect "each person's religious views," but it merely reinforced the principle embodied in the Constitution of 1815 in asserting that "public education is an object of continual concern of the government" (Art. 194).[83] This gave little comfort to those who were seriously involved with the promotion of traditional religious education.

The lack of satisfaction with the law of 1806 led to agitation for new legislation which would do away with the monopoly of education by the state and accomplish other reforms.[84] A new law, passed in 1857, provided that "subsidies may be granted to private schools on the part of the communal, provincial or state authorities. Schools thus assisted shall be open to all children, without distinction of religious creed. . . . "[85] Art. 23 emphasized that the school system should be adapted toward the "training in all Christian and social virtues" and added that public schoolrooms should be made available to denominations for religious instruction outside the regular school time. Of great significance was the abolition of the old requirement, dating from 1801, for permission from the state for the founding of religious schools.

For the most part, the law of 1857 was satisfactory. The complaint by the religious groups, however, was that they still had to pay for their own schools. And so the Liberals and later the Socialists on one side and the Calvinists and the

---

[83] Quoted in Wouters and Visser, op.cit., p. 280.

[84] L. C. T. Bigot and Gilles van Hees, "Verleden en heden: beknopte geschiednis van opvoeding en onderwijs" (Groningen: Wolters, 1951), p. 212.

[85] Anna T. Smith and C. H. Plugge, "Netherlands, Education in the," in Paul Monroe, editor, "A Cyclopedia of Education," Vol. IV (New York: Macmillan, 1913), p. 418.

Catholics on the other carried on the struggle over financing of the private schools. With the law of 1878, the Liberals introduced the idea of state regulation in return for any subsidy to religious schools. But the religious authorities were more pleased by the Mackay Law (1889) which allowed state, not communal, subsidies up to 30% of the private school's total expenditure. As a compensation to the Liberals, the Conservatives consented to the principle of compulsory education enacted in the law of 1900.[86] From this time on, both the Socialists and the Liberals gradually gave up their opposition to the equality of public and non-public education,[87] thus paving the way for a settlement or "Pacificatie"[88] after some "80 years of hard struggle (1840-1920)."[89]

A leading authority on Dutch education points out that it took over a century, from the Constitution of 1815 to that of 1917, for the adjective "public" to be removed from the statement specifying governmental concern for education.[90] The new document, which now stated that "education is a matter of continuous concern of the government," also recapitulated the need for respecting everyone's religious views in public education. In addition, it proclaimed that private primary schools may receive public funds and must be regulated by standards according to law, but they are granted freedom in educational

[86] *Ibid.*

[87] Diels, *op.cit.*, p. 268.

[88] I. Van der Velde, "Onderwijsvernieuwing op de lagere school en haar organisatorische problemen" (Groningen: Wolters, 1946), p. 171.

[89] Helena W. F. Stellwag, "Problems and Trends in Dutch Education," *International Review of Education,* III, No. 1, 1957, p. 61.

[90] P. J. Idenburg, "Schets van het nederlandse schoolwezen" (Groningen: Wolters, 1960), p. 52.

methods and teacher appointments.[91] The way was now clear for the enactment of the law of 1920. In this legislation, which was the "life work" of the Minister of Education, Arts, and Sciences, Dr. J. Th. de Visser, and the solution to the long controversy, "the financial equalization [of public and non-public schools] was perfectly worked out."[92] The costs of instruction in the private schools would be borne jointly by the national government, which is responsible for the teachers' salaries, and by the municipal authorities, who pay for the school buildings, textbooks, and so forth. There is no unreasonable control by the public authorities of the private schools.[93]

A school system such as that prevailing in Holland is bound to be far more expensive than one which does not support private education. The Dutch, however, feel that the results are worth the price. They place a premium upon religious freedom, which they hold higher than a single, national system of public schools as the essential of a democratic nation. As Idenburg remarks, "Freedom is freedom only if people are economically able to use it."[94] When parents pay their taxes for the public schools and then must find funds for the type of school

[91] *Ibid.*, pp. 4-5; "Dutch School System" ([The Hague:] Ministry of Education, Arts, and Sciences, 1960), p. 7.

[92] Idenburg, *op.cit.*, p. 53.

[93] Details on the administration of the system of state subsidies to religious schools may be found in Philip J. Idenburg, "Education in the Netherlands" (The Hague: Netherlands Government Information Service, 1951), pp. 23-26.

[94] P. J. Idenburg, "Financial Equalization in the Netherlands," in Robert K. Hall and J. A. Lauwerys, editors, "Education and Economics: The Year Book of Education: 1956" (Yonkers, N. Y.: World Book Co., 1956), p. 418.

they prefer, then the term "freedom" loses its basic meaning, stresses this Dutch educator, who, incidentally, is a high government official, a professor of education at the Municipal University of Amsterdam, and a Protestant.

The rationale for the distinctive Dutch solution of the school finance question may be discerned from the ideas expressed in a recent bill: "As education of the children is by nature in the first place the right and duty of the parents, freedom of education in the sense wished for by parents, ought to come first. This starting point, however, means that interference of the State is strictly limited. Because instruction and education cannot well be separated, interwoven as they are, the family ought to have a central place in the concept and the functioning of the law. If anywhere, the rule should be applied here that the task of the Government must be restricted to the affording of possibilities for the parents to accomplish this personal and educational task."[95]

To pretend that there are no problems and difficulties in the equalization of *openbaar onderwijs* and *bijzonder onderwijs* (private education) is to shut one's eyes to the events and writings in Holland during the past four decades. Apart from the matter of the economics of maintaining a pluralistic system of schools, there is the fundamental question of the status of the public schools. Time and again, American and other critics have expressed fears that the reduction of the percentage of public schools in relation to the total number in the country is a serious danger to Dutch democracy and national unity. There is no doubt of the decline of the

---

[95] Quoted in Stellwag, *op. cit.*, pp. 61-62.

public school from the standpoint of percentage: in 1921, the public elementary schools were 56% of the entire total of Dutch schools, whereas in 1959 they went down to 32%. Among the private schools, the Catholic rose from 21% (1921) to 37% (1959) and the Protestant from 22% (1921) to 29% (1959). In the category of advanced primary education (*uitgebreid lager onderwijs*, or U. L. O.), public schools constituted only 28% of the combined number of institutions in 1959. In 1958-59, 36% of all students were in preparatory higher and secondary schools of the public type. On the other hand, 79% of all graduates in higher education obtained their degrees in public universities.[96]

Another important factor in the national educational picture is that of cost per pupil. In 1920, the cost per public school pupil was 115 florins and 82 for a pupil in a denominational school. In 1952, the figures were 227 and 201, respectively.[97] If the public schools are low in the percentage column, they are not discriminated against financially.

The question of social, spiritual, and cultural isolation has been mentioned as a result of the operation of the Dutch educational system.[98] But this, according to Idenburg, has been partially compensated for by the intellectual unity of the country and by the conviction that "only through recognition of variety and respect for it can our

---

[96] The figures are taken from "Dutch School System," *op.cit.*, pp. 25, 37, 52, 90.

[97] Idenburg, "Financial Equalization in the Netherlands," *op.cit.*, p. 420.

[98] *Ibid.*, p. 418; P. J. Idenburg, "The Netherlands: Social and Historical Analysis," in Lauwerys and Hans, "Year Book of Education: 1951," *op.cit.*, pp. 487-489; Ralph H. Lane, Letter to the Editor, *New York Times*, March 19, 1961.

people find unity."[99] Even if "many people in the Netherlands are concerned about this [isolation] . . . few would for that reason abandon a system which they conceive as a consequence of democracy—of all political systems still the least obnoxious."[100] This sentiment is re-echoed by the Dutch citizens and officials, orally and in writing. Finally, the equal treatment of public and non-public schools in Holland has been defended as "an interpretation of the democratic principles of liberty and equality in the field of education, which has nowhere in the whole world been thought out so completely and carried out so constantly."[101] It would require considerable proof of an uncontestable nature before Holland can be looked upon as other than a democratic nation of the highest order.

GERMANY

Church, state, and school traditionally have been intertwined through the entire history of Germany. In his famous sermon in 1530, "On the Duty of Sending Children to School," Martin Luther, the great reformer, demanded that the state (Obrigkeit) "should force its subjects to keep their children in school."[102] Anyone familiar with Luther's views is aware that, to him, education was religious in nature. The idea of a church school under state control was furthered by followers of Luther and others in the 16th and later centuries. Thus, Duke Ernst the Pious

    [99] Idenburg, "The Netherlands: Social and Historical Analysis," op.cit., pp. 488-489.
    [100] Idenburg, "Financial Equalization in the Netherlands," op.cit., p. 418.
    [101] Idenburg, "The Netherlands: Social and Historical Analysis," op.cit., p. 487.
    [102] Quoted in Fredrich Heman and Willy Moog, "Geschichte der neueren Pädagogik" (Osterwieck: Zickfeldt, 1921), p. 51.

of Gotha, in his *Schulmethodus* of 1642, which set up compulsory school attendance in his realm, called upon the teachers *(Schuldiener)* to inculcate the principles of religion in children in as kind and benevolent a way as possible and to keep in mind the special significance of religious education for the church.[103] The views of Duke Ernst, which actually were written down by a school rector, Andreas Reyher,[104] on the basis of the thinking of Comenius, "did much to further the state-supported church school in conformity with the ideas of the Protestant reformers."[105] Forty years later, Friederick William, the Great Elector of Brandenburg, ordered that "the church and community authorities should go to great pains in establishing every so often well-organized schools in villages, market-towns, and cities."[106] According to a thorough and careful student of the history of church-state relations in German education, "this ordinance is the key to the future development of the Prussian educational system. The state orders and makes the laws, but they are to be implemented and administered by the churches and the local communities."[107]

The 18th-century viewpoint of King Frederick II (the Great) is deserving of some attention because of its anticipation of the basic Catholic argument at present. "Der alte Fritz" maintained

---

[103] Portions of this document are found in Kurt Rassfeld and Hermann Wendt, "Grundriss der Pädagogik" (Leipzig: Teubner, 1918), pp. 366-367. See also pp. 305-307.

[104] Heman and Moog, *op.cit.,* p. 139.

[105] Ernst C. Helmreich, "Religious Education in German Schools: An Historical Approach" (Cambridge: Harvard University Press, 1959), p. 24.

[106] Quoted in C. Müller, "Grundriss der Geschichte des preussischen Volksschulwesens" (Osterwieck: Zickfeldt, 1910), p. 9.

[107] Helmreich, *op.cit.,* pp. 24-25.

that "it is criminal coercion, when one takes
from fathers the right according to their desire
to educate their children . . . ; it is a criminal
coercion if you send the children to a school run
according to the precepts of natural religion,
when the fathers want the children to become
Catholics like themselves."[108] This remark was
consistent with his ordinance in 1765 for the
establishment of state-supported schools for the
Catholic population of Silesia, which he had
just taken over from Austria.

As the 18th century passed its mid-point, the
rationalism, secularism, and tolerance of the *Auf-
klärung* began to exert an impact on educational
administration. Until this time, the church exercised supervisory control over the Prussian
schools. This monopoly was broken in 1787
when the Prussian minister of education, Baron
Karl Abraham von Zedlitz, instituted the *Ober-
schulkollegium* (Secondary School Board) which
placed the right of inspecting secondary schools
under the control of the state. This marked the
official recognition "in principle [of] the separation of the church from the school."[109] As later
events showed, however, this incipient separation
never was carried through fully, either in
Prussia or in Germany.

But there was no denial of the fact that a
basic change had come about. The *Allgemeines
Preussisches Landrecht* of 1794, a historical school
code which influenced education for well over a
century afterward, proclaimed that "schools and
universities are state institutions aiming at in-

[108] Quoted in *ibid.*, p. 29.
[109] Müller, *op.cit.*, p. 79. *Cf.*, Heman and Moog,
op.cit., p. 256; and R. H. Samuel and R. Hinton Thomas,
"Education and Society in Modern Germany" (London:
Routledge and Kegan Paul, 1949), p, 91.

struction of youth in useful knowledge and science" and that such institutions can be established "only with the foreknowledge and approval of the state."[110] It guaranteed access to public education without regard to religious belief and freed members of minority faiths from religious instruction in the public schools. Art. 12 required active co-operation by the local minister of religion, "not only through supervision, but also through his own instruction of the schoolmaster and of the pupils toward the attainment of the purpose of the schools."[111] The function of supervision was to be shared by the school inspector and the pastor.

It is tempting to trace in detail the interesting history of church-state-school relations in Germany during the 19th and 20th centuries, but a good part of it has been done already by Helmreich. Consequently, only a few facts need to be stressed in this chapter. New geographical changes in the early part of the century resulted in the organization of the *Simultanschule* (interdenominational school) in the Duchy of Nassau in 1817. This type of school, which also was known as the *Paritätische Schule* and later the *Gemeinschaftsschule,* was intended to take the place of the denominational or confessional school (*Bekenntnisschule*). In time, it became the bone of contention between religious and secular groups down to the present. The *Simultanschule* provided religious instruction according to denomination in the same building. Thus, in the larger cities, there were religious classes for Catholic, Protestant, and Jewish pupils at the same time, but the rest of the curriculum

---

[110] Quoted from the document as given in Müller, *op.cit.,* p. 87.
[111] *Ibid.,* p. 90.

was in non-denominational classes. Later on, there were demands for a *weltliche Schule* or *Weltanschauungsschule* (secular school), and Germany thus developed a triple educational system. But the German solution could not have been described at any period as one which was in accordance with a principle of real church-state separation.

The Weimar Republic, which was for a time at least under socialist influence, was unable to weaken the impact of religion on German public education. Art. 146 of the Constitution of 1919 required the teaching of religion in all public schools except the secular, guaranteed the continuation of the faculties of theology in the state universities, and allowed the establishment of primary denominational schools for parents desiring them.[112] Signficantly, all public school teachers, even the clergymen who taught religion, were put under the civil service by Art. 143, while the following article declared that "the entire school system is under the supervision of the state"— public and private, secular and religious instruction.[113] Repeated debates took place between 1919 and 1933 in connection with efforts to enact legislation on the church-state problem in education, but the status quo remained by the time Adolf Hitler came to power.[114]

During the early months of the Nazi regime, Hitler promised in his Reichstag speech of March 23, 1933, that "the National Government

---

[112] Erich Hylla, "Germany: Legal Status of Religious Education," in Kandel, "Educational Yearbook . . . 1932," *op.cit.*, pp. 204-205.

[113] *Ibid.*, p. 205.

[114] Reinhold Lehmann, "Germany: The Federal School Law and Religious Education," in Kandel, *ibid.*, pp. 233-261.

will allow and secure to the Christian Confessions the influence which is their due both in the school and in education."[115] The early acts of the Nazis, including the Concordat of 1933 with Pope Pius XI, indicated that they were intent upon fulfilling Hitler's promise. As time went on, however, there was a decided change in policy. Minister of Education Bernhard Rust decreed on July 9, 1935, that students in secondary schools could not be compelled to attend religious services and celebrations of any kind, on weekdays or Sundays, in school buildings or in nearby churches.[116] From 1938 on, the confessional schools, which supposedly were guaranteed for the Catholics by the Concordat of 1933, were eliminated and replaced by the interdenominational schools.[117] There were other measures, such as the closing of many Catholic monastic schools in Bavaria; the curtailment of religious instruction in the secondary schools from two hours to one hour per week in the last four years; the withdrawal of the right of Jewish and Seventh Day Adventist students to be absent without penalty from Saturday classes; and the order in Württemberg that the New Testament was to be taught according to the principles of racism. That the Nazis made a travesty out of religion in education was clear, perhaps never so much as in the case of the school inspector in Thuringia who issued a circular ordering that Julius Streicher's newspaper, *Der Stürmer,* which promoted sex and anti-Semitism simultaneously,

---

[115] Quoted in Helmreich, *op.cit.,* p. 154. This sentence was subsequently omitted from official versions of the speech. See p. 334, note 3.

[116] This document is in A. Kluger, editor, "Die deutsche Schule im Grossdeutschen Reich" (Breslau: Hirt, 1940), p. 308.

[117] Helmreich, *op.cit.,* pp. 174-175.

"should be given the 'most widespread application' in the teaching of religion."[118]

Hitler's persecution of religion and of religious education was undone at the end of World War II, except that the Concordat continued in effect. The relations of the church, state, and school were now directed by the constitutions and laws of the various *Länder* (state governments) and by the Basic Law (provisional constitution) adopted by the Federal Republic of Germany in May, 1949. Art. 7 of the latter document placed "the entire educational system" under state supervision; required religious instruction as a "regular subject" in all public schools, except the *bekenntnisfreie Schulen* (secular schools), with no pupil or teacher being forced to take part in it; and permitted private schools of the interdenominational *(Gemeinschaftsschule)*, denominational *(Bekenntnisschule)*, or non-religious *(Weltanschauungsschule)* type.[119] The Basic Law is particularly strict with regard to regulating the private schools. Whenever a private school offers a kind of instruction which is not provided adequately by a state school, it receives public subsidies. Such institutions are designated as "private schools of a public type."[120] Art. 37 of the Württemberg-Baden Constitution of 1946 declared that "the public elementary schools are Christian and interdenominational."[121] Art. 131 of the Bavar-

---

[118] Samuel and Thomas, *op.cit.*, p. 108.

[119] Reinhold Mercker, editor, "Grundgesetz für die Bundesrepublik Deutschland vom 23. Mai 1959" (Stuttgart: Reclam-Verlag, 1956); "Basic Law for the Federal Republic of Germany" (Bonn: Deutscher Bundestag [1960]), p. 7.

[120] Franz Hilker, "Die Schulen in Deutschland (Bundesrepublik und West-Berlin)" (Bad Nauheim: Christian-Verlag, 1954), p. 24.

ian Constitution of 1946 proclaimed that "the highest objectives of education are reverence for God," among other values.[122] The constitutions of all the states stressed religious education and tolerance in the spirit of the Basic Law. Whatever the form of organization, denominational or interdenominational, as practiced in the individual states, it is very clear that religion is an officially recognized part of the public school curriculum. In addition, religious devotions are usually a part of the public school program throughout the country.[123]

Communist East Germany, or the German Democratic Republic as it is officially known in Eastern Europe, separated church from state and church from school through the "Law for the Democratization of the German School," July 27, 1945. This law stressed that the state has exclusive control of the school and that religious instruction is a private church matter.[124] Although the G. D. R. Constitution of 1949 reiterated in Art. 40 that "religious education is a function of the religious associations," it also stated that "the right of the church to give religious instruction on school premises shall be guaranteed" (Art. 44).[125] Nevertheless, in actual practice, this guarantee often was denied and protests were given no attention by local authorities.[126] In general, the German Communist government has tried to discourage religious education in

[121] "Germany, 1947-1949: The Story in Documents," Publication 3556, U. S. Department of State (Washington: U. S. Government Printing Office, 1950), p. 552.
[122] Ibid., p. 553.
[123] Helmreich, op.cit., p. 253.
[124] Document in Wilhelm Schneller, "Die deutsche demokratische Schule" (Berlin: Volk und Wissen, 1955), p. 28; Helmreich, op.cit., pp. 256, 268.
[125] Quoted, Helmreich, op.cit., p. 259.
[126] Ibid., p. 271.

many ways.[127] The abolition of the private
school, in accordance with Art. 38 of the G. D. R.
Constitution, is perhaps one step in this direction. However, by and large, it may be doubted
if the Communist authorities of East Germany
really have exerted themselves with sufficient
vigor, as the Soviet Union has done, to abolish
religious education. The fact that the universities still retain the faculties of theology is an
indication that the German Communists are not
ready as yet to make a full break with the educational tradition of Germany.

SWITZERLAND

The Federal Constitution of Switzerland
(1848) specifies that primary education is under
the sole supervision of the cantonal authorities,
that the public schools must be open to adherents of all faiths without injury to their "freedom of creed and of conscience," that no child
should be forced to take religious instruction,
and that parents and guardians are responsible
for religious education up to the age of 16.[128] It
will be noted that there is no explicit requirement of a secular public school in the Constitution. In actual practice, religion in the form of
Bible history is taught in most public schools,
generally by a lay person or a minister under
public school supervisors. The schools are interdenominational or confessional, depending upon
the nature of the population of the district.
Thus, the Canton of St. Gall has had, by way of
tradition, denominational primary schools, while

---

[127] M. G. Lange, "Totalitäre Erziehung: Das Erzieh-
ungssytem der Sowjetzone Deutschlands" (Stuttgart: Ring-
Verlag, 1954), pp. 106-107.
[128] Quoted in Martin Simmen, "Die Schulen des
Schweizervolkes" (Frauenfeld: Huber, 1946), pp. 15, 19
(Articles 27, 49).

Canton Freiburg has had public Catholic schools in industrial areas.[129]

The private religious schools have a right to exist, provided they do not become aggressive toward other faiths. No public funds are granted them, since there is widespread feeling that such payments are "contrary to the spirit of the Constitution" of Switzerland.[130] The basic law of the land, however, cannot be said, in view of the religious teaching in the public schools, to reflect a policy of real separation of church and state.

ITALY

The laic trend in Italian education originated in the enlightened decades of the late 18th century and gathered momentum during the first half of the 19th century. From the time of unification on, the new Italian state passed legislation which eased out the Catholic Church from its privileged position in the schools. The *Legge Casati* of 1859 did not really forbid religious teaching in the schools, but it declared that it was not the basis of instruction.[131] In 1872, those few faculties of theology in the universities which managed to survive were closed down in a drive "to make higher education completely secular."[132] The Coppino laws of June 23 and July 15, 1877, abolished religious instruction in

---

[129] *Ibid.*, pp. 18-19. See also Elisabeth Rotten, "Schweiz," in Erich Hylla and W. L. Wrinkle, editors, "Die Schulen in Westeuropa" (Bad Nauheim: Christian-Verlag, 1953), pp. 474-475; and Gottfried Herzfeld, "Das Schweizer Erziehungswesen" (Wiesbaden: Pädagogische Arbeitsstelle, 1950), p. 45.

[130] Rotten, *op.cit.*, p. 474.

[131] L. Minio-Paluello, "Education in Fascist Italy" (London: Oxford University Press, 1946), p. 8.

[132] Lamberto Borghi, "Educazione e autorità nell' Italia moderna" (Florence: La Nuova Italia, 1951), p. 25.

secondary and elementary schools, respectively.[133]
From about 1875 to 1910, various tendencies—
socialism, democracy, positivism, and freemason-
ry—tended for the most part to keep church and
public education separated. Demands by Catholic parents resulted in the Orlando Law of 1904
which allowed religious instruction by parental
request, but the Council of State laid down the
principle that religion could be taught outside
regular class hours only.[134] This change — and
in a momentous year for French education —
proved to be one of the steps in the growing
rapprochement between the Vatican and the
Italian government.

By the time Benito Mussolini inaugurated the
Fascist regime, the climate was favorable for a
new deal in church-state relations in Italy. The
Gentile Reform of 1923 reintroduced Catholic
education into the elementary schools, the Code
of 1928 strengthened the position of the church
by making the teaching of religion increasingly
dogmatic and catechetical, and the Concordat
between Mussolini and the Holy See (1929) resulted in the introduction of religious instruction into the secondary schools.[135]

Il Duce labeled the Gentile Reform as the
most Fascist of reforms ("La più fascista delle
riforme"), but time and circumstance caused the
government to take a second look at the spirit
underlying the school. A new school charter,
introduced in 1939 by Giuseppe Bottai, the
minister of education, aimed to bring education
more directly under the aegis of the corporate
state. The *Carta della Scuola*, which echoed to

[133] Ernesto Codignola, "Italy," in Kandel, "Educational
Yearbook . . . 1932," *op.cit.*, p. 302.
[134] *Ibid.*, pp. 302-303.
[135] *Ibid.*, pp. 304-314.

a large extent the ideology of Bottai's Labor Charter of 1927, is noteworthy because of its radical departure from the religious terminology of the Gentile Reform. No longer was there any thought about Catholic doctrine being "the foundation and crown of elementary education in all grades." Instead, Bottai's document began with the statement that the Fascist schools look upon "education as an instrument for the formation of the adult mind, recognise the principle of a popular culture, inspired by the eternal values of the Italian tradition, grafting it through work to the tangible activities of handicraft, the arts, professions, science and a knowledge of military matters."[136] The curriculum "aims at the moral and cultural formation" of the character of boys and, in accordance with the educational principles of the Fascist youth movement, "at their political and military training."[137] Although the word "moral" might be interpreted possibly as religious, there is nowhere any mention of religious instruction or Catholicism. It cannot be assumed that this important document took religion out of the public schools, especially when one realizes that World War II made it impossible for Bottai's reform to be put into full operation. But it is quite clear that Facism, like Nazism, used Catholicism for its own political purposes in the schools and then was ready to dispense with it when the aims were considered to have been achieved. As a close student of Fascist education has remarked, in the *Carta della Scuola* "only very vague hints were made about the relation between family, religious, and state education, and only a few

---

[136] "The School Charter in Italy" (Rome: Laboremus, 1939), p. 12.
[137] *Ibid.*, p. 13.

rhetorical words were used to explain the content and ideals of education."[138] The writing on the wall was plain to see.

Had Italy emerged from World War II with a Fascist orientation, it is very likely that its schools would have de-emphasized Catholic teaching. As it was, in 1945, "Religion and art continue to be the backbone of the Italian elementary school . . . [and] the teaching of the Christian Doctrine, according to the form that has come down from Catholic tradition, constitutes the cornerstone and the crowning point of all subjects studied in all grades of the elementary school."[139] The postwar period, indeed, saw the Catholic Church gain in political and legal strength and, consequently, in educational power. By what might be considered a curious coalition of the Communists and the conservative Catholic parties, the Constituent Assembly voted on March 25, 1947, by the large majority of 350 to 149, to reconfirm the Lateran Pact of 1929 and to make the state and the Catholic Church "independent and sovereign," in their respective spheres.[140] This provision became Art.

---

[138] Minio-Paluello, *op.cit.*, p. 207. For more details on religion and education during the Fascist era, see D. A. Binchy, "Church and State in Fascist Italy" (London: Oxford University Press, 1941), pp. 434-495. A useful overall reference is A. C. Jemolo, "Chiesa e stato in Italia" (Torino: Einaudi, 1949), translated as "Church and State in Italy, 1850 to 1950" (Oxford: Blackwell, 1960).

[139] Howard R. Marraro, "The Democratization of the Italian Elementary School," *School and Society*, June 23, 1945, p. 402. Marraro's phraseology is more or less identical with the language of the Gentile Reform as expressed in Art. 25 of the Royal decree of Oct. 1, 1923. *Cf.*, Codignola, *op.cit.*, pp. 304-305. Note also the close similarity to Art. 36 of the law of May 27, 1929, which approved the Concordat, *ibid.*, p. 311.

[140] Leicester C Webb, "Church and State in Italy: 1947-1957" (Carlton, Victoria: Melbourne University Press, 1958), pp. ix, 17, 22.

7 of the new Constitution, which went into effect on Jan. 1, 1948.

The Constitution guaranteed full equality before the law to all religious creeds in Art. 8 (*Tutte le confessioni religiose sono egualmente libere davanti alla legge*), as well as in Articles 3, 19, and 20.[141] Since Art. 7 also insured the special status of the Catholic Church, it is evident that religion would be taught in the public schools as heretofore. Thus, it is no surprise to read in the introduction to the primary school syllabus of 1955 that "the foundation and the crown" of the primary curriculum is "the teaching of Christian doctrine, in the form received by catholic [sic] tradition."[142] It is not difficult at all to recognize the terminology of the laws of 1923 and 1929 in the statement of aims of 1951.

Since the Constitution was adopted, there have been reports of violations of the provisions of equality of all faiths before the law.[143] On the other hand, there also have been specific acts by the Italian government to make certain that the rights of religious minorities in education would be preserved. Thus, a decree in 1956 by the Ministry of Public Instruction ordered that no written examinations should be administered on Saturdays, so that candidates of such groups as the Jewish and Seventh Day Adventist may not be deprived of their right to observe their day of rest. Recently, in 1960, Giuseppe Medici,

---

[141] For the text of the Constitution, see "Manuale di educazione popolare" (Rome: Istituto Poligrafico dello Stato, 1950), pp. 3-32. The articles on religion have been translated in Webb, *op.cit.*, p. 26.

[142] Quote in Enzo Petrini, "Education in Italy" (Paris: Unesco, 1959), p. 4.

[143] *E.g.*, Webb, *op.cit.*, p. 27, including documentation in note 51.

Minister of Public Instruction, issued instructions to school superintendents all over Italy to make it possible for Jewish and Seventh Day Adventist candidates for teaching positions in the public schools to take the oral examinations, now given on Saturday, on other days.[144]

The new 10-year plan for the reform of Italian education, adopted in 1958, includes funds for the construction of *scuole materne* (nursery schools and kindergartens), most of which are under the jurisdiction of Catholic groups. Such public aid "does not appear to be consistent with the principle of separation of church and state."[145] Actually, no such principle is stated or implied in the Constitution, when one considers the recognition in Art. 7 of the Concordat of 1929. What Art. 33 says is that "private" schools may be set up, but "without state support." Evidently, the Constitution denies public aid to private religious schools, but not to public schools where Catholic doctrine is "the foundation and the crown" of the curriculum. By no stretch of terminology can this combination be construed as church-state separation.

SPAIN

Spain has been a classical example of a country where church and state have been almost inextricably intertwined. Except for relatively minor deviations, such as under the Bourbon monarchy in the 18th century, under the impact of the occupation by a French revolutionary army early in the following century, and under the Republic of the 1930's, Catholicism and Spanish edu-

---

[144] "World Report," *Liberty*, November - December, 1960, p. 31.

[145] Lamberto Borghi and Anthony Scarangello, "Italy's Ten-Year Education Plan," *Comparative Education Review*, June, 1960, p. 29.

cation have been synonymous.[146] After his successful counterrevolution in 1939, Gen. Francisco Franco, "nuestro illustre Caudillo," reconfirmed the Concordat with Rome (1851) by which instruction in all the public schools must be in accordance with Catholic doctrine.[147] In 1945, the new primary education law, signed by Franco himself, declared in the preamble that the Spanish school, in harmony with long-time tradition, "has to be, above everything else, Catholic."[148] This statement is spelled out in more detail with regard to the rights of the Catholic Church and the nature of religious instruction in the public schools (Articles 3 and 5).

The Spanish government has had the policy of paying the salaries of teachers in the private schools, which are also Catholic in spirit and content, as well as half of the cost of erecting and maintaining private school buildings.[149] The position of the church was further strengthened through the Concordat of 1953, according to which compulsory Catholic instruction is guaranteed by the state in both public and private schools. However, there is a stipulation that non-Catholic children "shall be dispensed from such lessons at the request of their parents or guardians."[150] It would appear that all is fine in Spain, from the standpoint of the church, but

---

[146] For an overview of the history of Spanish education, see José Castillejo, "Education and Revolution in Spain" (London: Oxford University Press, 1937).

[147] Bates, "Religious Liberty: An Inquiry," *op.cit.*, pp. 18-19.

[148] "Ley de Educación Primaria de 17 de Julio de 1945" (Madrid: Ministero de Educación Nacional, 1952), p. 38.

[149] Thomas Dubay, "Philosophy of the State as Educator" (Milwaukee: Bruce, 1959), p. 119.

[150] Quoted in *ibid.*, p. 88.

recent events indicate that there might be a church-state conflict in the field of labor.[151]

SCANDINAVIA

The Elementary Education Act of 1937, still in force, states that the teaching of the doctrines of Lutheranism, the established church of Denmark, is required in all public elementary schools, with the customary conscience clause.[152] Private elementary schools, some of them conducted by Catholics and other religious groups, receive as much as 80% of their expenses, according to the law of 1946, but they are under the same supervision as the public schools.[153] Religious instruction also is a required subject in the secondary schools.

The situation in Norway may be grasped quickly by taking note of the name of the central administrative agency in charge of schools: The Royal Norwegian Ministry of Church and Education (*Kyrkje- og undervisningsdepartementet*). The Constitution of 1814 declared that the Evangelical Lutheran religion constituted the established church and required all professing Lutherans to bring up their children in the faith. This obligation could be carried out by private instruction or by the compulsory religion courses in the public primary, secondary, and

---

[151] *New York Times*, Jan. 1, 1960. Pfeffer calls attention to the problem of persecution of Protestants, the limitations upon public worship by Jews, and the lack of religious liberty for the Catholic as an individual, *op.cit.*, pp. 29-31.

[152] Ministry of Education, "Survey of Danish Elementary, Secondary and Further (Non-Vocational) Education" (Copenhagen: Schultz, 1951), p. 8; "Undervisningsvejledning for Folkeskolen," Betaenkning No. 253 (Copenhagen: Statens Trykningskontor, 1960), p. 112.

[153] Ministry of Education, "Survey of . . . Education," *op.cit.*, p. 18; C. F. Vorbeck, "Danemark," in Hylla and Wrinkle, *op.cit.*, p. 506.

normal schools. The religious teaching in the public schools, from which dissenting pupils may be exempt at their parents' request, is under the supervision of the clergy. The few special schools patronized by nonconformists receive no public support, but children of the Seventh Day Adventist belief who are absent on Saturdays from the public schools make up the lost work by private lessons or special instruction provided and financed by the public schools. In general, the religious teaching (*Kristendomskunnskap*) of the Evangelical Lutheran Church predominates the spirit of the Norwegian public school system, with the notable exception of continuation and vocational schools.[154]

The Norwegian state does not support financially the orthodox Lutheran schools of divinity, but their work is recognized as equivalent to that of a university faculty of theology. On the other hand, the orthodox normal school, which parallels the public institution, has received public funds.[155] Folk high schools, some of which are under religious auspices, are supported publicly and are under governmental supervision with no apparent loss of spiritual independence.[156] Incidentally, religion is taught in the

---

[154] Einar Sigmund, "Norway," in Kandel, "Educational Yearbook . . . 1932," *op.cit.*, pp. 371-377; Helga Stene, "Norway," in Lauwerys and Hans, "The Year Book of Education: 1951," *op.cit.*, pp. 505-510; Helen Huus, "The Education of Children and Youth in Norway" (Pittsburgh: University of Pittsburgh Press, 1960), pp. 36-39, 66, 162. See also Normal plan ("Mönsterplan for landsfolkeskulen") (Oslo: Aschehoug, 1954), p. 23; and Den Högre Almenskolen etter Lov av 10. Mai 1935, "Undervisnings Planer" (Oslo: Bröggers Boktrykkeris Forlag, 1950), p. 11.
[155] Sigmund, *op.cit.*, p. 380.
[156] Stene, *op.cit.*, p. 512.

folk high schools which are not identified with denominational sponsorship.[157]

The Constitution of Sweden, by insisting in Art. 2 that the king must profess "the pure evangelical faith," makes it clear that Lutheranism is the established church. In the public school system, consequently, it is logical to expect provision for religious education (*Kristendomskunskap*). The law of Oct. 31, 1919, stated that religion was to be taught in the elementary schools, while the laws of 1914 and 1928 required this study in the normal schools and secondary schools, respectively. In fact, according to the law of 1873, every pupil and student in Sweden, regardless of religious belief, had to attend classes in religion. Should a nonconformist or member of a minority faith neglect to make certain that his child receives instruction in religion, the local school board can force the pupil to take religious (that is, Lutheran) instruction in the public schools. Religion is taught by lay teachers, all of whom are supposed to be members of the Lutheran Church. The clergy may visit the public schools to check on religious instruction, but they are only permitted to forward their criticism to the Royal Central Board of Education.[158]

---

[157] Huus, *op.cit.*, p. 106.

[158] B. J.:son Bergqvist, "Sweden," in Kandel, "Educational Yearbook . . . 1932," *op.cit.*, pp. 400-410; Ture Casserberg, "Schweden," in Hylla and Wrinkle, *op.cit.*, pp. 100-101; Frithiof C. Borgeson, "The Administration of Elementary and Secondary Education in Sweden" (New York: Bureau of Publications, Teachers College, Columbia University, 1927), p. 22; Ingemar During, "The Swedish School-Reform: 1950" (Uppsala: Appelberg, 1951), p. 35; "Oversikt av Skolevasendet i Sverige" ([Stockholm:] Kungl. Skolöverstyrelsen, 1957), pp. 25, 35-36, 42, 47; "Survey of the School System in Sweden (Stockholm: Royal Board of Education in Sweden, 1958), pp. 26, 36-37, 43, 48.

Since all pupils in Sweden must study religion, it is obvious that the private schools would be expected to include this subject as do the public schools. In 1924, those private schools meeting the standards of the Royal Central Board of Education received public support "from more than one-third to three-fifths of the total income of such schools."[159]

Finland has two established churches: the Evangelical-Lutheran State Church, of which 95% of the population are members, and the Greek Orthodox State Church, which only has some 74,000 members. Children of these faiths must take appropriate religious instruction in the public elementary and secondary schools. Private primary schools located in districts where the linguistic minority (Swedish) is very small obtain funds from the state. According to the law of 1950, private secondary schools receive from the government about 70% of their annual operating expenses and are subject to supervision by the Central Board of Schools. Folk high schools, some of which are conducted by religious groups, are publicly subvented to the extent of 70% of their annual expenses.[160]

Few countries have had as consistent a record of democracy in actual practice as have those in Scandinavia. On the basis of their experiences, there is no necessary validity to the argument that democracy only can thrive in a state which

[159] Borgeson, *op.cit.*, p. 211; Fr. Sandberg and Borije Knos, "Education and Scientific Research in Sweden" (Stockholm: Bonnier, 1938), pp. 27-28.

[160] R. H. Oitinnen and Matti Koskenniemi, "Education in Finland" (Paris: Unesco, 1960), pp. 3-7.

is dedicated to the separation of church and state. The Scandinavian nations teach religion in the public schools and subvent to some extent private religious schools. The proposition as to the correlation between separationism and democratic education requires, consequently, a rationale of greater depth.

U. S. S. R.

Of the tsarist institutions, the Russian Orthodox Church alone "has survived, virtually intact, after 40 years of Soviet rule, despite the fact that its basic aims are contrary to those of the Communist regime. This staying power is derived from close to a thousand years of existence as the main religion of Russia. From 1861 until the Revolution of 1917, indeed, the Orthodox Church was the established church of the empire and the tsar was its head.[161] The counter-force to the church, Communism, drew its doctrine regarding religion from the sacred scriptures of Karl Marx. In the words of Lenin in 1909, "Religion is the opium of the people—this dictum of Marx's is the cornerstone of the whole Marxist view on religion."[162]

The October Revolution enabled the Bolsheviks to put their ideology into practice. A decree signed by Lenin on Jan. 21, 1918, stated that "the church is separated from the state. . . . The

---

[161] John S. Curtiss, "Church and State," in Cyril E. Black, editor, "The Transformation of Russian Society: Aspects of Social Change since 1861" (Cambridge: Harvard University Press, 1960), p. 405.

[162] Quoted in Committee on Un-American Activities, House of Representatives, 86th Congress, First Session, "Facts on Communism: Volume I, The Communist Ideology" (Washington: U. S. Government Printing Office, 1959), p. 133.

school is separated from the church."[163] It also prohibited religious instruction in all public and general private schools, but allowed the private teaching of religion. This was followed by a series of decrees and instructions: on Aug. 24, 1918, the Commissar of Justice, D. Kurskii, reiterated that religious instruction was not permitted in any school except the "purely theological establishments" and ordered the nationalization of all religious schools;[164] the Commissar of Public Education, Anatol V. Lunacharski, sent out a circular on March 3, 1919, declaring that "teaching religious doctrine to persons younger than eighteen years is not permitted,"[165] ostensibly in organized class form, and on other occasions proved himself to be most zealous in urging all Communists to wage a war of propaganda against religion; the 1923 Criminal Code of the R. S. F. S. R. stated that "imparting of religious instruction in state or private educational institutions to children or minors, is punishable by forced labor up to a year," a regulation which also appeared in the Criminal Code in 1938.[166]

Lunacharski's crusade against religion was answered in the formation, in 1925, of the Society of the Militant Godless and in the publication of its organ, *Bezbozhnik (Godless)*. This

---

[163] E. N. Medinskii, "Narodnoe obrazovanie v SSSR" (Moscow: Uchpedgiz, 1947), pp. 15-16. The document is printed in V. Z. Smirnov, editor, "Khrestomatiya po istorii pedagogiki" (Moscow: Uchpedgiz, 1957), pp. 441-442; and, in English, in Boleslaw Szczesniak, editor, "The Russian Revolution and Religion" (Notre Dame: University of Notre Dame Press, 1959), pp. 34-35.

[164] Document in Szczesniak, *op.cit.*, pp. 45-46.

[165] Quoted in John S. Curtiss, "The Russian Church and the Soviet State: 1917-1950" (Boston: Little, Brown, 1953), p. 76.

[166] Document in Szczesniak, *op.cit.*, p. 107. See also Paul B. Anderson, "People, Church and State in Modern Russia" (New York: Macmillan, 1944), pp. 18-19.

propagandistic organization attained a membership of 3,500,000 in 1941, but it apparently was made to stop its work in the fall of 1941, not long after the Nazi invasion of the Soviet Union, an occasion which brought about some sort of understanding between the church and the state.[167] In the meantime, the literature and the activities of the Society of the Militant Godless had obtained the *imprimatur*, hardly surprisingly, from the Commissar of Public Education (the *Narkompros*), who put into all subjects (including mathematics and foreign languages) on all levels a generous amount of anti-religious ideology. Of special value to the curriculum makers, suggested the educational commissar, was the periodical, *The Godless in the School*, published under the auspices of *Besbozhnik*.[168]

The prohibition of all religious teachings and practices in the government schools and the abolition of private schools by the law of Dec. 18, 1923, would seem to have been adequate measures toward the extirpation of all religious belief in due time in the Soviet Union. Nevertheless, in spite of all these actions and of the introduction of anti-religious courses and seminars in higher educational institutions,[169] there was ample evidence of official awareness that success was still far away. Thus, in 1928, Lunacharski himself made the "damning admission" of the weakness of the attack on religion: "Religion is like a nail, the harder you hit it the

---

[167] John N. Hazard, "The Soviet System of Government" (Chicago: University of Chicago Press, 1957), p. 128.
[168] William W. Brickman, "The Historical Setting after the Revolution," in George Z. F. Bereday, William W. Brickman, and Gerald H. Read, editors, "The Changing Soviet School" (Boston: Houghton Mifflin, 1960), pp. 60-61.
[169] Julius F. Hecker, "Religion and Communism: A Study of Religion and Atheism in Soviet Russia" (London: Chapman and Hall, 1933), pp. 254-256.

deeper it goes into the wood."[170] In order to save its basic ideological program, the Soviet regime timed its intensification of the anti-religion campaign to coincide with the beginning of the Five-Year Plan in 1929. One important step was an amendment to the Constitution striking out the provision of the freedom of religious propaganda and permitting the anti-religious type only (April 14, 1929).[171] A "basic decree," or rather, a compilation of decrees, restated the prohibition of "the teaching of any form of religious belief" in public school or through private teaching, except in theological schools.[172] In other ways, too, this law made it clear that the official policy was that religion must disappear from the U. S. S. R.

The Stalin Constitution of 1936 devoted Art. 124 to the matter of religion: "In order to ensure to citizens freedom of conscience, the church in the U. S. S. R. is separated from the state, and the school from the church. Freedom of religious worship and freedom of anti-religious propaganda is recognized for all citizens."[173] It is to be noted that this "new" constitution recapitulated its predecessor of 1929 in that freedom of pro-religious teaching was denied. Furthermore, Art. 123 guaranteed the "equality of rights of citizens of the U. S. S. R., irrespective of their nationality or race," but not of religion. In point of actual fact, however, all religious groups are oppressed by the regime, with the Jews consti-

---

[170] Quoted in Bernard Pares, "Russia" (New York: New American Library, 1949), p. 110. *Cf.,* Sir Bernard Pares, "A History of Russia," fifth edition (New York: Knopf, 1947), p. 507.

[171] Pares, "Russia," *loc. cit.*

[172] Document in Robert Tobias, "Communist-Christian Encounter in East Europe" (Indianapolis: School of Religion Press, 1956), p. 289.

[173] Quoted in Anderson, *op.cit.,* p. 225.

tuting "a special target of Communist persecution" because of the official suspicion of their "attachment to the religious tenets of Judaism" and related reasons.[174]

During World War II, as already stated, there was a kind of rapprochement between the regime and religion. The government set up, in October, 1943, within the Council of Ministers, a Council for Affairs of the Orthodox Church and shortly afterward a council for all the minority faiths. During the following year, it also allowed the resumption of organized religious education for the priesthood and of private religious training by priests.[175]

The ideological and constitutional principles for the separation of church and state in the U. S. S. R. are as old as the regime itself. Specific and clear-cut as they are, unlike the presumed separationism of the U. S. Constitution, it is difficult to appreciate the relation of the Council for the Management of Religious Cults *(Soviet po delam religiozni kultovna)* with its two divisions governing the Russian Orthodox Church and all the other religions, respectively.[176] The Council helps churches obtain new buildings and other material needs but furnishes no money. All church buildings belong to the state, but the congregations have the right of unlimited use. Religious groups also enjoy the freedom, according to an official of the Council, to

---

[174] Select Committee on Communist Aggression, House of Representatives, 83rd Congress, Second Session, "Treatment of Jews under Communism," Special Report No. 2 (Washington: U. S. Government Printing Office, 1954), p. 33.

[175] Hazard, *op.cit.,* p. 128.

[176] This paragraph is based on an interview between Pavel A. Zadarozhnii, member of the Council, with the writer and a special committee of the Comparative Education Society, August, 1958, Moscow.

publish Bibles and prayer books, but there is a quota on ink and paper. They must decide on what they wish — Bibles, prayer books, or any other religious publication. In visiting churches and synagogues, one is impressed by the scarcity and advanced age of Bibles and prayer books.[177] This observation has been corroborated by others.

Just how much of a church-state separation is there in the Soviet Union? Obviously, there is some recognition and even support of churches, even if religious instruction is still banned in every form except theological training and private teaching. The existence of a special subcouncil on church affairs within the Council of Ministers lends proof to the hypothesis that the state is officially controlling the churches. Any resemblance to actual separation seems to be merely verbal.

There can be little disagreement with the proposition that the Communist regime never stopped having its troubles with the liquidation of religion. After World War II, a new approach was adopted in an attempt to solve the perplexing problem of the persistence of faith. In 1949, the All-Union Society for the Dissemination of Scientific and Political Knowledge, which replaced the defunct Society of the Militant Godless, undertook a campaign to convince youth and adults of the incompatibility of religion and science. Museums for the propagation of atheism were reopened to bring this fact home to young people and the adult public, and classes of school children made frequent pilgrimages to these shrines of anti-religion.[178] That these

---

[177] The writer visited Soviet schools, universities, churches, mosques, and synagogues in 1957, 1958, and 1960.

[178] Hazard, op.cit., p. 129. Cf., New York Times, April 2, 1961.

efforts did not attain the desired results is evident from the regretful confession by Academician M. B. Mitin, president of the All-Union Society, in *Voprosi filosofii* (1957), that there was a revival of religious activities in the Soviet Union.[179] One is reminded of Lunacharski's wry comment nearly two decades earlier. Clearly, the bitter disappointment of Mitin also was an acknowledgment of the failure of the special antireligious campaign inaugurated in July, 1954, by the Communist Party.[180] It testified, in addition, to the weakness of the atheistic propaganda spread among Soviet youth following the decree by the Central Committee of the Communist Party, signed by N. K. Khrushchev on Nov. 10, 1954, on the "mistakes of the Party's scientific-atheistic propaganda among the population."[181] To what extent the magazine *Nauka i Religiya (Science and Religion)* and the Dom Ateista (House of the Atheist) will advance the atheistic cause is yet to be determined. Certainly, the scientific-atheistic instruction has been stepped up in the schools in recent years. On the basis of the writer's observations in 1960 in the Soviet Union, the walls of the school corridors and the classrooms had an abundance of scientific-atheistic exhibits, more than he ever had seen before.

But history seems to be repeating itself in demonstrating the profundity of Lunacharski's dictum over 30 years ago about the futility of the attempt to abolish religion. A dispatch from

---

[179] Alessio U. Floridi, "Antireligious Education of Soviet Youth," in George Z. F. Bereday and Jaan Pennar, editors, "The Politics of Soviet Education" (New York: Praeger, 1960), p. 99.

[180] Helmut Neubauer, "Kirchen and Religionsgemeinschaften," in Hans Koch, editor, "Sowjetbuch" (Cologne: Deutsche Industrieverlag, 1958), p. 333.

[181] Floridi, *op.cit.*, p. 90.

Moscow, dated Feb. 8, 1961, stated that Soviet educators still fear that "atheistic education in the schools is not taking hold and that religion may retain a stubborn foothold."[182] The Komsomol and other party groups have been ordered to fight against the trend among young people to join Protestant sects. Another report, written by Seymour Topping and datelined March 25, 1961, in Leningrad, reveals that even if religion appeared to be losing ground gradually among the youth in this city, it was giving atheism a strong battle. "The faithful still flock to the sixteen Russian Orthodox Churches, one Roman Catholic church, one Baptist church, one synagogue, and one Moslem mosque tolerated by the Leningrad City Soviet."[183]

The government allows a number of theological seminaries for the Russian Orthodox, the Baptist, and the Moslem groups. One Jewish seminary with a registration of 19, for a minority of about 3,000,000, has been in existence since 1956. In general, the government sets up the rules for these institutions along the lines of those under the aegis of the Ministry of Higher Education. The Soviet regime seems to be somewhat partial toward the Russian Orthodox and the Moslem faiths, probably for political reasons. At the same time, also because of political motivation, it is especially hostile toward the Roman Catholics and the Jews.[184]

At present, the U. S. S. R. is nominally committed to a policy of church-state separation in education and all other aspects of society. Actually, this means that religious teaching is almost universally forbidden and private schools with

[182] *New York Times,* Feb. 12, 1961.
[183] *New York Times,* April 2, 1961.
[184] Hazard, *loc.cit.*

religious content cannot exist. It does not mean, however, that there is an official hands-off policy with regard to the churches. The government controls all churches, as it does all other institutions. The current concern by the Communists with the resurgence of religion may lead to even more stringent controls over the churches and perhaps also to a return to the atheistic corners in the classrooms of the 1920's. In any event, the Soviet experience justifies the conclusion that a separationist policy has no necessary relationship to democracy.

OTHER COMMUNIST COUNTRIES

Poland, with 95% of the population Roman Catholic, has worked out in 1960 a *modus vivendi* with its ecclesiastical authorities. Under this agreement, Catholic religious instruction would be given in the public schools and the government would support the Catholic schools. The policy of supporting religious schools, of course, goes back to prewar Poland.[185]

The Constitution of the Polish People's Republic proclaims that "the Church is separated from the State" (Art. 70), but this does not prevent priests from giving religious instruction in the state schools; such instruction, however, is not compulsory.[186] Prior to the fall of 1956, when the Polish hierarchy signed another agreement with the new Gomulka government reinstating religious education in the primary schools and *liceums* (secondary schools), there was a period of church-state conflict during which "the teaching of religion was gradually but steadily re-

---

[185] Clifford R. Barnett, *et al.*, "Poland: Its People, Its Society, Its Culture" (New Haven: HRAF Press, 1958), p. 340; *cf.*, Zygmunt Parnowski, "Education in Poland" (Warsaw: Polonia Publishing House, 1958), p. 41.

[186] Parnowski, *op.cit.*, p. 9.

duced until it was practically nonexistent."[187] In the higher level, the Catholic University of Lublin is the only such institution recognized by the state, which furnishes no financial aid but exercises control to such an extent as to deprive the university practically of its Catholic character. The Catholic faculties of theology of the Jagiellonian University of Cracow and the University of Warsaw were abolished in 1954 and replaced by the Communist-controlled Academy of Catholic Theology in Warsaw.[188] Thus, the Communist government of Poland utilizes the constitutional policy of church-separation in a variety of ways in order to further its own ideological ends. If it is in practice more liberal than the U. S. S. R., it probably is no less so in theory. In all likelihood, it is biding its time for a day of reckoning with the Catholic Church.

Czechoslovakia, by a tradition going back to the laws of 1867, 1868, and others, has recognized religious instruction in the public schools on an interdenominational basis and has granted public funds to private religious schools.[189] These principles also prevailed during the democratic phase of Czechoslovakia's history, from 1919 to 1939 and from 1945 to 1948. If religion were a compulsory subject in the elementary, secondary, and normal schools, there was a conscience clause for the dissenters.[190] Unlike the other Communist countries, Czechoslovakia did

---

[187] Barnett, op.cit., p. 337.

[188] Joseph Bronars, "Higher Education in Poland: Some Aspects of Its Sovietization" (Washington: Catholic University of America Press, 1957), pp. 8-9.

[189] Emanuel Lippert, "Czechoslovakia," in Kandel, "Educational Yearbook . . . 1932," op.cit., pp. 117-118.

[190] Severin K. Turosienski, "Education in Czechoslovakia," Bulletin 1935, No. 11, U. S. Office of Education (Washington: U. S. Government Printing Office, 1935), p. 4.

not insert a statement of church-state separation in its Constitution of June 9, 1948. In fact, in the Education Act of April 21, 1948, Sec. 19 provided for religious instruction in the public schools under church supervision, but with the Ministry of Education reserving its right of "supreme direction and supervision."[191] Religious instruction in public schools is optional and was given in 1950 to 80-90% of the children by teachers who were paid by the government. The theological seminaries of the Protestant, Orthodox, and Catholic denominations also are under state control.[192] What the future will hold for this church-state relationship cannot be predicted with accuracy, but it is possible that the Czech Communists found the power of history too strong in the early stages of their regime.

The Constitution of the Hungarian People's Republic, Aug. 18, 1949, stated in paragraph 54 that "in the interest of the assurance of conscience-freedom, the Hungarian People's Republic separates the Church from the State" after having guaranteed freedom of conscience and the right of free exercise of religion to the citizens.[193] Only the year before, the Communist regime had nationalized all private schools, thus appropriating to itself 5,437 church schools of a total of 7,791 schools in Hungary, according to a report by the Ministry of National Education.[194] During the year of constitutional separation, religious instruction was made optional in the public schools without affecting the Communist insistence that church and state were

[191] Document in "School Reform in Czechoslovakia" (Prague: Orbis, 1949), p. 16.
[192] Tobias, op.cit., p. 514.
[193] Quoted in ibid., p. 478.
[194] "International Yearbook of Education" (Geneva: International Bureau of Education, 1953), p. 182.

apart.[195] Notwithstanding government agreements with the Protestant, Catholic, and Jewish groups for public religious instruction, the use of public classrooms for church classes and services, and the furnishing of state funds to the churches,[196] it did not take long to see that the Hungarian Communists were more interested in stifling than in supporting religious education. Evidently, the agreements were valid in theory but frequently were not carried out in practice— so frequently, in fact, that the difficulties in teaching religion in the public schools prompted the church groups "to make special efforts to provide religious instruction in the homes, or in church buildings."[197] This was an effort to escape from the clutches of the government which had decreed separation but was acting as if church and state were one—under the state. The picture of a Ministry of Public Worship opposing a theological faculty in the university is another indication of a very peculiar situation under church-state separation. That freedom of religion was at least questionable could be inferred from the disagreement between Jewish groups who claimed that Jewish pupils were forced to attend public schools on Saturday, while the Hungarian government disclaimed any discriminatory practices.[198]

According to Art. 84 of the Constitution of the People's Republic of Rumania (1948), "the school is separated from the Church. No religious creed, congregation or community may open or maintain institutions of general educa-

---

[195] *Ibid.*, p. 188.
[196] See the documents in Tobias, *op.cit.*, pp. 468-487.
[197] *Ibid.*, p. 460.
[198] Charles D. Ammoun, "Study of Discrimination in Education" (New York: United Nations, 1957), p. 56.

tion, but only special schools for training the personnel of the cult."[199] Nothing is said about the separation of the church from the state, and, indeed, there is no separation. The basic purpose of the Ministry of Religions (Cults) is "to combat superstitions and deleterious sects, to expose the intrigues of the Vatican."[200] Should any denomination go along with this aim, it will receive government support and will be permitted to issue theological publications in limited quantity. Religious education is forbidden in the public schools, which present, according to the Education Reform Act of 1948, a "secular" education based on "democratic, popular and realist scientific principles."[201] As in the Soviet Union, however, the only religious education given on the non-seminary level is in the homes.

Art. 78 of the Constitution of the People's Republic of Bulgaria (1947) states clearly that "the Church is separate from the State,"[202] but Art. 15 of the Law on the Churches (Feb. 24, 1949) insists on control of the organization and curriculum of the theological schools by the Ministry of Foreign Affairs.[203] Formal education of a religious nature is forbidden by Art. 20 of the same law: "The education of children and young people and the establishment of youth organizations is under the special care of the State, and is outside the scope of activity of the churches and the ministers."[204] However, it is possible "in the intimate family circle, in Bible

---

[199] Quoted, *ibid.,* p. 55.
[200] Quoted in Tobias, *op.cit.,* p. 337.
[201] Quoted in *ibid.,* p. 339.
[202] Quoted in *ibid.,* p. 367.
[203] *Ibid.,* p. 373.
[204] Document in *ibid.,* p. 374.

study, in the pastoral visits of the clergy, in small groups of children meeting in homes. . . . "[205]

Albania nationalized all schools in 1933 and closed those Catholic schools which did not consent to public supervision and control. During the Italian occupation in World War II, the Catholic institutions were given more generous treatment. Under the Constitution of Communist Albania (1946), "the Church is separated from the State," but several sentences later the same document declared that "the state may give material aid to the religious communities."[206] The abolition of religious instruction came the following year and the nationalization of schools in 1948. In the Church Law of Nov. 26, 1949, this blunt statement occurred in Art. 23: "The education of youth is conducted by the State, and religious institutions have nothing to do with it."[207]

Prior to World War II, religion was a compulsory course in all public schools of Yugoslavia—primary, secondary, vocational, and civic. The law of 1935 introduced the idea of prayers in class before and after instruction and the requirement of elementary and secondary pupils to fulfill the obligations of their respective faiths. The government provided funds for the theological seminaries of the recognized faiths—the Greek Orthodox, the Catholic, and the Moslem.[208] With the advent of Marshal Tito's Communist regime, religious instruction became optional, according to the desire of the parents. The state allows the teaching of religion after

[205] *Ibid.*, p. 364.
[206] Quoted in *ibid.*, p. 381.
[207] Quoted in *ibid.*, p. 382.
[208] Sevenin K. Turosienski, "Education in Yugoslavia," Bulletin 1939, No. 6, U. S. Office of Education (Washington: U. S. Government Printing Office, 1939), p. 10.

school time in the public school buildings.[209]
Faculties of theology are at three of the five
Yugoslav state universities.[210] The General Law
on Education (1958) made no mention of religious instruction. Art. 7 provides that "all citizens, regardless of nationality, sex, social origin
or religion, shall enjoy equal rights to education
under the same conditions."[211] This might seem
to imply that private religious schools can co-
exist with the public schools, but such an interpretation hardly will be entertained by the
authorities. The fundamental objective of education in Yugoslavia can be found in Art. 14:
"Education shall be based upon the premises of
sciences and principles of pedagogy, upon the
achievements of the history and culture of the
people of Yugoslavia and other peoples, and
upon ideological foundations and the humanist
spirit of socialism."[212]

The situation at present is that religion is no
longer even an optional subject in the public
schools in Yugoslavia, but it may be taught in
churches. Religious groups may open theological
schools to train priests. All this is explainable
under the constitutional separation of church
and state.[213] From the recent developments in
Yugoslavia, it appears that this Communist
country is well on the road toward separationism.

Before turning to a Communist country on

---

[209] Ammoun, op.cit., p. 52.
[210] "The University in Socialist Yugoslavia" (Belgrade:
National Commission of the FPR [Federal People's Re-
public] of Yugoslavia for Unesco, 1955), p. 71.
[211] "General Law on Education in Yugoslavia" (Belgrade: Jugoslavija, 1959), p. 53.
[212] Ibid., p. 55.
[213] Bogdan Osolnik, "The Development of the School
System in Yugoslavia" (Belgrade: Jugoslavija, 1959), p. 5.

another continent,[214] it would be well to pause and reflect on the similarities and differences within the Marxist microcosm. There are all grades and levels of church - state separation — from no religion (save atheism) in public education, as in the U. S. S. R., to the compromise of religion in public schools made by Poland. The private religious school and religious liberty in general have fallen prey to Communist ideology—of that there can be no possible doubt. The Communist area may not be uniform in all details regarding its attitude toward religion and religious education, but it is united in one respect at least: first to control and then to get rid of both with impunity, as soon as circumstances permit.

The question of church-state relations was of virtually no concern to the Confucianists, Taoists, and Buddhists in the Republic of China (Nationalist) prior to the Communist Revolution. Only the Christian community, among the major religions in China, looked upon the government regulations as interference with the freedom of religion. It apparently was the regulations of the Ministry of Education in 1917, prohibiting compulsory religious teaching and ceremonies in the Christian primary schools, that touched off controversy. These rules were restated several times during the 1920's, culminating in the Regulations for Private Schools (Aug. 29, 1929) by the Ministry of Education.[215] But the official attitude was by no means the strictest; the left wing of the Kuomintang party, in accordance with Communistic ideology, advocated

---

[214] Communist East Germany was discussed in a previous section under Germany.
[215] Herman C. E. Liu, "China," in Kandel, "Educational Yearbook . . . 1932," op.cit., pp. 85-104.

that the property of the Christian schools be confiscated,[216] thus presaging government action after 1949.

In the People's Republic of China—mainland or Communist China—the Constitution of 1954 contained the statement that "Citizens . . . enjoy freedom of religious belief."[217] This claim must be assessed in the light of these facts: "Confucianism has disappeared without a trace," Taoism and Buddhism are on the road to extinction, Islam is regarded as a nationality rather than as a religion, and an anti-religious campaign has been under way since 1950 against Christianity. The Chinese Communists have been utilizing all sorts of methods, delicate and brutal, in their struggle to uproot the Christian belief. The state took over the Christian theological seminaries and, instead of closing them, trained ministers of religion whose primary loyalty was to communism. "With the further stabilization and growth in power of the Communist government, prospects are that formalized religion in China will continue to decline and wither away as an institution in the life of the Chinese people."[218] The withering-away process is standard Marxism, and the Chinese Communists are at least as Marxist as any other group. Undoubtedly, they are for a strict separation of church and state, a policy which would not prevent them from

[216] *Ibid*, p. 89.

[217] Liu Shao-Chi, "Report on the Draft Constitution of the People's Republic of China: Constitution of the People's Republic of China" (Peking: Foreign Languages Press, 1954), p. 97.

[218] Chang-tu Hu, *et al.*, "China: Its People, Its Society, Its Culture" (New Haven: HRAF Press, 1960), p. 139. Most of the paragraph is derived from pp. 116-139. *Cf.*, Harold C. Hinton, "China," in George M. Kahin, editor, "Major Governments of Asia" (Ithaca: Cornell University Press, 1958), p. 103.

making use of all tactics to liquidate religion and religious persons.

THE MIDDLE EAST

The Ottoman Empire was based on the principle of church-state unity with full autonomy in worship and education enjoyed by Christians and Jews. The founding of the Republic of Turkey in 1923 by Mustapha Kemal Ataturk resulted in the adoption of the idea of church-state separation and in the closing of the Moslem schools. "Religious teachings have been erased from the school programs."[219] A change of policy came about, however, in 1950, when the Council of Ministers decided "that religion be taught in elementary schools in order to meet the religious needs of the Turkish children same [sic] as in all other fields."[220] Parents who do not wish that religion be taught to their children may request exemption. This action constitutes, by implication at least, an acknowledgement of the need for compromise. Private religious schools run by Christians and Jews are controlled but not financed by the authorities. In recent years, religion has been on the ascendency, to judge from the erection of 5,000 mosques since 1950, the establishment of a faculty of theology at the University of Ankara, the opening of secondary schools to train imams and preachers, and other indications.[221]

The State of Israel, which came into being on May 14, 1948, drew upon the governmental re-

---

[219] "Public Instruction in the Republic of Turkey" (Ankara: Ministry of the Interior, 1936), p. 18.

[220] Quoted in Abul H. K. Sassani, "Education in Turkey," Bulletin 1952, No. 10, U. S. Office of Education (Washington: U. S. Government Printing Office, 1952), p. 17.

[221] *New York Times,* Feb. 28, 1960.

ligious and educational policies that had prevailed under the Ottoman Empire and the British Mandatory in Palestine, as well as upon the ancient traditions of the Bible and Talmud. The proclamation issued upon the birth of the state declared that the new government "will be based on the principles of freedom, justice and peace as envisaged by the Prophets of Israel. . . . will ensure complete equality of social and political rights to all its inhabitants irrespective of religion, race, or sex; . . . will guarantee freedom of religion, conscience, language, education, and culture; . . . will safeguard the Holy Places of all religions. . . ."[222] The State Education Law of 1953, which instituted a national school system, recognized the coexistence of the state school and religious state school (Beth Sefer Mamlakhti Dathi). The latter is defined by the law as a public school which is religious as to "way of life, curriculum, and teachers."[223] In addition, there is the Hinukh Atzmai (independent education), a system of religious schools, the secular programs of which are under state control but which receive a large public subvention. Public Christian and Moslem schools are supervised by the Ministry of Education and Culture and receive full financial support.

What is of special interest in the educational system of Israel is that the syllabus of the public primary (secular) schools contains religious material in various subjects, making it obvious that the government's objective is "to instruct Jewish pupils in the basic traditional lore and values of the Jewish people."[224] The statement

---

[222] Quoted in William W. Brickman, "Religion in the Israeli Public Schools," Tradition, Spring, 1960, p. 240.

[223] Quoted in ibid., p. 242.

[224] Ibid., p. 256.

of aims makes it clear that the Bible *(Tanakh)* is "the basic book of Jewish culture" which provides the children with "the basic values of Judaism as expressed in the commands and laws"; that the pupils are "to acquire the basic knowledge of the spiritual image of the nation and of its struggle for physical and spiritual existence as the bearer of the word of God in the ancient, idol-worshipping world"; and that they should be given the opportunity "to acquire love and reverence for the Book and the desire to read it constantly, and the inner stimulus to derive inspiration from it."[225] In this program of a secular school there seems to be more religious thought and content than in many a religious school in another country.

With the exception of Lebanon, the Arab countries in the Middle East recognize Islam as the state religion and teach the Moslem faith in their public schools.[226] Koran and religion are regular subjects in the primary schools of the United Arab Republic, Yemen, Iraq, Jordan, Libya, Bahrein, and Kuwait; Koran, Bases of Moslem Religion, and Moslem Law in those of Saudi Arabia; and noncompulsory religion in Lebanon.[227] One of the characteristics of education in the Middle East for the past century or so was the presence of foreign mission schools in which all pupils were generally required to study Christianity even if it were not their

[225] Misrad Hahinukh Vehatarbut, "Tokhnit halimmudim l'beth hasefer hayesodi hamamlakhti v'hamamlakhti-hadati: Kitot Alef-Daleth" (Hakiryah: Hamadpis Hamemshalti, 1954), p. 1.

[226] Roderic D. Matthews and Matta Akrawi, "Education in Arab Countries of the Near East" (Washington: American Council on Education, 1949), p. 529.

[227] "Compulsory Education in the Arab States" (Paris: Unesco, 1956), pp. 49-52.

parents' faith. Egypt, in 1948, enacted a law prohibiting the private school from imparting "religious instruction to its pupils of other denominations, even if the parents give their consent."[228] Private schools, many of which were religious, received public funds from the time of the decree by the Ministry of Education (1934).[229] In 1954, the Egyptian government allowed in the schools the teaching of Christianity to Christian children, with public funds for this instruction but with Moslem teachers interpreting the Christian religion.[230] In Iraq, as in Egypt, the government gave financial aid to private sectarian schools which adopted the official curriculum and were subject to inspections.[231]

CENTRAL ASIA

The significance of Islam in Pakistan may be seen in frequent statements made in government documents and in official statements. The Constitution of the Islamic Republic of Pakistan (1949) stated that it derived its authority from "Allah Almighty alone."[232] That the principles of Islamic democracy and social justice were to inspire the public school system was the desire

[228] Quoted in Sati El Hussri, "Arab States," in Lauwerys and Hans, "The Year Book of Education: 1951," op.cit., pp. 599-600.

[229] Amir Boktor, "Egypt," in I. L. Kandel, editor, "Educational Yearbook of the International Institute of Teachers College, Columbia University: 1937," (New York: Bureau of Publications, Teachers College, Columbia University, 1937), p. 136; Matthews and Akrawi, op.cit., p. 111.

[230] Ammoun, op.cit., p. 50.

[231] Paul Monroe, editor, "Report of the Educational Inquiry Commission" (Baghdad: Government Press, 1932), p. 48.

[232] Quoted in Keith Callard, "Pakistan," in Kahin, op.cit., p. 402.

of educators and officials from 1948 on.[233] The introduction to the new plan of educational development laid down the policy that the education of Pakistan must be "inspired by Islamic values, for these values constitute a valid and coherent philosophy pervading all aspects of life."[234] It is not surprising, therefore, that religious education is compulsory in Pakistan.

From the mid-19th century onward, there were many instances of the teaching of religion in the public schools of India and grants of public money to private denominational schools.[235] The existence of many religious groups all over India has doubtless operated against a national attitude toward religious education,[236] as did the tendency toward secularism.[237] Nevertheless, on the state level, there are various provisions which encourage the teaching of religion. Thus, the Primary Education Act of Bombay State (1947) offered grants to approved private schools, as did the government of Mysore.[238] Madras insists that "public funds should not be utilized for imparting religious instruction," but it does facilitate the organization of religious classes in the public schools either before or after instruction hours, presumably at the expense of the parents or the denominations.[239]

----

[233] Muhammad S. Huq, "Compulsory Education in Pakistan" (Paris: Unesco, 1954), p. 92.

[234] "Six Year National Plan of Educational Development for Pakistan: Part I" (Karachi: Government of Pakistan Press, 1952), p. 5.

[235] J. M. Sen, "India," in Kandel, "Educational Yearbook . . . 1932," op.cit., pp. 284-292.

[236] S. N. Mukerji, "Education in India—Today andTomorrow" (Baroda: Acharya, 1950), p. 193.

[237] K. G. Saiyidain, J. P. Naik, and S. A. Husain, "Compulsory Education in India" (Paris: Unesco, 1952), p. 97.

[238] Dubay, op.cit., p. 121.

[239] Ibid., p. 152.

Ceylon has given generous aid to all denominational schools, including the Christian, and it allows religious instruction, subject to the recognized democratic safeguards, in the public schools.[240] But, in 1960, the movement to nationalize the entire school system, which had been quite strong a decade earlier, gained considerable momentum.[241] Late that year, the nationalist-minded government introduced legislation to take over the 2,500 private schools, most of which were operated by the Roman Catholics.[242] The new plan, which went into effect on Dec. 1, 1960, evoked the vigorous opposition of the Catholic bishops. In January, 1961, however, the bishops issued a declaration that they would be "most willing to accept a national system of education provided the Government insured for Catholics that no harm would thereby befall their religious interests."[243] There are no signs of a separation of church and state, merely the weakening of Hindu and Christian influence in the educational process in favor of that of the Buddhist majority. The Buddhists, it is interesting to note, are reported as having favored the nationalization of the minority religious schools.

THE FAR EAST

The relation of religious education to government in the history of Japan does not appear to be entirely clear to a Westerner. The Elementary School Act of 1905 excluded religious instruction from public elementary schools and even

[240] K. Neshiah, "Ceylon," in Lauwerys and Hans, "The Year Book of Education: 1951," op.cit., pp. 587-88.

[241] K. S. Arulnandhy, "Ceylon," in J. A. Lauwerys and N. Hans, "The Year Book of Education: 1952" (London: Evans, 1952), pp. 542-543.

[242] New York Times, Oct. 23, 1960.

[243] Quoted in New York Times, Jan. 19, 1961.

forbade such teaching in private schools financed by denominational schools.[244] This followed Edict No. 12 of the Department of Education, Aug. 3, 1899, which separated education from religious doctrine and ceremonies in all schools on all levels.[245] A decade earlier, the first Constitution of 1889 pronounced the freedom of religion in Art. 28, but set up Shrine Shinto "as a national rite—not a religion—so that believers of all religions were claimed to owe loyalty to the shrines and the national rites."[246] From the Japanese point of view, there was no contradiction between religious freedom and loyalty to Shinto.

The famous and influential Imperial Rescript on Education, Oct. 30, 1890, with its mention of "Our Imperial Throne coeval with heaven and earth,"[247] seemed to acknowledge an identification between government and religion in education. This document has been recognized by Japanese and foreign commentators as religious doctrine, and its constant ceremonial use in the public schools until 1946 constituted religious instruction and worship.[248] Also of religious educational significance was the required reading of *Kokutai no Hongi* ("The Cardinal Principles of the National Entity of Japan") in all institutions

---

[244] K. Ashida, "Japan," in Kandel, "Educational Yearbook . . . 1932," *op.cit.*, pp. 325-326.

[245] *Ibid.*, p. 327; H. Sasaki, "Moral-Erziehung in Japan" (Leipzig: Akademische Verlagsgesellschaft, 1926), p. 159.

[246] "Religions in Japan" ([Tokyo:] Religious Affairs Section, Ministry of Education, 1959), p. 83.

[247] Document in Ronald S. Anderson, "Japan: Three Epochs of Modern Education," Bulletin 1959, No. 11, U. S. Office of Education (Washington: U. S. Government Printing Office, 1959), p. 215.

[248] *Ibid.*, p. 13; Ashida, *op.cit.*, p. 317; Robert K. Hall, "Shushin: The Ethics of a Defeated Nation" (New York: Bureau of Publications, Teachers College, Columbia University, 1949), p. 37.

above the secondary level and by all teachers as part of their in-service education. This official statement concerning the nature of the state, published on March 30, 1937, by the Bureau of Thought Control of the Ministry of Education, emphasized the divine origin, characteristics, leadership, and mission of the Japanese emperor, government, and people.[249] Another document, *Shimmin no Michi* ("The Way of the Subject"), issued in 1941 by the Bureau of Thought Control, helped to complete the trilogy of theological-national works which were used for indoctrination purposes in public education on all levels.[250] In the primary school, these ideas were propagated by means of the course in *Shushin* ("ethics").

The defeat of Japan in World War II broke down the state-religion partnership. On Dec. 15, 1945, the Supreme Commander for the Allied Powers (SCAP) issued a directive ordering the "Abolition of Governmental Sponsorship, Support, Perpetuation, Control, and Dissemination of State Shinto." Included in the directive was the prohibition of the circulation of *Kokutai no Hongi, Shimmin no Michi,* and similar publications.[251] Subsequently, the Ministry of Education banned the Imperial Rescript from the public schools and the ceremonies during which chil-

[249] Hall, "Shushin: The Ethics of a Defeated Nation," *op.cit.,* pp. 52-59; Robert K. Hall, editor, "Kokutai no Hongi: Cardinal Principles on the National Entity of Japan," translated by John O. Gauntlett (Cambridge: Harvard University Press, 1949).

[250] Hall, "Shushin: The Ethics of a Defeated Nation," *op.cit.,* pp. 68-70. For a translation of this booklet, see Appendix A in Otto D. Tolischus, "Tokyo Record" (New York: Reynal & Hitchcock, 1943).

[251] The full document is in "Religions in Japan" (Tokyo: Civil Information and Education Section, SCAP, 1948), pp. 185-189.

dren bowed in the direction of the palace and shouted, *"Tenno Heika Banzai"* ("Long Live the Son of Heaven").[252]

The new Constitution, which was adopted in 1946 and went into effect the following year, proclaimed religious freedom for all and specified that "the State and its organs shall refrain from religious education or any other religious activity" (Art. 20).[253] In addition, it stated that "no public money or property shall be appropriated for the use, benefit or support of any system of religion, or religious institution or association, or for any charitable, educational or benevolent purposes not under the control of public authority" (Art. 89).[254] According to the occupation authority in 1948, "Articles 20 and 89 of the new Constitution provide guarantees of separation of religion and state which are as clear and unequivocal as those contained in any of the written constitutions of the world" and "today, the separation of religion and state in Japan is as complete as in any country in the world."[255] One wonders if this complete separation was not, in part at least, due to the convictions and zeal of American authorities who found it easier to effectuate this situation in Japan than in their own country.

But this perfect condition apparently was breached as early as December, 1949, with the passage of the Private School Law after consternation among the private schools which had suffered as a result of the war.[256] The govern-

---

[252] *Ibid.*, p. 133.
[253] Quoted in Robert K. Hall, "Education for a New Japan" (New Haven: Yale University Press, 1949), p. 405.
[254] Quoted in "Education Reform in Japan" ([Tokyo:] Japan Education Reform Council, 1950), p. 102.
[255] "Religions in Japan," SCAP, *op.cit.*, p. 135.
[256] "Education Reform in Japan," *op.cit.*, pp. 102-115.

ment now shares control of the private schools and universities, many of which are under religious auspices, with the private school and university councils. At the same time, the law provided subsidies to these institutions for construction and operation and to the private school personnel's mutual aid association, so that teacher benefits and protection would be about equal for both public and private school teachers.[257] In this way, it appears that public funds are permissible to private religious schools which are "under the control of public authority" (Art. 89) and which are not "organs" of the state (Art. 20). Separation is thus maintained and religious schools receive governmental benefits under what is regarded as an agreeable *modus vivendi*.

The Republic of China (Taiwan) maintains in its Constitution of 1946 that "all citizens shall have an equal opportunity to receive education" (Art. 159) and that all public and private schools shall be "subject to State supervision" (Art. 162).[258] Public subsidies are to be given to "private educational enterprises in this country which have a good record."[259] There is no indication that such aid is restricted to secular schools, nor is there any evidence that religion is taught in the public schools.

The Japanese occupation of Korea (1910-45) was a period of strict separation between religion and education in the Korean elementary schools and the prohibition of religious teaching in the

---

[257] Anderson, *op.cit.*, pp. 85-86.

[258] Quoted in Abul H. K. Sassani, "Education in Taiwan," Bulletin 1956, No. 3, U. S. Office of Education (Washington: U. S. Government Printing Office, 1956), p. 6.

[259] Quoted in *ibid.*, p. 7.

private mission schools.[260] However, the Japanese authorities followed the example of their mother country by introducing the emperor worship inherent in *Shushin.*[261] With liberation came a new approach to religion-education relations. The educational legislation of 1949-51 (Laws No. 86 and 178) emphasized that "no national or public school shall offer sectarian religious education" (Sec. 1, Art. 5).[262] On the other hand, Christian schools do teach religion. Catholic instruction is given after school hours with no apparent compulsion of non-Christians, and in Protestant schools the Bible is part of the curriculum and non-Christians are compelled to join the other pupils at prayer meetings.[263]

Christian secondary mission schools, which usually are regarded as among the best in Korea, are "sometimes favoured by important financial subsidies enabling them to select superior teachers" and are under government control in any case.[264] It is by no means surprising that private schools are not subsidized by the government as a rule, inasmuch as in 1955 some 50-75% of the operating funds of the primary schools were raised by the contributions of the parents' associations.[265] Nor do private universities receive any funds from a national or provincial source.

SOUTHEAST ASIA

In Thailand, "All private schools, irrespective of religion and nationality, are entitled to the

---

[260] Clara H. Koenig, "The Republic of Korea" ([Athens, Ohio: American Association of Collegiate Registrars and Admissions Officers], 1958), pp. 24-25, 27.
[261] "Rebuilding Education in the Republic of Korea" (Paris: Unesco, 1954), p. 24.
[262] Quoted in *ibid.,* p. 35.
[263] *Ibid.,* p. 56.
[264] *Ibid.,* p. 55.
[265] Koenig, *op.cit.,* pp. 13-14.

various kinds of help given by the Ministry of Education if they comply with the rules of high quality, and apply for such aid."[266] The subsidies include a portion of the salaries of the private school teachers.

Laos recognizes Buddhism as the established religion and the public schools teach its doctrines. On the other hand, the Pali schools, which are under the Ministry of Public Worship rather than the Ministry of Education, have added the secular subjects of French and arithmetic to their curriculum. There is "a consensus of opinion in favour of interpenetration" of the two elements, but few seem to know "how it may best be accomplished."[267]

Under the Netherlands East Indies Government, Indonesian private religious schools received public subsidies until about 1890, by which time the strictly neutral policy in matters of religion became fully established. However, in 1920, at the time when the mother country passed its famous law aiding religious schools, this policy was revised. The subsidies also were made available during the Japanese occupation. The new Indonesian Ministry of Education kept up the subsidies, in some cases as much as 100% of the total expenses of a school meeting official standards.[268]

According to Art. 41 of the Provisional Constitution of the Republic of Indonesia (1950), the school authorities must make "provision within school hours of the opportunity for reli-

---

[266] M. L. Manich Jumsai, "Compulsory Education in Thailand" (Paris: Unesco, 1951), p. 81.

[267] Charles Bilodeau, Somlith Pathammarong, and Le Quang Hong, "Compulsory Education in Cambodia, Laos and Viet-Nam" (Paris: Unesco, 1955), p. 108.

[268] M. Hutasoit, "Compulsory Education in Indonesia" (Paris: Unesco, 1954), p. 67.

gious teaching in accordance with the parents' wishes," and "the pupils of private schools which conform to the standards laid down by the law for public schools shall have the same rights as are accorded to the pupils of public schools."[269] Art. 18 guarantees "freedom of religion, of conscience and of thought" to all, while Art. 43 proclaims that "the State is founded on belief in Divine Omnipotence" and again assures freedom of religion. Further, "Aid in any form given by the authorities to ministers of religion and to religious denominations or organizations shall be on a basis of equality."[270] This indicates the official approval of the idea of a subsidization of religious schools.

When the Philippines came under the control of the U. S. at the beginning of the 20th century, the Spanish policy of church-state identification underwent a change. The Filipinos adopted the view of Gov. Gen. William Howard Taft that there was no constitutional violation of church-state separation if the teaching of Catholicism were given in the public school after school hours.[271] Subsequently, the Constitution approved optional religious instruction in the public schools, with permission for local priests to teach religion in the school buildings (Art. XIV, Sec. 5).[272] This provision, according to a prominent Filipino educator, is consistent with the "fundamental political theory of our democ-

---

[269] Quoted in *ibid.*, pp. 39, 40. In 1951, the Minister of Education and the Minister of Religious Affairs agreed jointly to start religious instruction in the fourth grade and to continue through the secondary school. See p. 79.

[270] Quoted in *ibid.*, p. 79.

[271] Antonio Isidro, "The Philippine Educational System" (Manila: Bookman, 1949), pp. 399-400.

[272] *Ibid.*, p. 400; Ammoun, *op.cit.*, p. 51.

racy—the principle of separation of Church and
State."[273]

AUSTRALIA AND NEW ZEALAND

The church-state question in Australian education, well over a century old, has been marked
by controversy and conflict between the Protestants and the Catholics. In New South Wales,
the Public Schools Act of 1866 made religious
education compulsory in the public schools.
Under the Public Instruction Act of 1880, the
term "secular instruction" signified the inclusion
of "general religious teaching as distinct from
dogmatical or polemical theology."[274] The latter
act discontinued, from 1883 onward, all public
aid to the denominational schools.

Sec. 116 of Australia's Commonwealth Constitution (1901) is reminiscent of the First Amendment of the American Constitution: "The Commonwealth shall not make any law for establishing any religion, or for imposing any religious
observance, or for prohibiting the free exercise
of any religion, and no religious test shall be
required as a qualification for any office or
public trust under the Commonwealth."[275] It
will be noted that the prohibition of "imposing
any religious observance" is rather explicit and

---

[273] Isidro, op.cit., p. 253.

[274] D. C. Griffiths, editor, "Documents on the Establishment of Education in New South Wales: 1789-1880" (Melbourne: Australian Council for Educational Research,
1957), p. 164. On the history of the problem in Australia,
see also Brother Ronald Fogarty, "Catholic Education in
Australia: 1806-1950," 2 vols. (Carlton, Victoria: Melbourne University Press, 1959), and J. S. Gregory, "Church
and State, and Education in Victoria, to 1872," in E. L.
French, editor, "Melbourne Studies in Education: 1958-
1959" (Parkville, Victoria: Melbourne University Press,
1960), pp. 3-88.

[275] Quoted in Leicester Webb, "Churches and the
Australian Community," in French, ibid., p. 110.

would make legally impossible some of the practices now prevalent in many public schools in the U. S. To an Australian authority, the Australian constitutional separation is not generally regarded by the people "as a vitally important element in their national tradition."[276] A Gallup Poll in 1955 indicated that over 70% of the Australians favored some kind of religious teaching in the public schools, while some 51% believed that the government should aid denominational schools.[277]

At present, the church schools are not subsidized, although they are under the inspection of the state education departments.[278] General religious instruction of a nonsectarian nature may be given by public school teachers in all states, except Victoria, where it may be given by clergymen and visiting teachers. Four of the six states—New South Wales, Queensland, Tasmania, and Western Australia—have organized "a double-barreled system of religious instruction, general and special, by teachers and visiting instructors."[279] The interpretation of separation in the Commonwealth Constitution, accordingly, is a rather broad one and does not seem to disturb the Australian citizenry. A visiting American scholar, however, noted a concern "just below the surface" about the church-state-school relationship in Australia and predicted the possibil-

---

[276] *Ibid.*, p. 113.

[277] *Ibid.*, p. 115.

[278] "Compulsory Education in Australia" (Paris: Unesco, 1951), pp. 93, 98.

[279] George S. Browne, "Australia," in Kandel, "Educational Yearbook . . . 1932," *op.cit.*, p. 12. *Cf.*, A. P. Elkin, "Australia," in Lauwerys and Hans, "The Year Book of Education: 1951," *op.cit.*, p. 405.

ity in the future of the eruption of a religious conflict to "plague" Australian education.[280]

The separation of church and state in education in New Zealand was brought about by the Education Act of 1877. Under this law, instruction in the primary schools was supposed to be "entirely of a secular character."[281] Actually, however, as in the U. S., there developed a wide hiatus between principle and practice, and the Nelson system made it possible after 1896 for religion to be taught in the public schools at the beginning of the day "through the device of not declaring the school open till religious instruction was over."[282] In the secondary schools, moreover, there are such practices as hymn singing, the Lord's Prayer, and Bible reading. The Act of 1877, it is worth noting, was passed after clauses for Bible reading, the recitation of the Lord's Prayer, and grants to religious schools had been stricken out.[283] Although private schools do not receive any direct grants from the state, they are given primary school textbooks, other school publications, and health services, and pupils may use free public transportation under certain circumstances.[284] To judge from a recent overwhelming resolution by the New Zealand Educational Institute, there will be no radical change in the custom of religious instruction and devotional exercises in the

---

[280] R. Freeman Butts, "Assumptions Underlying Australian Education" (New York: Bureau of Publications, Teachers College, Columbia University, 1955), pp. 23-26.

[281] Quoted in G. W. Parkin, "New Zealand," in Lauwerys and Hans. "The Year Book of Education: 1951," op.cit., p. 420.

[282] Ibid., p. 421.

[283] "Compulsory Education in New Zealand" (Paris: Unesco, 1954), p. 23.

[284] Ibid., pp. 42-43.

235

public schools during regular school hours.[285] There are parallels between the Australia-New Zealand solution and that of the U. S., and all three countries are democracies.

UNION OF SOUTH AFRICA

From the 17th century on, Protestantism has played a prominent role in South African education. "As far as the school was concerned the State was the Church and the Church was the State."[286] Various laws in all provinces made compulsory the Lord's Prayer, Bible reading, and religious instruction. Thus, Law No. 25 (1907) of the Transvaal Province required prayers, Bible reading, and Bible instruction at the beginning of the public school day, but it forbade sectarian dogmas.[287] A recent syllabus offers details of Bible and church history which pupils should master and points out that *Godsdiens-onderwys* ("religious instruction") should stress hymns, psalms, and sacred songs in all classes in the primary schools.[288] Private denominational schools have been under state supervision, but they also have received grants with no control over religious instruction.[289] Only the mission schools for the Negroes have been abolished (Bantu Education Act of 1954) on the ground that the work of such schools was too good: they had been preparing the natives for a status in

[285] *Times Educational Supplement,* May 22, 1959.
[286] E. G. Malherbe, "Union of South Africa," in Kandel, "Educational Yearbook . . . 1932," *op.cit.,* p. 415.
[287] *Ibid.,* p. 422; J. Chr. Coetzee, "Onderwys in Transvaal," in J. Chr. Coetzee, editor, "Onderwys in Suid-Afrika: 1652-1956" (Pretoria: Van Schaik, 1958), p. 280.
[288] Transvaalse Onderwysdepartement, "Voorgestelde leerplanne vir die laerskool" (Pretoria: Die Staatsdrukker, 1952), pp. 8-9. This publication is in Afrikaans and English.
[289] Malherbe, *op.cit.,* p. 428.

society which they never could attain in South Africa.[290]

LATIN AMERICA

An established church may be found in Argentina, Bolivia, Colombia, Costa Rica, the Dominican Republic, Haiti, Paraguay, Peru, and Venezuela. Church - state separation has been brought about in Brazil, Chile, Cuba, Ecuador, El Salvador, Guatemala, Honduras, Mexico, Nicaragua, Panama, and Uruguay.[291] However, with the possible exception of Mexico and contemporary Cuba, there does not seem to be any clear-cut line of demarcation between church and state in education in Latin America.

Separationism in Mexico goes back to the Constitution of 1857, under which the ideology of *laicismo* brought about the abolition of religious instruction and ceremonies in the public schools.[292] These provisions were so restated and strengthened in the Constitution of 1917[293] that even private religious schools were discouraged. In fact, after the Constitution was adopted, over 2,500 primary and secondary religious schools were forced to close.[294] It was evident, from the legislation of 1931 and other actions, that the Mexican government was intent upon the com-

---

[290] George W. Carpenter, "African Education and the Christian Missions," *Phi Delta Kappan*, January, 1960, p. 193, *Cf.*, A. L. Behr, "Onderwys aan Nie-blankes," in Coetzee, *op.cit.*, pp. 441-442.

[291] William W. Pierson and Federico G. Gil, "Governments of Latin America" (New York: McGraw-Hill, 1957), pp. 435-447.

[292] Manuel Barranco, "Mexico," in Kandel, "Educational Yearbook . . . 1932," *op.cit.*, pp. 362-363.

[293] Russell H. Fitzgibbon, editor, "The Constitutions of the Americas" (Chicago: University of Chicago Press, 1948), pp. 498-499.

[294] George F. Kneller, "Education of the Mexican Nation" (New York: Columbia University Press, 1951), p. 45.

plete secularization of all the schools within its borders.[295] In actual practice, however, the full realization of this aim proved impossible. It is true that, although 90-95% of the Mexican population is Catholic, only a small percentage of Catholic children attend the 2,002 religious schools. Obviously, then, the government must shut its eyes to the existence of the Catholic schools as it does to the schools maintained by the Protestants and Jews.[296] Recent straws in the wind point to a possible reconsideration by the Mexican government of the prohibition of religious education in the public schools and of the entire matter of church-state relations.[297]

In the Caribbean area and Central America, religion is taught in the public schools of the Dominican Republic, Haiti, Costa Rica, Honduras, Guatemala, Panama, and Colombia. Public subsidies are granted to private religious schools in the same countries (plus Venezuela).[298] On June 7, 1961, the Castro government of Cuba issued a law nationalizing education, thus providing legal support for the earlier closing down of Catholic schools.[299]

Brazil enforced a policy of separation since its establishment as a republic in 1889. The revolution of 1930, however, introduced religious in-

---

[295] Barranco., op.cit., pp. 365-367.

[296] Mathias C. Kiemen, "Catholic Schools in the Caribbean," in A. Curtis Wilgus, editor, "The Caribbean: Contemporary Education" (Gainesville: University of Florida Press, 1960), p. 115; Ammoun, op.cit., p. 54.

[297] New York Times, June 19, 1960; Dec. 8. 1960.

[298] Kiemen, op.cit., pp. 110, 113-114; John H. Furbay, "Education in Colombia," Bulletin 1946, No. 6, U. S. Office of Education (Washington: U. S. Government Printing Office, 1946), p. 18; George A. Dale, "Education in the Republic of Haiti," Bulletin 1959, No. 20, U. S. Office of Education (Washington: U. S. Government Printing Office, 1959), p. 64; Dubay, op.cit., p. 159.

[299] New York Times, June 8, 1961.

struction in public primary, secondary, and normal schools.[300] The current Constitution of 1946 states that all levels of government are forbidden "to establish or subsidize religious sects or to embarrass their exercise" and "to have relations of alliance or dependence with any sect or church without prejudice to reciprocal collaboration in furtherance of the collective interest" (Art. 31).[301] What this form of separationism amounts to is made clear by Art. 168, which states that "religious instruction shall be a part of the teaching schedule of official schools, and shall be administered in accordance with the religious confession of the pupil, manifested by him, if he is capable, or by his legal representative or person responsible for him."[302]

Although Art. 2 of the Constitution of 1853 provided for the support of the Catholic Church by Argentina, religious classes, according to the law of 1884, could be conducted in the public school buildings after regular hours only. During the Juan Peron regime, on Dec. 31, 1943, a governmental decree made religious instruction an integral part of the public school program.[303] In 1946, a law gave the church control of education,[304] while in 1949 the new Constitution reiterated the policy that Catholicism was the

---

[300] Webster E. Browning, "Latin America," in Kandel, "Educational Yearbook . . . 1932," op.cit., pp. 347-350; "Educação, Ação social e política," Revista Brasileira de Estudos Pedagógicos, October-December, 1958, pp 87-88.

[301] Fitzgibbon, op.cit., p. 67.

[302] Ibid., p. 98.

[303] John J. Kennedy, "Dichotomies in the Church." Annals of the American Academy of Political and Social Science, Vol. 334, March, 1961, p. 60; and John J. Kennedy, "Catholicism, Nationalism, and Democracy in Argentina" (Notre Dame: University of Notre Dame Press, 1958), pp. 186-201.

[304] Alfred B. Thomas, "Latin America: A History" (New York: Macmillan, 1956), p. 309.

official religion of Argentina.[305] After the death
of Eva Peron (1952), the textbooks placed more
emphasis on her as the "Jefa Espiritual de la
Nación" than upon Jesus, Mary, and the
saints.[306] This must have been a shadow cast by
the happenings of the future, for in 1955 Peron
dismissed 100 priests from their position as
teachers in the public schools, discontinued religion as a subject, got the congress to separate
the Catholic Church from the state, and decreed
that all religious institutions would lose their
exemption from taxation.[307] There was little
doubt that Peron, like many another dictator,
tried to make use of the church for the furtherance of his own ideology (*peronismo* and *justi-
cialismo*) and power. As in the case of other
dictators, his attempt boomeranged.

According to the Chilean Constitution of 1925,
there is a full separation of church and state,
but the law of 1929 provided for Catholic instruction in the public primary schools.[308] Another accommodation to the religious interests
is the grant of some public funds to private religious schools.[309]

The government of Peru recognized in its
Constitution of 1946 the Apostolic Roman Catholic Religion as the state church, with all relations between the two realms to be based on a
concordat.[310] Accordingly, there is Catholic re-

---

[305] Austin F. Macdonald, "Latin American Politics and
Government," second edition (New York: Crowell, 1954),
p. 95.

[306] *E.g.*, the first-grade reader, "Evita," by Graciela
Albornoz de Videla (Buenos Aires: Lassere, n.d.).

[307] John F. Bannon and Peter M. Dunne, "Latin
America: An Historical Survey," revised edition (Milwaukee: Bruce, 1958), p. 379.

[308] Browning, *op.cit.*, pp. 344-346.

[309] Dubay, *op.cit.*, p. 118.

[310] Fitzgibbon, *op.cit.*, p. 693.

ligious instruction in the public primary, secondary, and normal schools, and subsidies are granted to private schools.[311] Apparently, the differences between a separationist country (Chile) and a church-established country (Peru) in the matter of religion in education are those of degree only.

CANADA

The history of the relations of church and state in Canadian education is long and complicated, and it has been described in detail in a number of documented monographs and studies.[312] Only a few salient facts need be mentioned here.

The basis of the present Canadian solution to the problem has its legal roots in the British North American Act of 1867, Canada's constitution. According to Art. 93, education is a provincial rather than a national function and no law "shall prejudicially affect any right or privilege with respect to denominational schools" already in force. The Act also extended the system of separate schools in Ontario to Quebec and provided the right to appeal for redress to the

[311] Cameron D. Ebaugh, "Education in Peru," Bulletin 1946, No. 3, U. S. Office of Education, (Washington: U. S. Office of Education, 1946), pp. 15, 23-24, 26, 29; "Programas para la Educación Secundaria: Ciclo Basico" (Lima: Ministerio de Educación Pública, 1960), pp. 8-9.

[312] E.g., C. B. Sissons, "Church and State, in Canadian Education: An Historical Study" (Toronto: Ryerson Press, 1959); John S. Moir, "Church and State in Canada West, 1841-1867" (Toronto: University of Toronto Press, 1959); George M. Weir, "The Separate School Question in Canada" (Toronto: Ryerson Press, 1934); J. G. Hodgins, "The Legislation and History of Separate Schools in Upper Canada" (Toronto: Briggs, 1897); "Report of the Royal Commission on Education in Ontario: 1950" (Toronto: Baptist Johnston, 1950), pp. 458-539, 803-894; and Charles E. Phillips, "The Development of Education in Canada" (Toronto: Gage, 1957), pp. 301-334.

Governor General and the national Parliament.[313] Ontario's Separate School Act of 1863, "a compromise which, though satisfying neither party [Catholics and Protestants], has been virtually sanctified by time."[314] It also appears that the dual system of Catholic and Protestant public schools has been satisfactory, by and large.[315] In 1905, when Alberta and Saskatchewan joined the older provinces in the Confederation, they, too, instituted the practice of separate denominational schools side by side with the public schools. The separate schools for minority faiths (*e.g.*, Protestant in Quebec and Catholic in Ontario) can be found in only four of the 10 provinces, but these four constitute about 75% of the total population of the entire country.[316]

Manitoba abolished its state-supported separate schools by the law of 1890. The appeals by the Catholics to national authority, in line with the British North America Act, resulted in some temporary compromise measures but in no change from the law which had set up a free, nonsectarian public school system.[317]

The system of public education in Newfoundland is unique even for Canada. In the newest province, with few exceptions, there are four types of sectarian schools—Roman Catholic, Church of England, United Church of Canada, and Salvation Army—under the direction of four Superintendents of Education. The costs of operating the schools are shared by the provincial

---

[313] Fitzgibbon, *op.cit.*, pp. 123-124.

[314] Moir, *op.cit.*, p. 180.

[315] *Cf.*, Phillips, *op.cit.*, p. 317; K. M. Glazier, "Canada: Religion and Morals," in Lauwerys and Hans, "The Year Book of Education: 1951," *op.cit.*, p. 377; Charles Bilodeau, "Canada: Quebec," in *ibid.*, p. 387.

[316] Glazier, *op.cit.*, pp. 376-377.

[317] Sissons, *op.cit.*, p. 181; Phillips, *op.cit.*, p. 319.

and local authorities.[318] Interestingly, "Under a system largely controlled by the religious bodies and with equal rights to all denominations there has been very little friction and next to no litigation."[319] Coming from a specialist who expresses frequently all through a study his disapproval of "segregation" of a denominational nature in education, it is obvious that this statement provides a reply to those who raise the bogey of divisiveness whenever public subsidies to private schools are discussed.

No province in Canada can be said to practice church-state separation in education. British Columbia and Manitoba do not allow public grants to denominational schools, but the latter makes provision for religious instruction at the end of the day by clergymen or qualified public school teachers. In the former province, the public schools are to be conducted, according to the Public Schools Act, "on strictly secular and nonsectarian principles," with "the highest morality" taught on a non-religious basis, but "the Lord's Prayer may be used in opening or closing school."[320] Moreover, permission is granted for "elective extra-mural high school courses in religion."[321] Other significant deviations from separationism in British Columbia are the long-term sites at nominal rentals for the construction of Protestant and Catholic theological colleges. "Apart from a virtually free grant of land they

[318] John F. Cramer and George S. Browne, "Contemporary Education: A Comparative Study of National Systems" (New York: Harcourt, Brace, 1956), p. 149; Sissons, *op.cit.*, pp. 392-393.

[319] Sissons, *op.cit.*, p. 396.

[320] Quoted in W. E. MacPherson, "Canada: General Statement," in Kandel, "Educational Yearbook . . . 1932," *op.cit.*, p. 62-63.

[321] Glazier, *op.cit.*, p. 377.

receive no financial support from the Province, although their divinity students now benefit from the federal grant."[322]

The provincial solutions may have been fine, as far as the major denominations were concerned, but they presented serious problems to the Jewish minority. In Ontario, the Jewish community complained that the conscience clause, which exempted dissenters from the religious instruction introduced into the public schools in 1944, was not a guarantee against religious injustice.[323] Instead of requesting separate schools, the Jewish leadership preferred to raise the issue of divisiveness, fragmentation, and avoiding the weakening of "the unifying bond of Canadianism."[324] Since this seemed to be a matter of relatively minor concern to the non-Jewish majority, it was apparent that articulate Canadian Jewry was "papstlicher als der Pabst." In dismissing the proposal that rabbis paid by the Jewish community teach religion to Jewish children in public schools where they predominate, one Jewish rabbinical leader stated that "no concession would mitigate the violence done to a basic democratic principle—the separation of Church and State."[325] Notwithstanding the evidence which he adduced of the permeation of the Ontario public schools with Christianity, the rabbi rejected the idea of a separate Jewish school or any arrangement for the teaching of Judaism in the public schools, as long as the

[322] Sissons, op.cit., p. 386.
[323] Abraham L. Feinberg, "Religious Instruction in the Public Schools of Ontario" (Toronto: Canadian Jewish Congress, 1945), p. 11.
[324] Ibid., p. 13.
[325] Abraham L. Feinberg, "Dilemma of Religion in the School," Congress Weekly, Feb. 7, 1949, p. 11.

imaginary principle of separation would be upheld.

The division of the public schools in the Province of Quebec into Catholic and Protestant also involved difficulties for Jews. In this instance, the Jewish pupils were classified as "Protestant" and the tax funds of the Jewish citizens went for the support of the Protestant schools. The prices paid by the Jews for their desire not to fragmentize public education further were dissatisfaction, protest, and litigation.[326] Incidentally, the Jewish religious day schools receive no tax funds, since they are regarded as private institutions. But recent events suggest that some part of the Canadian Jewish community at least is rethinking the question of separate, publicly supported Jewish schools.[327]

CONCLUSION

This review of the background and the current status of the various aspects of the church-state-school relationship has covered countries on six continents. The issue is a complicated one and must be studied from the standpoint of historical, religious, political, social, and economic traditions and conditions. An over-all, consistent pattern, other than the inevitability of conflict over the solutions, is very hard to discern.

Some general principles may be formulated, however. First, there have been changes in policy and practice in most countries over a period of years. Any solution to the church-state problem in education seems to be a function of time and circumstance. Compromise and conciliation seem

---

[326] Phillips, *op.cit.*, p. 318; Sissons, *op.cit.*, pp. 147-153; Pfeffer, *op.cit.*, pp. 43-45.
[327] Jewish Telegraphic Agency, Releases, Montreal, Feb. 20, 1961, and June 16, 1961.

to be characteristic of the development of the role of religion in education almost everywhere.

Without going into population statistics and counting countries, the general impression is that government schools all over the world include some form of religious instruction and observance in their programs. In conjunction with this, there usually is a conscience clause of more or less effectiveness for minority religious and secularist groups. To the extent that the conscience clause is effective, the principle of religious freedom tends to thrive. Few countries, such as the U. S. S. R. and France, actually forbid any and all forms of religious education in the public schools. Some, such as the U. S., declare themselves in favor of church-state separation but in actuality are nowhere near the realization of such a policy. There is no objective way of correlating the idea of separation with democracy.

Public support for private religious schools is more common than people have been led to think. Of course, this involves governmental supervision and control, but only of the secular studies as a rule. It is well to remember, however, that practically all countries control their private shcools regardless of whether they grant them public subsidies.

Scholars, students, public officials, clergymen, and citizens must familiarize themselves to a greater and more exact degree than heretofore with the facts and underlying ideas concerning church, state, and school in other countries. This is one method of evaluating in an experimental way the viewpoints and arguments advanced in any given area. It is not necessary to consider copying the solution of another nation; rather, it is essential to assess and appraise the situation in one's country in the light of the experiences abroad.

It is the belief of the writer that a fuller study of the church-state issue in various foreign cultures will disclose, as his own survey has done to him, that there is no absolute solution which is satisfactory for all times, places, and peoples. Decision-makers who are well informed, patient, tolerant, and flexible will arrive at a solution which will be of maximum benefit to majorities and minorities alike. In such societies, neither majorities nor minorities will be loath to impose their will and way of thought on the other.

Under such circumstances, religion might be taught in the public schools in countries where there is no policy of complete separation of church and state. Children of minority groups choosing to attend public school will receive full protection against indoctrination and discrimination, while others will be accommodated in private religious schools receiving public subsidies for performing a public service.

If church and state are fully separated, then there will be no religion in the public schools and no public aid to religious schools. However, as already shown, a complete and consistent church-state separation never has existed even in countries, such as the U. S. S. R., which have explicit constitutional declarations to that effect.

Religion has had a long history in education all over the world. Those who want it taught should receive encouragement, and those who wish to dispense with it should suffer no discrimination.

Appendix

Chronological Outline of Church-State Relations in American Education

WILLIAM W. BRICKMAN

THE FOLLOWING compilation of historical events is intended to furnish the framework for analyses of the historical and controversial aspects of church-state problems in education in the U.S., as well as a springboard for further research. Interesting hypotheses may be formed as a result of a close perusual of the facts in their own historical context and in the light of earlier and later developments. This reasonably representative, but hardly complete, listing is derived from primary sources (laws, court decisions, original writings); such documentary collections as those by Ellwood P. Cubberley, Edgar W. Knight, Knight and Clifton L. Hall, and Mark De Wolfe Howe ("Cases on Church and State in the United States," 1952); monographs by Samuel W. Brown, R. Freeman Butts, Richard J. Gabel, Alvin W. Johnson and Frank H. Yost, and others; detailed general works, such as Anson Phelps Stokes' "Church and State in the United States," 3 vols. (1950) and Leo Pfeffer's "Church, State, and Freedom" (1953); and writings on church and religious history, minority problems, and educational history.

In spite of the rich literature, or perhaps because of it (keeping in mind the multiplicity of biased publications), there is need for a closely documented, fully described, and objectively analyzed history of church-state-school relations in the U.S. There is still room for a large number of monographs and short studies.

SEVENTEENTH CENTURY

1606—The "Articles, Instructions and Orders" issued by King James I to the Virginia Company required that there should be provisions in all colonies and plantations that "the true word, and service of God and Christian faith be preached, planted, and used. . . ."

1619—Meeting of the first colonial legislative body in a church at Jamestown, Va.

1631—General Assembly of Virginia passed law requiring compulsory teaching of religion by ministers: ". . . upon every Sunday the mynister shall halfe an hower or more before evenenge prayer examine, catechise, and instruct the youth and ignorant persons of his parrish, in the ten commandments, the articles of the beliefe and in the Lord's prayer; and shall diligentlie heere, instruct and teach them the catechisme, sett forth in the booke of common prayer."

1642—Massachusetts law gave towns "power to take account from time to time of all parents and masters, and of their children, concerning their calling and implyment of their children, especially of their ability to read and understand the principles of religion and the capitall lawes of this country, and to impose fines upon such as shall refuse to render such accounts to them when they shall be required. . . ."

1643—Virginia law ordered the guardians and overseers of orphans "to educate and instruct them according to their best endeavors in Christian rudiments of learning and to provide for their necessaries according to the competents of their estate."

1647—Law passed by General Court of Massachusetts requiring towns to establish elementary and grammar schools to defeat the "one cheife piect of yt ould deluder, Satan, to keep men from the knowledge of ye Scriptures. . . ."

1647—Rhode Island Charter, granted in England to Roger Williams for the separation of church and state.

252

1649—Toleration Act in Maryland guaranteed religious liberty to Trinitarian Christians but not to non-Christians.

1665—Duke of York's Law in New York Colony specified that "the Constables and Overseers are strictly required frequently to Admonish the Inhabitants of Instructing their Children and Servants in Matters of Religion and the Lawes of the Country. . . ."

1700—Law of Province of New York ordered "perpetual imprisonment" for Catholic priests performing religious rites or teaching Catholic doctrine.

EIGHTEENTH CENTURY

Eighteenth Century until 1880—Parochial schools of the Reformed Church. By 1800, some 188 Reformed Churches had 144 parochial schools.

1704—Law in Maryland prohibited Catholic priests from baptizing children.

1716—Law in Maryland ordered severe punishment for public officials who attended Catholic mass.

1731—Opening of the first Jewish parochial school in America, Yeshibat Minhat Areb, by Congregation Shearith Israel in New York City.

1750—All but one of the Lutheran congregations in Pennsylvania had parochial schools. In 1820, there were 206 parochial schools in 84 congregations.

1754—Royal charter granted to King's College (Columbia University) forbade the college authorities "to exclude any person of any religious denomination whatever from equal liberty and advantage of education, or from any of the degrees, liberties, privileges, benefits, or immunities . . . on account of his particular tenets in matters of religion."

1764—The General Assembly of Rhode Island granted a charter to the College of Rhode Island (Brown University), founded by Baptists, providing that "youth of all religious denominations shall and may be freely admitted to the equal advantages, emoluments, and honor of the college or university, and shall receive a like, fair, generous, and equal treatment during their residence therein. . . ."

1768-74—"Period of the Great Persecution" of Baptists in Virginia. Baptists were whipped, jailed, and fined.

1770—The corporation of the College of Rhode Island declared that "the children of Jews may be admitted into this institution, and entirely enjoy the freedom of their own religion, without any constraint or imposition whatever."

c. 1776—Public Catholic worship only in Pennsylvania.

According to the Governor, such worship was illegal even in Pennsylvania.

c. 1776—Three years' prison term for the denial of the Trinity in Virginia. The state could deprive a Unitarian or a freethinker of the custody of his children.

1780—Massachusetts Constitution declared that the legislature could "authorize and require the several towns, parishes, precincts, and other bodies politic, or religious societies, to make suitable provision, at their own expense, for the institution of the public worship of God, and for the support and maintenance of public protestant teachers of piety, religion and morality, in all cases where such provision shall not be made voluntarily."

1782—First Catholic parochial school ("Mother School") in the U.S. opened by St. Mary's Church, Philadelphia.

1785—James Madison's successful pamphlet, "Memorial and Remonstrance against Religious Assessments," was instrumental in preventing the passing of "A Bill Establishing a Provision for Teachers of the Christian Religion" by the Virginia Assembly.

1786—The Virginia Assembly passed Thomas Jefferson's "Act for Establishing Religious Freedom" (introduced originally in 1779), thus disestablishing the Episcopal Church.

1787 (July 13)—Northwest Ordinance passed by Congress of the Confederation: ". . . religion, morality, and knowledge being necessary to good government and the happiness of mankind, schools and the means of education shall forever be encouraged."

1787 (July 23)—Congress authorized sale of Federal land to the Ohio Company, with the stipulation that "the lot No. 29, in each township, or fractional part of a township, . . . be given perpetually for the purposes of religion."

1789—Massachusetts law required participation of clergy in public school supervision and teacher certification and also required teachers on all levels "to impress on the minds of children and youth . . . the principles of piety, justice, and a sacred regard to truth. . . ." However, "no settled minister shall be deemed, held, or accepted to be a School-Master, within the meaning of this Act."

1790—Establishment of the Catholic hierarchy in the U.S., with John Carroll as the first bishop.

1790—In his letter to the Hebrew Congregation of Newport, R. I., President George Washington stated that the U.S. government "gives to bigotry no sanction, to persecution no assistance."

1791—First Amendment to the U.S. Constitution: "Congress shall make no law respecting an establishment of religion, or prohibiting the free exercise thereof."

1794—Gov. Samuel Adams, in his message (Jan. 16) to the Massachusetts legislature, urged that "such modes of education as tend to inculcate in the minds of youth the feelings and habits of piety, religion and morality" be established.

1795—Common School Act of New York State provided for funds to denominational charity schools (Protestant, Catholic, Jewish). In 1796, the grants were given for elementary education in religious academies.

1796—"Treaty of Peace and Friendship" with Tripoli stated that "the government of the United States of America is not, in any sense, founded on the Christian religion. . . ."

NINETEENTH CENTURY

1801—New York State legislature divided the school fund of New York City among its various religious denominations.

1802 (Jan 1)—Letter from President Thomas Jefferson to Danbury Baptist Association in Connecticut interpreted the First Amendment as "building a wall of separation between church and state."

1804—Ohio University (then Presbyterian) received grants from the state.

1805—Renewal of treaty with Tripoli omits statement that the U.S. government is not founded on the Christian religion.

1809—Miami University (then Presbyterian) received grants from the state.

1811—New York State law granted money to school of the Jewish Congregation Shearith Israel in New York City.

1817-21—Territorial government of Michigan established the "Catholepistemiad, or University of Michigania," with the Rev. John Monteith (Presbyterian) as president and the Rev. Gabriel Richard (Catholic) as vice-president. For a brief period, in 1821, Fr. Richard was acting president.

1827 (March 10)—Massachusetts law made it a duty for "all . . . instructors of youth . . . to impress on the minds of children, and youth . . . the principles of piety, justice, and sacred regard to truth. . . ."; and ordered that the town school committees "shall never direct any school books to be purchased or used, in any of the schools under their superintendence, which are calculated to favor any particular religious sect or tenet" (Laws of Massachusetts, 1826, chap. 143, sect. 7). In 1835, this law was revised, with the last clause modified to: "which are calculated to favor the tenets of any particular sect of Christians."

1829—The Catholic Church's First Provincial Council of Baltimore adopted the policy of parochial schools, especially because of the rising immigration from Ireland. The bishops adopted a canon stating that "we judge it absolutely necessary that schools should be established, in which the young may be taught the principles of faith and morality, while being instructed in letters."

1832—Land grants by U.S. Congress to Columbian College (today George Washington University), a Baptist institution.

1833—Disestablishment of the Congregational Church in Massachusetts.

1833—U.S. Congress passed law to give land grants to Georgetown College (today University), a Catholic institution.

1834—Samuel F. B. Morse, in a series of articles in the *New York Journal of Commerce*, urged the closing of the Catholic schools, which he described as part of a "plot" to take over the United States.

1834 (Aug. 11)—Burning by anti-Catholic mob of Ursuline convent school, Charlestown, Mass.

1835-44—Lowell, Mass., Plan by which Catholic schools received public funds, but religion was taught after school hours.

1838—Defeat of Benton Bill in the Senate to grant Federal land to the French University of St. Louis (today St. Louis University), a Catholic institution.

1839—In a lecture, "The Necessity of Education in a Republican Government," delivered to the Common School Convention, Horace Mann, secretary of the Board of Education in Massachusetts, defined education as "such a culture of our moral affections and religious susceptibilities, as in the course of Nature and Providence, shall lead to a subjection or conformity of all our appetites, propensities and sentiments to the will of Heaven."

1839—Resolution by American Bible Society to work in behalf of Bible reading in every public school classroom all over the country. Passed again in 1840.

1839—In his first report as secretary of the Board of Commissioners of the Common Schools of Connecticut, Henry Barnard stated, "I cannot but look upon the severance of the school interest from all other municipal and religious interests of society as one of manifest disadvantage. It has led, in part, to widespread apathy which prevails in regard to the condition and prospects of the common schools."

1840—Fourth Provincial Council (Catholic) in Baltimore ordered priests to see to it that Catholic children do not use the Protestant Bible or sing Protestant hymns in the public schools.

1840—Legislative message by Gov. William H. Seward of New York urged the establishment of public schools in which immigrant children "may be instructed by teachers speaking the same language with themselves and professing the same faith."

1841—Native American Party founded "to prevent the union of Church and State" and to "keep the Bible in the schools."

1842—New York State law stated that in New York City and County "no school . . . in which any religious sectarian doctrine or tenets shall be taught, inculcated, or practised, shall receive any portion of the school moneys to be distributed by this act, as hereafter provided."

1844—In *Vidal v. Girard's Executors* (2 How. 127), the U.S. Supreme Court, in the opinion of Justice Joseph Story, affirmed that Christianity was "part of the common law of the state," thus upholding Daniel Webster's argument that "general, tolerant Christianity, Christianity independent of sects and parties . . . is the law of the land."

1846-70—Presbyterians opened 264 parochial schools in 29 states.

1848—In his Twelfth Annual Report (the final one) as secretary of the Massachusetts Board of Education, Horace Mann said that "the Bible is the acknowledged expositor of Christianity. . . . This Bible is in our Common Schools, by common consent. Twelve years ago, it was not in all the schools" (p. 21).

1852—First Plenary Council (Catholic) of Baltimore urged bishops to open a school in every parish and that teachers be paid from parish funds.

1852—Massachusetts legislature's compulsory attendance law, the first in the nation, together with its compulsory Bible reading law (1855), constituted compulsory religion in the public schools.

1854—Mob action and violence against the Rev. John Bapst, S.J., and Catholic school property in Ellsworth, Me., over Catholic opposition to the reading of the Protestant version of the Bible in the public school.

1854—In *Donahoe v. Richards* (38 Maine 376), the Maine

Supreme Court ruled that the compulsory reading of the King James Bible did not infringe upon the religious freedom of a Catholic child, since "reading the Bible is no more an interference with religious belief, than would reading the mythology of Greece or Rome be regarded as interfering with religious belief or an affirmance of the pagan creeds."

1855—The national platform of the Know Nothing Party called for education "in schools provided by the state . . . and free from any influence or direction of a denominational or partisan character." However, since Christianity was "considered an element of our political system, and the Holy Bible is at once the source of Christianity and the depository and fountain of all civil and religious freedom, we oppose every attempt to exclude it from the schools thus established in the States."

1855—Massachusetts law required that the Bible "in the common English version" be read daily in the public schools.

1855—Constitutional amendment in Massachusetts stated that public funds "shall never be appropriated to any religious sect for the maintenance, exclusively, of its own schools."

1857—New York State grants of $25,000 to University of Rochester (Baptist) and St. Lawrence University (Universalist). This practice went back to the previous century and, during 1795-1815, Union College (Presbyterian) received over $350,00 from New York State.

1859—In *Commonwealth v. Cooke* (Am. L. Reg. 417), the Massachusetts Supreme Court decided that compulsory Bible reading in public schools, "without sectarian explanations, is no interference with religious liberty." It considered a Catholic child's petition to be exempt from compulsory Bible reading as a step in bridging "that heretofore impassable gulf which lies between Church and State. . . ."

1864-65, 1873—Statute of University of South Carolina (a state institution) provided for "a school of mental and moral philosophy, sacred literature and evidences of Christianity."

1865-71—Freedmen's Bureau spent more than $5,000,000 for Negro schools, most of which were operated by religious societies.

1866—Second Plenary Council (Catholic) in Baltimore ordered that a school be opened in every parish and that catechism classes should be organized in every church for Catholic children attending public schools.

1870—Congressional appropriation of $10,000 to Wilber-
force University, a Methodist institution.

1871—In *Watson v. Jones* (80 U.S. 679), the U.S. Supreme
Court stated that "in this country the full and free
right to entertain any religious belief, to practice any
religious doctrine which does not violate the laws of
morality and property, and which does not infringe
personal rights, is conceded to all. The law knows
no heresy, and is committed to the support of no
dogma, the establishment of no sect."

1872—*Board of Education v. Minor et al.* (23 Ohio St.
211). The Supreme Court of Ohio, in reversing the
judgment of the Superior Court, upheld resolutions
by the Cincinnati board of education prohibiting
Bible reading and religious instruction in the public schools.

1873—A South Carolina statute required the University
of South Carolina to open a "school of mental and
moral philosophy, sacred literature, and evidences
of Christianity."

1873-99—Poughkeepsie, N. Y., Plan by which the public
school board rented parochial school buildings and
paid from public funds the Catholic nuns who were
the teachers.

1875 (Sept. 29)—President U.S. Grant, in his address to
the Army of the Tennessee, Des Moines, Iowa, said:
"The centennial year of our national existence, I
believe, is a good time to begin the work of strengthening the foundations of the structure commenced
by our patriotic forefathers one hundred years ago
at Lexington. Let us all labor to add all needful
guarantees for the security of free thought, free
speech, a free press, pure morals, unfettered religious
sentiment and of equal rights and privileges to all
men, irrespective of nationality, color, or religion.
Encourage free schools and resolve that not one
dollar appropriated for their support shall be appropriated to the support of any sectarian schools.
Resolve that neither the state nor the nation, nor
both combined, shall support institutions of learning other than those sufficient to afford every child
growing up in the land the opportunity of a good
common school education, unmixed with sectarian,
pagan or atheistical dogmas. Leave the matter of
religion to the family altar, the church, and the
private school, supported entirely by private contributions. Keep the church and state forever separate. With these safeguards, I believe the battles,
which created the army of the Tennessee, will not
have been fought in vain."

1875 (Dec. 7)—President U.S. Grant's annual message to Congress recommended a constitutional amendment prohibiting the teaching in public schools "of religious, atheistic, or pagan tenets" and "the granting of any school funds or school taxes, or any part thereof, either by legislative, municipal, or other authority, for the benefit or in aid, directly or indirectly, of any religious sect or denomination. . . ."

1875 (Dec. 14)—Rep. James G. Blaine's Joint Resolution to Congress for a constitutional amendment: ". . . no money raised by taxation in any State for the support of public schools, or derived from any public funds therefor, nor any public lands devoted thereto, shall ever be under the control of any religious sect, or denomination; nor shall any money so raised or lands so devoted be divided between religious sects or denominations." The Blaine Amendment was passed overwhelmingly by the House of Representatives on Aug. 4, 1876.

1876 (Aug. 14)—The Senate, with less than the necessary majority of two-thirds, defeated the following version of the James G. Blaine Amendment: "No State shall make any law respecting an establishment of religion, or prohibiting the free exercises thereof; and no religious test shall ever be required as a qualification to any office or public trust under any State. No public property, and no public revenue of, nor any loan of credit by or under the authority of, the United States, or any State, Territory, District, or municipal corporation, shall be appropriated to, or made or used for, the support of any school, educational or other institution, under the control of any religious or anti-religious sect, organization, or denomination, or wherein the particular creed or tenets of any religious or anti-religious sect, organization, or denomination shall be taught; and no such particular creed or tenets shall be read or taught in any school or institution supported in whole or in part by such revenue or letter of credit; and no such appropriation, or loan of credit shall be made to any religious or anti-religious sect, organization, or denomination, or to promote its interests or tenets. This article shall not be construed to prohibit the reading of the Bible in any school or institution; and it shall not have the effect to impair rights of property already vested. Congress shall have power, by appropriate legislation, to provide for the prevention and punishment of violations of this article."

1878—In *Reynolds v. U.S.* (98 U.S. 145), the U.S. Supreme Court upheld a Congressional law prohibiting polygamy, in spite of the fact that the Mormon religion advocated the practice.

1882-90—Defeat of Sen. Henry W. Blair's bills for Federal aid to public schools only.

1884—Third Plenary Council of the Roman Catholic Church in Baltimore ordered that a parochial school be established in every parish and that "all Catholic parents are bound to send their children to the parochial schools."

1887—Founding of American Protective Association, Clinton, Iowa, to fight Catholic "subversion" of the public school system.

1888—"Religious Educational Amendment," by Sen. Blair, provided for "a system of free public schools" in every state with instruction "in the common branches of knowledge, and in virtue, morality, and the principles of the Christian religion."

1888—U.S. government provided $29,500 for Presbyterian, Episcopalian, Catholic, and other mission schools in Alaska.

1889—Founding of National League for the Protection of American Institutions in New York City to protect public education against Catholic attempts to obtain public aid for their schools and particularly against Federal aid to Catholic mission schools for Indians.

1890—In *State ex rel. Weiss et al. v. District School Board of Edgerton* (76 Wis. 177), the Wisconsin Supreme Court ruled that compulsory Bible reading, "although unaccompanied by any comment on the part of the teacher, is 'instruction'" in the public school, and therefore contrary to the state constitution. Children of poor parents who are practically obliged to attend the public schools would, if such reading were permitted, be compelled to attend a place of worship, also unconstitutionally. "The fact that children . . . are at liberty to withdraw during the reading of the Bible does not remove the ground of the complaint." The Weiss family was Roman Catholic.

1891—The Rev. Thomas Bouquillon, professor of moral theology, Catholic University of America, argued in "Education: To Whom Does It Belong?" that "education belongs to men taken individually and collectively in legitimate association, to the family, to the state, to the Church, to all four together, and not to any one of these four factors separately."

1891-93—Faribault and Stillwater, Minn., Plan by which the Catholic schools, with nuns as teachers, were virtually under the control of the public school boards.

1892—In *Church of the Holy Trinity v. United States* (143 U.S. 457), the U.S. Supreme Court declared that "this is a Christian nation" (Justice David J. Brewer).

1892—Lutherans and Catholics in Wisconsin joined in repealing the Bennett Law of 1889 which ordered all private schools to follow the public school program or close up. The Lutherans had 380 parochial schools at the time.

1892—U.S. government gave $29,980 to mission schools in Alaska.

1896-97—Congress passed appropriation acts for District of Columbia prohibiting any funds for "any institution or society which is under sectarian or ecclesiastical control. . . ."

1899—Congress granted 25,000 acres to Tuskegee Normal and Industrial Institute, despite the fact that this institute offered theological training in its Phelps Hall Bible Training School and maintained a daily chapel service.

1899—In *Bradford v. Roberts* (175 U.S. 291), the U.S. Supreme Court approved a Congressional act which had provided Federal funds to a secular, nonsectarian hospital operated under the auspices of the Catholic Sisters of Charity.

TWENTIETH CENTURY

1903—Founding of the Religious Education Association (interreligious).

1908—In *Reuben Quick Bear v. Leupp* (210 U.S. 50), the U.S. Supreme Court declared that Federal money can be given to Indians for the education of their children in schools operated by the Bureau of Catholic Indian Missions, "because the Government is necessarily undenominational, as it cannot make any law respecting an establishment of religion or prohibiting the free exercise thereof."

1909—Michigan Constitution, Art. XI, Sect. 1: "Religion, morality, and knowledge being necessary to good government and the happiness of mankind, schools and the means of education shall forever be encouraged."

1909—McPherson College (Lutheran Baptist), McPherson, Kan., received $62,000 in public funds.

1909—St. Olaf College (Lutheran), Northfield, Minn., received $13,000 from the town government.

1914—Beginning of the Gary, Ind., Plan for Released Time in public school buildings on school time.

1917—Amendment to Massachusetts Constitution stipulated that "no grant, appropriation or use of public money or property or loan of public credit shall be made . . . for the purpose of founding, maintaining or aiding any school or institution of learning, whether under public control or otherwise, wherein any denominational doctrine is inculcated. . . ." This amendment prohibited public payments for sectarian instruction on a constitutional rather than on a mere statutory basis. Christian teaching, accordingly, was not illegal if it was not denominational. Bible reading remained compulsory while prayers and the fundamentals could be included in public schools, as desired by the local school boards.

1917—In the Smith-Hughes Act, Congress insisted that no money should be applied "directly or indirectly" to "any religious or privately owned or conducted school or college."

1920—Under the National Defense Act, a training school for chaplains was established.

1921—*Wilkerson v. City of Rome* (152 Ga. 763). The Georgia Supreme Court decided that a local law requiring the reading of the King James Bible and daily prayer did not conflict with the religious freedom of Catholic and Jewish pupils.

1922—*Smith v. Donahue* (202 App. Div. [N. Y.] 656). The Appellate Division of the New York State Supreme Court ruled that free textbooks to parochial pupils was unconstitutional, since there was no distinction between direct and indirect grants.

1923—In *Meyer v. Nebraska* (262 U.S. 390), the U.S. Supreme Court held that, under the religious liberty guaranteed by the Fourteenth Amendment, the state could not forbid or limit any teaching in the German language to pupils in the elementary (eight-grade) Zion Parochial School conducted by the Lutheran Church (Mr. Justice James C. McReynolds.) This decision applied also to *Bartels v. Iowa, Bohning v. Ohio* (262 U.S. 404).

1923, 1926—Maine legislature defeated proposed constitutional amendments to prohibit public funds to private and religious schools. The state continued aid to Baptist, Catholic, Methodist, Quaker, and other denominational schools until 1937.

1925—In *Pierce et al. v. Society of Sisters* (268 U.S. 510), the U.S. Supreme Court unanimously decided that a state law in Oregon compelling parents who had sent their children to Catholic and other private schools to send them only to public schools was unconstitutional. According to Mr. Justice McReynolds, who echoed the brief of Louis Marshall, "the child

263

is not the mere creature of the State; those who nurture him and direct his destiny have the right, coupled with a high duty, to recognize and prepare him for additional obligations." This decision provides the the the constitutional basis for parochial and private schools.

1925—Tennessee Anti-Evolution Act stated that "it shall be unlawful for any teacher in any of the universities, normals and all other public schools of the state which are supported in whole or in part by the public school funds of the state, to teach any theory that denies the story of the Divine creation of man as taught in the Bible, and to teach instead that man has descended from a lower order of animals."

1925-37—School of Religion, University of Michigan.

1927—Founding of the School of Religion, State University of Iowa.

1927—In *Farrington v. Tokushige* (273 U.S. 284), the U.S. Supreme Court upheld an injunction preventing the Territory of Hawaii from applying a law which closely controlled private (church-related) foreign language schools, especially those conducted in Japanese. The law was unconstitutional because its provisions "give affirmative direction concerning the intimate and essential details of such schools, intrust their control to public officers, and deny both owners and patrons reasonable choice and discretion in respect of teachers, curriculum and textbooks." This decision, moreover, may be regarded as a constitutional safeguard against excessive and unreasonable state control of parochial schools.

1927—*In Scopes v. State*, the Tennessee Supreme Court upheld the conviction of John T. Scopes, a high-school teacher of science, for teaching evolution in defiance of the Tennessee Anti-Evolution Act of 1925. The majority opinion said that "we are not able to see how the prohibition of teaching the theory that man has descended from a lower order of animals gives preference to any religious establishment or mode of worship."

1930—In *Cochran v. Louisiana State Board of Education* (281 U.S. 370), the U.S. Supreme Court decided that a state may furnish free textbooks to parochial school pupils on the theory of child benefits.

1934—In *Hamilton v. Regents of the University of California* (293 U.S. 245), the U.S. Supreme Court held that the religious freedom of Methodist students was not abridged unconstitutionally when the university expelled them for refusing, on religious grounds, to register in a required course in military training. In his concurring opinion, Mr. Justice Cardozo maintained that "the religious liberty protected by the First Amendment against violation by the Nation is protected by the Fourteenth Amendment against invasion by the states."

1935—National Youth Administration aided students through payment for work projects in denominational schools and colleges, including theological seminaries.

1937—Harrison-Black-Fletcher Bill for Federal aid to education. For the first time, Catholics supported the principle but also demanded aid for parochial schools.

1938—The Report of the President's Advisory Committee on Education recommended that pupils in non-public schools receive "reading materials, transportation, and scholarships . . ." and that "local public schools receiving Federal aid be authorized to make local health and welfare services available to pupils in nonpublic schools," under conditions subject to determination by the state or local authorities.

1940—In *Cantwell v. Connecticut* (310 U.S. 296), the U.S. Supreme Court ruled that the Fourteenth Amendment makes the state legislatures as "incompetent" as Congress in making "no law respecting an establishment of religion or prohibiting the free exercise thereof" (First Amendment).

1940—In *Minersville School District v. Gobitis* (310 U.S. 586), the U.S. Supreme Court decided that the compulsory flag salute in public schools did not violate the religious freedom of children belonging to the Jehovah's Witnesses. Mr. Justice Frankfurter, in the majority opinion, stated that "national unity is the basis of national security. . . . The flag is the symbol· of our national unity, transcending all internal differences, however large, within the framework of the Constitution."

1941—Beginning of released time classes for public school children in New York City under the McLaughlin-Coudert Law of 1940.

1941—*Chance v. Mississippi State Textbook Board* (190 Miss. 452). The Mississippi Supreme Court held constitutional a state law granting free textbooks to all pupils in public, private, and religious elementary schools. The decision emphasized that "the state which allows the pupil to subscribe to religious creed should not, because of his exercise of this right, proscribe him from benefits common to all. . . . Such

265

would constitute a denial of equal privileges on sectarian grounds. . . ."

1941—Oregon law furnished free textbooks to pupils attending private and parochial elementary schools.

1943—In *Murdock v. Pennsylvania* (319 U.S. 105), the U.S. Supreme Court stated that the Fourteenth Amendment made the First Amendment "applicable to the states."

1943—In *West Virginia State Board of Education v. Barnette* (319 U.S. 624), the U.S. Supreme Court reversed the Gobitis Decision. In the majority opinion, Mr. Justice Jackson pointed out that "those who begin coercive elimination of dissent soon find themselves exterminating dissenters. Compulsory unification of opinion achieves only the unanimity of the graveyard."

1944—*Commonwealth v. Bey* (92 Pittsburgh Legal Journal 84). Pennsylvania court decided that a Moslem parent must send his children to public school on Friday and that such attendance does not violate the principle of freedom of religion.

1944—G. I. Bill of Rights supported study by veterans at denominational schools and colleges, including theological study at theological seminaries.

1946—A survey by the National Education Association on "The State and Sectarian Education" revealed no agreement among the states as to what was permissible and what was forbidden in practice in church-state-school relations. Free textbooks were given to parochial school pupils in Louisiana, Mississippi, New Mexico, Oregon, and West Virginia.

1946—National School Lunch Act. Federal funds were made available for free lunches to pupils in private and parochial schools.

1946-51—Under the Hill-Burton Hospital Survey and Construction Acts, denominational hospitals received Federal funds: $58,000,000 to Catholic, $16,000,000 to Protestant, and $2,000,000 to Jewish hospitals.

1947—In *Everson v. Board of Education* (330 U.S. 1), the U.S. Supreme Court held that states may offer public bus transportation to parochial school pupils, in spite of its insistence that the "slightest breach" would not be tolerated in the wall of separation between church and state, which "must be kept high and impregnable" (Mr. Justice Black). In his dissenting opinion, Mr. Justice Jackson argued that the "undertones" of the majority decision favoring "complete and uncompromising separation of Church and

State were utterly discordant with its conclusion yielding support to their commingling in education."

1947—North College Hill, Ohio, public schools discontinued Catholic control.

1948—Founding of Protestants and Other Americans United for Separation of Church and State in opposition to all public aid to parochial schools.

1948—In *McCollum v. Board of Education* (333 U.S. 203), the U.S. Supreme Court prohibited released time classes during school time in public school buildings. Mr. Justice Black, for the majority, stressed again that the wall of separation must be kept "high and impregnable." To Mr. Justice Frankfurter, "Separation means separation, not something less." The only dissenter, Mr. Justice Reed, maintained that "cooperation between the schools and a non-ecclesiastical body [such as the Champaign Council of Religious Education] is not forbidden by the First Amendment."

1949—Controversy between Francis Cardinal Spellman and Mrs. Eleanor Roosevelt over the Barden Bill for Federal aid to public education only.

1951—The New Mexico Supreme Court, *Zellers v. Huff* (55 N.M. 501), ruled that religious garb could not be worn by public school teachers, but that Catholic nuns and brothers may serve in public schools if their teaching is not sectarian, and that free textbooks to parochial pupils were forbidden by the state constitution.

1952—In *Doremus v. Board of Education* (342 U.S. 429), the U.S. Supreme Court, by refusing to review the New Jersey statute requiring the daily reading of five verses from the Old Testament in the public schools, thereby upheld the reading of the Old Testament.

1952—In *Zorach v. Clauson* (343 U.S. 306), the U.S. Supreme Court permitted released time classes on school time outside public school buildings. According to Mr. Justice Douglas, in the majority opinion, "The First Amendment within the scope of its coverage permits no exception; the prohibition is absolute. The First Amendment, however, does not say that in every and all respects there shall be a separation of Church and State. . . . We are a religious people whose institutions presuppose a Supreme Being. . . . to find in the Constitution a requirement that the government show a callous indifference to religious groups . . . would be preferring those who believe in no religion over those who do believe. . . . We cannot read into the Bill

267

of Rights . . . a hostility to religion." In his dissent, Mr. Justice Black argued that the New York practice of released time "is not separation but combination of Church and State." In another dissent, Mr. Justice Jackson called the practice "a governmental constraint in support of religion" and, hence, unconstitutional. He warned against mixing "compulsory public education with compulsory godliness."

1957—Survey by Michigan State University indicated prayers in half of the state's public elementary and high schools, with lesser numbers practicing hymn singing and Bible reading.

1958—California voters defeated an amendment to reimpose a property tax on private and parochial schools. New York State Supreme Court declined to prevent the display of the Nativity scene on the grounds of a public high school.

1958—National Defense Education Act, under which parochial schools received Federal loans for improving the teaching of science, mathematics, and foreign languages.

1959—Maine Supreme Court invalidated Augusta's law allowing public transportation of parochial school pupils. Federal District Court in Philadelphia ruled unconstitutional a Pennsylvania state law requiring Bible reading and the Lord's Prayer in the public school.

1959—In *Hanauer v. Elkins* (79 Sup. Ct. 536), the U.S. Supreme Court upheld the practice of compulsory military training at the University of Maryland, despite the constitutional plea by conscientious religious objectors.

1960—Connecticut Supreme Court of Errors upheld the constitutionality of a state law permitting towns to provide public bus transportation to parochial school pupils.

1961—The State Supreme Court of Vermont ruled unconstitutional the tuition payments to Catholic high schools in other towns by towns lacking their own high schools.

1961—The U.S. Supreme Court upheld the Everson Decision of 1947 in dismissing "for want of a substantial Federal decision" an appeal from the Connecticut Court of Errors validating a state law which permitted communities to furnish public bus transportation for parochial school pupils.

1961—In *Chamberlin, Resnick, et al. v. Dade County Board of Public Instruction et al.*, the Circuit Court of Dade County, Fla., declared that "the State law requiring the reading of the Bible, without sectarian comment, in the public schools coupled with the defendant school board's ruling of a student being excused from the exercise when requested is not unconstitutional." Also approved by the court were the recital of the Lord's Prayer, the display of religious symbols, and baccalaureate programs. On the other hand, the court ruled as unconstitutional religious holiday observances which depict the birth or crucifixion of Christ, regular Bible instruction in the public school buildings after school hours, and the exhibition of religious motion pictures in public schools.

1961 (May 29)—In *Braunfeld v. Brown* (......U.S.......) and in *Gallagher v. Crown Kosher Market* (......U.S.......), the U.S. Supreme Court upheld the validity of Pennsylvania and Massachusetts laws, respectively, prohibiting the retail sale of certain commodities on Sunday and maintained that these laws did not interfere with the free exercise of religion by Orthodox Jews, who observe Saturday as their Sabbath. The Supreme Court also upheld on the same day the Sunday closing laws of Maryland in *McGowan v. Maryland* (......U.S.......) and of Pennsylvania in *Two Guys from Harrison v. McGinley* (......U.S.......).

1961 (June 19)—In *Torcaso v. Watkins* (......U.S.......), the U.S. Supreme Court unanimously declared unconstitutional a Maryland religious test which was required for holding public office, since this practice involved an invasion of "the appellant's freedom of belief and religion."

1961 (July 14)—In *Engel v. Vitale,* the New York State Court of Appeals, in a 5-2 decision, declared that the Board of Education, New Hyde Park, N. Y., could constitutionally require the daily recital of the prayer recommended by the State Board of Regents in all the public schools. According to Justice Ch. J. Desmond, "Belief in a Supreme Being is as essential and permanent a feature of the American governmental system as is freedom of worship, equality under the law and due process of law."

1961—The Alaska Supreme Court declared that the state constitution forbade the appropriation of public funds for bus transportation to parochial schools, since the schools are benefited directly.

Selected Documents on the Church-State-School Issue

WILLIAM W. BRICKMAN

ᴇDUCATIONAL, RE-
ligious, and other groups habitually have been
issuing resolutions, statements of position, and
analyses in the area of relations between church
and state in education. During 1960-61, in connection with the presidential campaign and the
subsequent possibility of the passage of a Federal
law for educational aid, such documents multi-
plied rapidly. Some of these were publicized in
the press, while others were read in restricted
circles.

The student of this problem should have
access to a variety of original statements. Consequently, a few have been brought together to
show, to some extent, the opinions and supporting proof of different groups and individuals.
Since it was not practical to print all statements
in full—particularly because they tended to over-
lap and to be repetitious—it was thought advisable to abridge them somewhat. It is hoped that
this space-saving did not result in any distortion
of a specific point of view.

1. National Council of the Churches of Christ in the United States of America

The following policy statement was adopted by the General Board of the NCCC on Feb. 22, 1961:

PUBLIC FUNDS FOR PUBLIC SCHOOLS

The churches comprising the National Council of Churches hold in common with many other American organizations, religious and secular, certain convictions and concerns about the role of public education in a free society. All citizens share responsibility for the general education of all children in our society. The public school, supported by the taxes of all citizens, is the main and indispensable agency for this purpose. Non-public schools, however valuable to their patrons and to society, cannot fulfill the responsibility of the whole society for educating all children.

As a nation it is our duty to encourage the full development of the talents and abilities of all of our citizens. The provision of general education for all requires the mobilization of the best resources of our society to support the public school system, which in many areas is already inadequate to cope with the rate of our population growth and the rapid increase of knowledge.

New public school buildings must be planned and built. More teachers must be recruited and trained. Better methods of education must be perfected and applied. This is a mammoth and long-term effort. Where there is inability or unwillingness in any community to provide adequate educational opportunities for all children, such failure must be remedied by society as a whole.

Sharing these concerns with a wide range of our fellow citizens, the members of the churches which comprise the National Council of Churches have in addition convictions which rise more directly out of their faith in Jesus Christ. That the Kingdom of Christ transcends all nations, that no government of men is independent of God, that the survival of our society depends ultimately upon the Providence of God, that no man should be prevented from responding in faith and obedience to God as He is revealed in Jesus Christ: these are some of the specifically Christian convictions that bear upon our attitude toward questions of educational policy in the United States.

Thus, while supporting as Americans the public system of elementary and secondary schools with a host of our fellow citizens, as Christians we stand for the right of all parents, all citizens, and all churches to establish and maintain non-public schools whose ethos and curriculum

271

differ from that of the community as a whole. (The Constitution of the United States as presently interpreted guarantees this right.)

In principle Protestant and Orthodox Churches claim the right for themselves to establish and maintain schools in any community where the ethos of the public school system is or becomes basically inimical to the Christian education of our children. But we believe that to encourage such a general development would be tragic in its results to the American people.

The elementary and secondary schools of general education related to or operated by constituent communions of the National Council of the Churches of Christ in the U.S.A. value their freedom and independence to witness to the Lord of the Church, and to nurture their pupils in the Christian faith. We do not, however, ask for public funds for elementary or secondary education under Church control. If private schools were to be supported in the United States by tax funds, the practical effect would be that the American people would lose their actual control of the use of the taxes paid by all the people for purposes common to the whole society. We therefore do not consider it just or lawful that public funds should be assigned to support the elementary or secondary schools of any Church. The assignment of such funds could easily lead additional religious or other groups to undertake full scale parochial or private education with reliance on public tax support. This further fragmentation of general education in the United States would destroy the public school system or at least weaken it so gravely that it could not possibly adequately meet the educational needs of all the children of our growing society.

We reaffirm our support of the public school system as an indispensable means of providing educational opportunity for all children; we urge provision of increased resources for the operation and improvement of the public schools; we declare our whole-hearted support of the principle of public control of public funds.

THEREFORE
1. We favor the provision of federal funds for tax-supported elementary and secondary public schools under the following conditions: (a) that the funds be administered by the states with provision for report by them to the U. S. Commissioner of Education on the use of the funds; (b) that there be no discrimination among children on the basis of race, religion, class, or national origin; (c) that there be adequate safeguards against federal control of educational policy.
2. We oppose grants from federal, state, or local tax funds for non-public elementary and secondary schools.

3. We oppose the payment from public funds for tuition or "scholarships" for children to attend private or church-related elementary or secondary schools, or grants to their parents for that purpose.
4. We are opposed to "tax-credits," "tax-forgiveness," and exemption from school taxes or other taxes for parents whose children attend non-public elementary or secondary schools.
5. We favor the supplying of dental or medical services, lunches, and other distinctly welfare services to all children, whatever school they may be attending, provided such services are identifiable by recipients as public services, and the expenditures are administered by public authorities responsible to the electorate.

We are concerned to promote and safeguard the principles already expressed, and to avoid the infringement of religious liberty which arises when taxes paid under compulsion by all the people are used to aid non-public schools.

87 FOR, 1 AGAINST, 0 ABSTENTIONS

2. Synagogue Council of America and the National Community Relations Advisory Council

These extracts are taken from "Safeguarding Religious Liberty" (1957), a compilation of policy statements formulated by the Joint Committee of the two groups. The Synagogue Council of America is the co-ordinating group for three rabbinical and three congregational organizations representing Reform, Conservative, and Orthodox Judaism. The constituent groups of the NCRAC are the three congregational organizations, three secular Jewish bodies, and numerous Jewish local and state agencies. Some orthodox groups, such as Torah Umesorah and Agudath Israel of America, have issued statements in favor of some form of public aid to religious day schools.

STATEMENTS OF POSITION
Religion and Public Education
Teaching of "Moral and Spiritual" Values

Insofar as the teaching of "spiritual values" may be

273

understood to signify religious teaching, this must remain as it has been the responsibility of the home, the church and the synagogue. Insofar as it is understood to signify the teaching of morality, ethics and good citizenship, a deep commitment to such values has been successfully inculcated by our public schools in successive generations of Americans. The public schools must continue to share responsibility for fostering a commitment to these moral values, without presenting or teaching any sectarian or theological sources or sanctions for such values.

"Objective" or "Factual" Teaching About Religion
The public schools must and should teach with full objectivity the role that religion has played in the life of mankind and in the development of society, when such teaching is intrinsic to the regular subject matter being studied. We are opposed to attempts by the public elementary and secondary schools to go beyond this, and teach about the *doctrines* of religion. Without passing upon the question of whether or not such teaching is inconsistent with the principle of separation of church and state, we believe that factual, objective and impartial teaching about the doctrines of religion is an unattainable objective. Any attempt to introduce such teaching into the public schools poses the grave threat of pressures upon school personnel from sectarian groups and compromises the impartiality of teaching and the integrity of the public educational system. Our opposition to such teaching rests on these grounds.

Teaching of a "Common Core"
We are opposed to any public school program that seeks to inculcate as doctrine any body of principles, beliefs or concepts that is represented as the "common core" of several or all religious faiths. The effort to extract from the religions current among us such a common denominator or "common core" can lead only to a watering down, a vitiation, of all that is spiritually meaningful in every religious faith. We submit, moreover, that attempts at religious inculcation in the public schools, even of articles of faith drawn from all religions and endorsed by representatives of all, violate the traditional American principle of separation of church and state.

Use of School Premises for Religious Purposes
We are opposed to the use of public school premises during school hours for religious education, meetings, or worship. Where public school premises are made available after school hours to civic groups outside the school system, they should be made available on the same basis to religious groups.

Religious Practices and Observances;
Joint Religious Observances

Mindful of the dangers inherent in any violation of the traditional American principle of separation of church and state, we are opposed to religious practices or observances in the public elementary and high schools, including:

The reading or recitation of prayers

The reading of the Bible (except as included in a course in literature)

The distribution of Bibles or religious tracts

The singing of religious hymns

The granting of school credits for religious studies

The wearing of any type of clerical garb by public school teachers on school premises

The holding of public school classes on the premises of religious institutions

The taking of a religious census of pupils

We are opposed to the observance of religious festivals in the public elementary and high schools because in our view such observance constitutes a violation of the traditional American principle of the separation of church and state.

Joint religious observances, such as Christmas-Chanukah and Easter-Passover, are in our opinion no less a breach of the principle of separation of church and state and violate the conscience of many religious persons, Jews and Christians alike.

Where religious holiday observances are nevertheless held in public schools, Jewish children have a right to refrain from participation. We recommend that local Jewish communities take such action as may be appropriate to safeguard this right of non-participation.

Released Time and Dismissal Time

We believe that Jewish communities are justified in objecting to released time or dismissal time programs.

Inherent in dismissal time are many, though not all, of the faults of released time. Nevertheless, when confronted with the necessity of a choice, we regard dismissal time as less objectionable.

Where a program of released time or dismissal time is in effect, or may be adopted, the Jewish community shall insist upon the following safeguards against possible abuses:

1. No religious instruction shall be given on public school premises;

2. The administrative machinery of the public school system shall not be employed to record or encourage attendance at religious instruction centers of students who avail themselves of either program;

275

3. There shall be no proselytizing on school premises;
4. All children participating in such programs shall be dismissed together, and all grouping, separation, or identification by religion or by participation or non-participation in such programs shall be avoided;
5. Children shall not be assembled on public school premises for the purpose of being led to religious instruction centers nor shall any representative of such religious instruction center meet the children on such premises to facilitate the operation of either program.

Governmental Aid to Religiously Controlled Schools

We are opposed to governmental aid to schools under the supervision or control of any religious denomination or sect, whether Jewish, Protestant, or Catholic, including outright subsidies, transportation, text-books and other supplies. We are not opposed to the use of any school for the provision of lunches, medical and dental services to children.

Closing of Public Schools on Jewish High Holy Days

It is our view that whether or not public schools should be closed on Jewish High Holy days is exclusively an administrative question to be decided by the public school authorities in the light of their own judgment as to the advantages or disadvantages involved. In some communities the public school authorities might find that the large number of absences of Jewish children and teachers make it impossible to engage in any fruitful educational work and therefore justifies keeping the schools closed in the interests of economy and efficiency. In other communities, public school authorities may reach a different conclusion. In either event, the Jewish community can have no special interest in the decision.

Therefore, we recommend:

1. It should be the concern of the Jewish community that no Jewish child or teacher shall be penalized for remaining away from school on a Jewish religious holiday.
2. That Jewish organizations or leaders should not request the public school system to close the schools on Jewish religious holidays.
3. Where the public school system, as a matter of school administration, wishes to close the schools on Jewish holidays, and requests an opinion from Jewish organizations or Jewish community leaders, no objection should be interposed by such Jewish representatives, provided the record is made clear that the decision was made purely for administrative reasons and that the Jewish community has not requested such action.

3. American Civil Liberties Union

The ACLU filed, on March 23, 1961, a statement with both houses of Congress. This extract is the major part of the document:

The American Civil Liberties Union has carefully reviewed S. 1021 and H. R. 4970, bills "to authorize a program of federal financial assistance for education." The general question of federal aid lies outside our scope, but we find no civil liberties barrier to this proposed legislation, because Section 102 of both bills limits the financial assistance to "*public* elementary and secondary education*" (italics ours), and Section 103 sets up strong safeguards against the type of federal control of public school policies and programs which the Union would oppose on academic freedom grounds.

The Union opposes any authorization of grants or loans to church-controlled elementary and secondary schools, just as it supports their right to exist so long as they meet the standards set by the compulsory education laws of the several states. We believe that the latter question was properly and definitively settled by the United States Supreme Court in 1925 in the case of *Pierce vs. Society of Sisters*, when it condemned as unconstitutional an Oregon Compulsory Education Act requiring all school-children to attend public schools. The Court held that the Oregon statute violated the "liberty of parents and guardians to direct the upbringing and education of children under their control." We believe that the Court could not have decided otherwise without ignoring that part of the First Amendment which forbids any law "prohibiting the free exercise" of religion.

But the Founding Fathers in the same first sentence of the First Amendment moved to forbid any law "respecting an establishment of religion." We believe that, if Congress were to authorize the making of long-term federal building loans to church-controlled elementary and secondary schools, it would be supporting not one, but various, establishments of religion—not only Catholic, but Lutheran, Episcopalian, Quaker, Jewish, etc.

* * *

President Kennedy stated in his press conference of March 8, 1961:

"The problem of loans to secondary education does constitute serious constitutional problems. I do not think that anyone can read the Everson case without recognizing that the position which the Court took, minority and majority, in regard to the use of tax funds for non-public schools, raises serious constitutional questions."

With President Kennedy, we point out that long-term loans to church-controlled elementary and secondary schools would involve "the use of tax funds." Such federal loans at low-interest rates would constitute basic support; if this were not so, they would not be sought. We therefore think it impossible to draw a constitutional line between loans and grants: both are financial aid.

We take no position on anything but the civil liberties problem involved in the debate over public vs. private (especially parochial) schools. But our belief that subsidization of church-controlled schools would violate the "establishment" clause rests upon the very nature, and understandable purpose, of church-controlled schools. They are devoted in considerable degree to religious instruction, or indoctrination. They are created for the precise purpose of communicating a body of religious teaching. They are meant to nurture and fortify the faith of children already linked with the religious group. They have additional functions to be sure; they engage in secular educational work, organized play, and the like. But they exist primarily to assure that children of school age will receive religious instruction and will be shielded from competing ideologies and values. So long as this is true, they must be regarded as a religious activity even though not devoted exclusively to religious exercises. A church does not cease to be a church because at times its basement may be used as a recreation hall by members of the congregation. No more does a religious school cease to be a religious activity because at times its premises may be used for the secular teaching which, by state law, is exacted as the price of keeping children away from the educational institutions the public has provided for them.

It has been argued by the advocates of federal loans to church-controlled elementary and secondary schools, that the expenditure of tax funds, local, state or national has in the past been authorized for the benefit of such schools. Congress did indeed pass the School Lunch Act, in 1946, extending the benefits of the Act to needy children registered in non-public schools. Considering this to be clearly a welfare aid to the child, the ACLU saw no constitutional violation there. On the issue of bus transportation for children attending sectarian schools, the ACLU took exception to the Supreme Court's 5-4 decision in the Everson case in which it was held that a state could, without violating the First Amendment, authorize the expenditure of local tax moneys for such a purpose. Though the question is debatable, it would seem to us that bus transportation, as contrasted with free school lunches, is more of an aid to the school than to the child per se. At any rate, when it comes to the supplying by a state of textbooks to church-controlled schools, we insist that since textbooks are essential to the educational process, their provision by any state to church-controlled schools is a breach of the "establishment" clause. We are therefore supporting our Oregon affiliate in a suit designed to challenge the state law which authorizes the expenditure of public funds for this purpose. We anticipate that this case will reach the Supreme Court and we will at that time ask the Court to reconsider the decision handed down as long ago as 1930. At that time the Court approved a similar Louisiana law.

The only type of federal financial aid now being provided to church-controlled elementary and secondary schools, other than funds expended for school lunches, is loans for the improvement of instruction in science, mathematics and modern foreign languages, authorized in the National Defense Education Act of 1958. Since legislation has been introduced calling for a five-year extension of the NDEA beyond its expiration date, June 30, 1962, the ACLU is at present studying the constitutionality of those provisions.

Proponents of long-term loans to church-controlled lower schools have further argued that to deny financial aid to such schools is to treat children who attend such schools, and their parents, as "second-class citizens." But no one is "a second-class citizen" or can be said to be "discriminated against," who is allowed free choice of action and equal opportunity. Every American is free to send his child or children to the public schools, which are provided for all children; or, alternatively, to send them to a church-controlled or another type of private school.

It has been urged, in the name of "distributive justice," that parents who wish to send their children to religious schools are penalized for the "free exercise" of their religion because they must both pay taxes for public schools and tuition to the religious schools. But all citizens must be prepared to pay in one way or another for their convictions or preferences.

* * *

The ACLU asks Congress to consider most seriously the basic constitutional issue involved, should amendments to S. 1021 and H. R. 4970 be proposed, or should separate bills be drafted providing for long-term building loans to church-controlled elementary and secondary schools. Such legislation, which could be tested in the courts only with the greatest difficulty, would carry the country a long way toward nullification of the "establishment" clause of the First Amendment. The process of attrition was begun, the ACLU has held in the past, with the Everson decision of 1947 approving free bus transportation for parochial school children, and carried further, in 1952, by the Zorach decision (340 U.S. 1952*) approving the release of some children from public schools to attend religious classes conducted off the premises while other children were kept at work in the public schools.

The ACLU speaks as the watchdog of the Bill of Rights. Since its founding in 1920, the Union has had as its sole mandate the safeguarding of that charter of liberties, which with the Thirteenth, Fourteenth, Fifteenth and Nineteenth Amendments, protects the basic rights of all Americans as citizens.

Since the Fourteenth Amendment guarantees equal protection of the laws to white and colored citizens, as interpreted by the Supreme Court decisions of 1954 and 1955, the Union urges that there be included in S. 1021 and H. R. 4970 a provision withholding federal funds from public schools in which segregation is practiced as a matter of policy.

4. Department of Education, National Catholic Welfare Conference

On March 14, 1961, the Rt. Rev. Msgr. Frederick G. Hochwalt, director, gave the following testimony before the Senate Subcommittee on Education:

My name is Frederick G. Hochwalt. I am the Director of the Department of Education of the National Catholic Welfare Conference. It is the function of my Department to coordinate the national interests of the parochial school system in the fifty states.

This school system includes 10,300 elementary schools, and approximately 2,400 high schools. These schools are staffed by more than 102,000 teachers, 40,000 of whom are laymen. The parochial elementary and secondary schools together enroll more than five million students.

These schools are established, operated, and maintained by Catholic citizens, by people of the same income group as those living about the neighboring public schools. Catholic schools, like public schools, aim for a proper balance of character building, scholarship and bodily development and are founded on the conviction that moral training is an essential part of education. These schools are no alien growth, but a sturdy native plant. They were first in the field of education in this country and are intimately a part of its development, deeply intertwined with its traditions and tied closely with the aspirations of our people.

---

* 343 U.S. 306—Editors' note

They are integrally a part of what is basically a dual system. Public and private schools form a necessary partnership for the fruitful service of this country. We are one people and it is in our national interest that both systems make their full contribution in the service of our children. Any other attitude would be extremely short-sighted and self-defeating.

Although the parochial schools are not governmentally sponsored and operated, they perform a public function, supplying large numbers of children with an education accepted by the state as fulfilling its requirements of compulsory education and meeting its specific standards.

In meeting these standards the parochial schools teach that true patriotism cannot exist in theory alone. It must be put into practice in the performance of the duties of citizenship. These duties include not only the virtues of obedience, sacrifice, and brotherly love, but those particular duties which arise from the responsibilities of democratic self-government.

Catholic parents and Catholic school administrators have for the past thirty years or more followed with interest the proposals of involving the Federal Government in the support of America's schools. Some of our Catholic citizens have feared the coming of federal aid as a prelude to federal control. The question of whether or not there ought to be federal aid is a judgment to be based on objective, economic facts connected with the schools of the country and consequently Catholic citizens should take a position in accordance with the facts. As on many questions there is a division of Catholic conviction in this area. A great many parents of parochial school children would welcome federal aid as a necessary help to them in a time of financial strain. They do feel the double burden of supporting two school systems and are apt to inquire much more pointedly now than heretofore why the proponents of federal aid do not take into consideration their needs. They point out that the classroom shortage exists as demonstrably in the private school system as it does in the public school system.

Recently my department made a spot check of ten dioceses across the country from coast to coast and the story in all of them was the same. Next fall, when the schools open, a shortage of parochial school classrooms in the thousands will be reported. Those children will be turned away from parochial schools to seek elsewhere for their education.

Earlier I stated that individuals must decide for themselves about the necessity of federal aid to education. To make that judgment one can look at the record. The federal aid to education which has come from the government in the past seems in the main part to have been a reasonable form of government assistance. The original and the later amended land-grant allocations, the provision for college housing, the school lunch program, the G. I. bill and the National Defense Education Act are good examples of how a government can interest itself in the welfare of its people.

This body of legislators now has before it an impressive list of proposed measures to strengthen American education by federal assistance; and a great deal of emphasis is placed in these proposals on schoolhouse construction. I am particularly interested in S. 1021, the Administration's educational bill. With reference to it may I emphasize that the decision to have federal funds for schoolhouse construction is one for the American people and the American legislators to make on the basis of sound evidence. If that evidence is sound and if the voice of the people is heard in a request for federal aid, then surely it will come about. But if it does, should not the American people be concerned about all of the schools of this great nation? If an intellectual and scientific breakthrough is to be realized, if excellence is to be achieved, who can tell whence will come the leadership for the nation, from the public schools, or from their partners in education, the private schools.

What can be done for the private school and, in particular, the parochial school? We have the courageous example of government aid to our colleges without discrimination. My petition today points up the need to grant similar assistance to the elementary and secondary schools by way of long term, low-interest rate loans, with the interest rate computed on an annual basis. To grant federal assistance to only part of the American educational effort is to deny to the other parts the chance to grow. In fact it hinders parents in that free choice of education which is essentially theirs. The federal government ought not to take any steps which would force the private schools out of business or, in effect, to deny to parents the right to choose their kind of schools.

We regard ourselves as an enlightened democracy giving leadership to western civilization, and yet other lands, guided by democratic principles, have solved this problem of educational assistance and have not been confused by elements extraneous to the main issue of human rights. Systems of education under the auspices of church groups, subsidized in whole or a great part by the government, are operated with success in England, Ireland, Scotland, Belgium, Holland, several provinces of Canada and elsewhere. After all, the manner in which the government offers assistance can be so arranged that the possibility of any educational chaos or irresponsible endangering of the state system or of private systems can be avoided.

282

I am here today to ask the legislators to think in balanced terms of the problems before us, for if federal aid is necessary, if it is to come and if it is to be granted to the states and to public school systems, then, in the interest of all of our citizens I would urgently plead for a consideration of the present plight and the future needs of our private schools, especially our parochial schools. In the name of educational freedom they must be continued. Under the concept of a pluralistic society they must be treasured and appreciated and in the name of the common good and the common welfare they must be given all of the assistance which is constitutionally acceptable.

It is unthinkable that this great nation would embark for the first time on a massive program of federal encouragement to education by leaving out of consideration that dedicated group of parents and educators who have contributed so much to the welfare of this nation. We are proud of the products of the parochial school system. They are first-class citizens and their children and their children's children ought to be treated as such.

The Contributors and Their Biographical Background

STANLEY LEHRER

ℭONTRIBUTORS TO this book include college and university professors of education, English, and political science; the former educational director, Ethical Culture Schools, New York City; the executive director, Department of Religion and Public Education, National Council of the Churches of Christ in the U. S. A.; the secretary of schools, The Lutheran Church-Missouri Synod, St. Louis; and the program co-ordinator, National Community Relations Advisory Council, New York City. The background of every contributor is covered in the following brief biographies.

WILLIAM W. BOYER, associate professor of political science, University of Pittsburgh, was born in Verona, Pa., Dec. 10, 1923. He received his education at the College of Wooster, Ohio (B.A., 1947), and the University of Wisconsin (M.A., 1949; Ph.D., 1953). His teaching career has included posts at the University of Florida, 1950; Grinnell College, 1951-52; and University of Connecticut, 1954. He also has served as assistant to the director, State of Wisconsin Governor's Commission on Human Rights, 1952-53, and administrative assistant to the Governor of Wisconsin, 1954-55. In addition to his current teaching chores at the University of Pittsburgh, he is director of the university's Foreign Specialists Programs in Public Administration. He is a member of the American Political Science Association, American Society for Public Administration, Society for Personnel Administration, and American Association of University Professors (president, University of Pittsburgh chapter, 1960-61). Among the periodicals that have accepted his writings are the *Wisconsin Law Review, Municipal Finance, American Bar Association Journal, School and Society, Personnel Administration, Bulletin* of the American Association of University Professors, *Midwest Journal of Political Science,* and *Religious Education.*

Born in New York City, June 30, 1913, WILLIAM W. BRICKMAN received his education at the College of the City of New York (B. A., 1934; M. S. in Education, 1935) and New York University (Ph. D., 1938). He has been serving in various capacities in the field of education: professor of educational history and comparative education (his present position), School of Education, New York University; president, Comparative Education Society, 1956-59; and, since 1953, editor, *School and Society,* and secretary, Society for the Advancement of Education. His contributions have appeared in the *Educational Forum, Religious Education, Tradition, American Historical Review, Modern Language Journal,* "Encyclopedia of Educational Research," "Encyclopaedia Britannica," and "Collier's Yearbook." The following books by him have been published: "Guide to Research in Educational History" (1949), "John Dewey: Master Educator" (co-edited by Stanley Lehrer, 1959, 1961), "The Changing Soviet School" (co-edited and co-authored by George Z. F. Bereday and Gerald H. Read, 1960), "The Countdown on Segregated Education" (co-edited by Stanley Lehrer, 1960), and "Religion, Government, and Education" (co-edited by Stanley Lehrer, 1961).

ROLFE LANIER HUNT was born in Milner, Ga., March 5, 1903, and educated at Millsaps College (B. A., 1924) and George Peabody College for Teachers (M. A., 1927; Ph. D., 1937). At present, he is executive director, Department of Religion and Public Education, National Council of the Churches of Christ, and lecturer in education, New York University. He has held the following positions: principal, Winona (Miss.) High School, 1924-26; superintendent, Bassfield (Miss.) Consolidated Schools, 1927-1929; associate editor in charge of youth materials, General Board of Christian Education, Methodist Episcopal Church, Nashville, Tenn., 1930-36; superintendent of schools, Louise, Miss., 1937-42, and Magnolia, Miss., 1942-45; editor, *Phi Delta Kappan,* 1945-52; and chief, Editorial Service, U. S. Office of Education, 1952-53. Among the organizations of which he is a member are the National Education Association, Religious Education Association, Comparative Education Society, American Academy of Political and Social Science, and Education

Writers Association. His articles have been featured in *Religious Education, Annals* of the American Academy of Political and Social Science, *International Journal of Religious Education,* and *School and Society.* He also contributed to the "Collier's Encyclopedia" and "Westminster Dictionary of Religious Education." His book, "Looking Toward High School" (co-authored by Paul Pearson), was published in 1960.

PHILIP JACOBSON, program co-ordinator, National Community Relations Advisory Council, New York City, was born in the same city, May 16, 1903. He received the L.L.B. from the School of Law of St. John's University, 1929. Prior to the present position, he served as director, Church-State Division, American Jewish Committee (1945-60). He is a member of the Religious Education Association, National Association of Intergroup Relations Officials, and Association of Jewish Community Relations Workers. Among the publications to which he has contributed are *Religious Education, Christian Century, School and Society,* and the 12th yearbook of the John Dewey Society.

BERNARD J. KOHLBRENNER, born in Syracuse, N. Y., Nov. 20, 1904, is now professor of education, University of Notre Dame. He earned the A. B. (1927) and A. M. (1928) at Syracuse University and the Ed. D. (1942) at Harvard University. Important posts that he has held include assistant professor of education, St. Louis University, 1939-40; professor of education and head of the department, College of New Rochelle, 1940-45; and associate professor of education, University of Notre Dame, 1945-49, after which he assumed his present duties. He was head, department of education, 1949-57. He belongs to the following organizations: Society for the Advancement of Education, Comparative Education Society, American Association of University Professors, History of Education Society, National Society of College Teachers of Education, National Catholic Educational Association, National Education Association, and Phi Beta Kappa. His writings have appeared in *School and Society, Catholic Educational Review, America, History of Education Journal, Social Studies, Thought,* and "Encyclopedia Americana." He is co-author of "A History of Catholic Education in the United States" (1937), "The American Apostolate" (1952), and "The Heritage of American Education" (1961).

On Oct. 4, 1900, WM. A. KRAMER was born in Frohna, Mo. For his education he attended Concordia Teachers College (B. S. in Education and Hon. Litt. D., the latter awarded in 1955) and St. Louis University (M. A. in Education, 1944). He has served as teacher, Grace Lutheran

School, Uniontown, Mo., 1922-28; principal and teacher, St. Paul's Lutheran School, Strasburg, Ill., 1928-40; and assistant secretary of schools (1940-57), associate secretary (1957-60), and secretary (since 1961), The Lutheran Church-Missouri Synod. He is a member of the Lutheran Education Association and National Education Association. *Lutheran Education, Lutheran Witness, This Day,* and the "Lutheran Cyclopedia" have published a total of more than 100 of his articles. His books are "Devotions for Lutheran Schools" (1934, 1946), "General Course of Study for Lutheran Elementary Schools" (editor, 1943), "Treasury of Christian Literature" (co-editor, 1949), "The Church through the Ages" (co-author, 1949), "Happiness Can Be Yours" (1952), "Living for Christ" (1952), "Teenagers Pray" (editor, 1955), and "Units in Religion for Lutheran Schools" (editor, 1955-58).

HAROLD H. PUNKE, professor of education, Auburn (Ala.) University, was born in Elliott, Ill., Nov. 11, 1900. The B.S. and M.S. were earned at the University of Illinois in 1924 and 1925. He received the Ph.D. at the University of Chicago in 1928. Major activities have included teaching at the University of Illinois, 1930-32, and in the University System of Georgia, 1933-42; civilian and military posts, U.S. government, 1942-49; and his present position at Auburn University which he assumed in 1949. He is on the membership rosters of Phi Delta Kappa, state and National Education Associations, and the American Association of University Professors. His writings comprise about 200 articles and four books — "The Courts and Public School Property," "Law and Liability in Pupil Transportation," "Community Uses of Public School Facilities," and "Teacher's Question and Answer Book on Guidance" (co-authored by Arville Wheeler).

Born in New York City, Aug. 20, 1923, J. STEPHEN SHERWIN studied at the University of Wisconsin (B.S., 1945), Teachers College, Columbia University (M.A., 1947), and New York University (Ed.D., 1954). A teaching career began in 1945 when he served as a substitute teacher of English, New York City high schools. During 1947-48, he was instructor in English, Sampson College. He then became lecturer in English, College of the City of New York, in 1950; assistant professor, State University of New York, College of Education, Geneseo, 1954-56; associate professor of English, State University of New York, College of Education, Buffalo, 1956-59; and professor of English at the latter institution in 1959, a position which he still holds. He has joined the following organizations: American Civil Liberties Union, American Association of University Professors, National Council of Teachers of English, Modern Language Association, Phi Delta Kappa,

Thoreau Society, and Emerson Society. Articles have been contributed to *School and Society*, *St. Louis Post-Dispatch*, *Journal of Communication*, *Journal of Educational Sociology*, and *Thoreau Society Bulletin*. He is the co-author of "A Word Index to WALDEN with Textual Notes" (1960).

V. T. THAYER, born in Tomora, Neb., Oct. 13, 1886, is the retired educational director, Ethical Culture Schools, New York City. The University of Wisconsin awarded him the A. B. (1916), M. A. (1917), and Ph. D. (1922). Professional services have embraced duties as superintendent of schools, Ashland, Wis., 1912-14 and 1918-19; instructor in philosophy, University of Wisconsin, 1919-22; principal, Ethical Culture Schools, New York City, 1922-24; professor of education, Ohio State University, 1924-28; and educational director, Ethical Culture Schools, New York City, 1928-48, a position from which he retired. But he has not remained inactive. Since 1948, he has assumed a number of teaching tasks: visiting professor, University of Hawaii and University of Virginia; John Hay Whitney Visiting Professor, Fisk University; and lecturer, University of Maryland, Johns Hopkins University, University of Wisconsin, Colorado State Teachers College, Ohio State University, University of Utah, and Teachers College, Columbia University. His organizational affiliations have included the National Education Association, John Dewey Society, Philosophy of Education Society, Phi Beta Kappa, Phi Delta Kappa, and American Civil Liberties Union. He has written for *School and Society*, *The Nation's Schools*, *Journal of Educational Research*, *Phi Delta Kappan*, *The Humanist*, *The New Leader*, *The Social Frontier*, *Harper's Magazine*, and *Journal of Higher Education*. He also is the author of several books: "Passing of the Recitation" (1928), "Supervision in the Secondary School" (co-authored by H. B. Alberty, 1931), "Reorganizing Secondary Education" (co-authored by Caroline B. Zachry and Ruth Kotinsky, 1939), "American Education under Fire" (1944), "Religion in Public Education" (1947), "The Attack Upon the American Secular School" (1951), "Public Education and Its Critics" (1954), and "The Role of the School in American Society" (1960).